Just a Job?

Just a Job?

*Communication, Ethics, and
Professional Life*

George Cheney, Daniel J. Lair,
Dean Ritz, Brenden E. Kendall

OXFORD
UNIVERSITY PRESS

2010

OXFORD

UNIVERSITY PRESS

Oxford University Press, Inc., publishes works that further
Oxford University's objective of excellence
in research, scholarship, and education.

Oxford   New York
Auckland   Cape Town   Dar es Salaam   Hong Kong   Karachi
Kuala Lumpur   Madrid   Melbourne   Mexico City   Nairobi
New Delhi   Shanghai   Taipei   Toronto

With offices in
Argentina   Austria   Brazil   Chile   Czech Republic   France   Greece
Guatemala   Hungary   Italy   Japan   Poland   Portugal   Singapore
South Korea   Switzerland   Thailand   Turkey   Ukraine   Vietnam

Published by Oxford University Press, Inc.
198 Madison Avenue, New York, New York 10016

www.oup.com

Oxford is a registered trademark of Oxford University Press.

Library of Congress Cataloging-in-Publication Data
Just a job?: communication, ethics, and professional life /
George Cheney ... [et al.].
p.   cm.
Includes bibliographical references and index.
ISBN 978-0-19-518277-4; 978-0-19-518278-1 (pbk.)
1. Occupations.   2. Professional ethics.   3. Success.
I. Cheney, George.
HF5381.J87 2009
174—dc22   2009008674

Printed in the United States of America
on acid-free paper

To the end of ethics as work

Acknowledgments

We are grateful to our colleagues, including Cliff Allen, Karen Lee Ashcraft, Kirsti Broadfoot, Connie Bullis, Dana Cloud, Lars Thøger Christensen, Charles Conrad, Stan Deetz, Shiv Ganesh, Rebecca Gill, Sasha Grant, James Hedges, Alison Henderson, Richard Johannesen, Tim Kuhn, Jill McMillan, Mette Morsing, Debashish Munshi, Majia Nadesan, Erin Ortiz, Juliet Roper, Matt Seeger, Mary Simpson, Cynthia Stohl, Katie Sullivan, Nikki Townsley, Sarah Tracy, Angela Trethewey, Roy Wood, Heather Zoller, and Ted Zorn, for their ideas, inspiration, and collaboration in professional ethics and related areas. We express deep thanks to Steve Goldzwig and Steve May for their careful reviews of the entire manuscript over the 2008–09 holidays. Thanks also to Helen Gamble for hosting an authors' retreat in September 2008, and to April Kedrowicz for helping us understand the engineering profession. Our editors at Oxford University Press, especially Catherine Rae, John Rauschenberg, and Brian Desmond, have been patient and helpful from start to finish. Our copy editor, Jackie Doyle, did a superb job! Finally, we express deep appreciation to our partners and families. George thanks Sally Planalp; Dan is grateful to Danielle De La Mare; Dean honors Carol Volpe; and Brenden dedicates his work on this project to his brother, Grant Kendall, and his parents, Mark and Roseann Kendall, for their inspiration and support.

Contents

Just a Job?

Introduction

The problem facing [the world] is the separation of the economy from society and the absence of any effective regulation of the market place.... [T]he critical issue is the absence of a set of professional ethics. (Turner, 1996, pp. xxxi–xxxii)

Why We Wrote This Book

Probing "Morality" and Prodding "Ethics"

Sometimes a word is worth a thousand words. Or an entire book. "Ethics" is one of those words, with no shortage of book-length treatments. The idea for a communication-centered investigation of ethics and its relationship to professional life arose during the opening session of George's ethics class in the spring of 2003. Although the students weren't terribly excited by the idea of ethics, they became much more animated when the discussion shifted to the term "morality."

They saw the latter term as more relevant to their lives, including work. In fact, many of these same students shared an implicit assumption that doing ethics is a *kind of work*—work in a pejorative sense. Was this merely a game of semantics? Or was it in fact more revealing? Further classroom discussion about the meanings students associated with each of those two labels proved very informative. A number of the students associated ethics with chores that were far from captivating. They suggested that ethics were dry, abstract, were suggestive of "don'ts" rather than "do's," and were unrelated to their everyday lives, including their careers. Talk of morality, on the other hand, got the students visibly excited: they recognized the prominence of the term in contemporary public discourse in the United States concerning everything from politics to entertainment; they also commented on the link to religion, values, and deep personal concerns. This single classroom episode said a lot, not only about the students but also about contemporary public discourse. The fact is that morality has come to trump ethics as a label: "(im)moral" has become more rhetorically compelling than "(un)ethical." In our everyday discourse we often consider moral questions without reference to ethics at all. As we will discuss throughout this book, the way we *frame* such issues, broadly speaking, has implications for which issues will be addressed, how salient they will be, and how they will be evaluated (Kellaris, Boyle, & Dahlstrom, 1994).

For us, of course, this classroom discussion is about much more than a preference for one term over another. It reminds us of the importance of *how we talk* about ethics—both with respect to specific issues (such as deception or confidentiality) and in terms of how we *frame* or approach ethics (or professional ethics) in general. That is, what sorts of things do we associate with ethics? Where do we position ethics vis-à-vis other dimensions of our lives? To which domains of activity do our ethical principles apply? When do we "locate" ethics in a distant place that we visit only occasionally, rather than as something integral to our day-to-day lives? In which situations do we call others' attention to ethics? What do we mean when we describe someone else as "an *ethical* person"? What does it mean for an organization or a profession to have *integrity?* How is *trust* central to the effective functioning of the market and, indeed, how does it reflect the health of our economy in general? (On the burgeoning interest in trust research, see Lewis & Einhorn, 2009.) Language, visual imagery, and communication in general are of great importance for ethics, as we will see. Now, let's consider why some people are paying greater attention to the study of ethics at work today, and just how they are talking about it. None of this is to suggest that symbols are everything, or that rhetoric is the whole of reality. Still, we will show how words and images make real practical differences in our pursuit of ethical grounding for a good life.

Appreciating the Power of Language

It is common to dismiss language or even visual images as being superficial, as not the "real stuff": by now, we are used to national political campaigns bombarding us with sound bites and spectacular images; yet, we are just as accustomed to denying their importance. Consumers regularly exhibit this tendency, when they report that *individual* ads don't affect them (*The Ad and the Ego*, 1999). At a certain level, though, we know their belief is false, or at least begs refinement. We can cite an array of examples from politics, business, religion, and other domains of our lives to demonstrate that what we often casually dismiss as "mere rhetoric" instead has powerful practical consequences. We would even reverse the question to this effect: action without talk should be as suspect as talking without action. For instance, as the social critic Slavoj Žižek (2008) observed after the global financial meltdown of October, 2008, it might have been helpful to upend the old adage to this effect: "Don't just do something: talk" rather than adopt quick fixes with little deliberation.

And so, we might ask, Who gets accorded the status of "leader," "hero," "star," "high performer," "visionary," "celebrity," "guru," and the like? In terms of ethics and morality, what practical differences do these word choices make? And why should we be concerned with such labels at all? This is precisely why the debate between the Democratically controlled U.S. Congress and the Republican administration of President Ronald Reagan in the 1980s amounted to far more than word play: to call the opposition forces in Nicaragua "freedom fighters" was to invoke the United States War of Independence and call for support; to term them "rebels" was to tie them implicitly to the losers in the U.S. Civil War and to suggest that they, who in this case called themselves "Contras," were not worthy of outside help. Today's often bitter debate over "undocumented workers," also called "illegal immigrants" or "illegal aliens," in the United States and elsewhere, has a similar dynamic, although the debate is not as clearly divided along party lines. Rather, the debate follows ideological lines: those who want cheap labor prefer "workers"; and those who fear the effect of foreign workers (or stoke fear of them) prefer "illegal aliens."

Ultimately, these and other distinctions are more than merely lexical choices, conscious or not. In everyday conversation and in public discourse, the promotion of one term over another often affects policies, patterns of behavior, and the scope of consideration. For example, consider how certain discussions—say, about new weapons systems—are steered toward technical assessments ("Does it work?") rather than moral ones ("Is it right?"). We can apply the same logic to new business initiatives: too often we ask only "How can we do it?" rather than "Should we do it all?" The global financial crisis that began in late 2007 also yielded the question, "*What*, in the broadest sense of the word, should we be doing?" Our language, our symbols, set up screens through which we view the world: some aspects of the world are inevitably featured, while others recede or are obscured from view (Burke, 1966). Words can alternately narrow or broaden our vision, just as optical lenses can do. Above all, the selection of one label, one category, over another implicates choice and thus is as much a matter of ethics as it is of fact. So it is with apparently technical terms, such as "efficiency," as it is with obviously value-oriented terms, such as "trust."

Engaging in Conversations about Ethics

When we move from the possibilities of language to the idea of *conversations* about ethics we can hear more clearly the ways we discuss ethics—or fail to—in various settings and at various levels. When we hear the word "conversation," we usually think of people talking one-on-one and face-to-face. And this is definitely one of the situations in which discussions of ethics are important. Think of cases where we consult with a family member, colleague, or friend about "the right thing to do." But, we also think about what might be called the larger conversation of ethics: not only about specific decisions but also about the role of ethics in our society. In the case of the popular television program *The Apprentice*, for instance, the lessons about ethics are not restricted to the specific decisions that characters or contestants make but also include how the program, as an entire set of messages, frames professional ethics as "just business." This is just one example in which the culture of ethics can be seen to extend far beyond the experience of individuals, groups, or organizations to point out the need to look for ethics in unusual places.

One of our purposes in writing this book is to promote such wide-ranging conversations about ethics, but to do so in a way that avoids as much as possible a rigid, formal treatment of ethical theories. Still, theory cannot be avoided altogether, as it inevitably informs our understandings of ethics, even when we don't notice it. Thus, as we engage theory, we consider not only the key concepts of various approaches but also how ethical commitments are understood from each perspective. In this way, it is helpful to revisit ethical theories and to connect them with folk or everyday ideas of ethical practice. For instance, we call for a revival of Aristotle's concept of *eudaimonia*, or flourishing, which brings together common notions of happiness with the idea of living a deeply good life: what philosopher Robert

Solomon (e.g., 1999) liked to call "A Good Life" rather than "The Good Life." As we will show, the revival of virtue ethics and the pursuit of *eudaimonia* are as valuable to the average worker, professional, executive, and consumer as to philosophers who spend time probing the value of such principles.

In terms of our work lives, we often speak of the importance of "being professional." At the same time, we recognize that many kinds of work and workers become invisible when we focus our attention on just those who typically *count* as professionals. Here, work is formalized in terms of codes, rules, and regulations. However, these guidelines are negotiated in practice and where they may or may not have traction. There are, for example, clear laws for modern war in the United Nations' charter, and in the "quaint" Geneva Convention (as Roberto Gonzales characterized it in a 2002 memo [see, e.g., BBC News, 2004] before he became the U.S. attorney general). The U.S. armed forces also have specific rules of engagement that dictate the circumstances under which military personnel may use lethal force. Yet one U.S. Marine has admitted to ordering his troops to "shoot first and ask questions later" in an assault in Haditha, Iraq, in 2005 ("Military Subpoenas," 2008). This retaliatory assault resulted in twenty-four noncombatant deaths. As experience shows us, rules in practice often diverge from rules on paper.

When we talk about "professional" in this book, we use that term self-consciously and critically, calling attention to how our society selects experts and how people aspire to, earn, or claim that label. We recognize that many kinds of work are not widely considered to be professional, and we are conscious of the status and class implications of the term. But we are not trying to perpetuate a strict division between, for example, "laborers" and "knowledge workers" because we believe both terms are sometimes misused. "Occupation" is another term we might use, as it is used in sociology, but this term is not as suggestive of questions of lifestyle, social pressures, and one's place in society—all of which we address in this book. In other words, we seek to probe intensively the meaning of professional*ism* in today's world, while bringing into full view the range of activities people do as work. Titles themselves are persuasive. People lean on one title or another according to the rhetorical and practical demands of a situation; they may use titles to avoid the appearance of a conflict of interest; and they invoke position to enhance authority and to foster a sense of mystery. Part of the "professionalization" of many lines of work is the upgrading of titles, but that can obscure as much as clarify what people actually do.

We are also concerned with the conversations on ethics found in everyday news, popular culture, and in our many dealings with one another on the street and outside of formal institutions. For instance, in a time of economic downturn, how do family, friends, neighbors, and colleagues talk about job loss? What do we say about ourselves when such misfortune strikes? "I wanted to stay home to take care of my kids." "I needed a change." "I'm between successes." "Work is overrated." "That company sucked, anyway." Also, what do these labels and stories say about how we view people and work (Hoffman, 2008)? In these and other instances, we engage in the process of crafting *accounts*, or specific narratives to explain ourselves (Scott & Lyman, 1968), especially when our judgment and actions are in question (as in the violation of a professional norm). When challenged about why we do things, we need to have excuses, which do not try to support the action; or we make justifications, which assert the value of the action. The same is true for institutions, as we saw in the hunt for culprits after the stock market crash of October 2008: "Who's to blame, and what did they do wrong?"

The ways we talk about our goals, as individuals, as communities of professionals, and as a society are important here—and not only as *individual* choices. The stories we tell about ourselves, our successes, our challenges, and our failures contribute to culture just as much as they reflect it. There's a fable that demonstrates the power of the stories we craft: A wealthy U.S. businessman takes a vacation in a small Mexican village on the coast. There, he sees a fisherman. The businessman watches this fisherman catch a few fish—enough for his family and a few extra to sell—noticing that the fisherman ends the day fairly early. The businessman approaches the fisherman and asks him what he loves about his work. The fisherman says he loves his contemplative time on the sea, the good food, and time with his family. The businessman asks the fisherman, "Why don't you have any ambition? You could work more hours each day, earn extra money, reinvest in your boat and tools, hire help, and, with luck, eventually manage a whole fleet of vessels. You could be rich; you could retire early!" The fisherman squints and replies, "But what would I do in my retirement?" The businessman replies, "Well, you could go fishing and have contemplative time on your boat, enjoy good food, and be with your family!"

As the parable of the fisherman and the businessman suggests, definitions of success vary widely at the individual level; so how can we begin to define success when abstracted to the level of a community, a nation, or a people? One question that probes how we define success at the collective level is, What do we mean when we say, "What's good for business is good for America—and its citizens"? A half-century ago, the American environmental writer Aldo Leopold (1949/1968) challenged that assertion: "Our bigger-and-better society is now like a hypochondriac, so obsessed with its own economic health as to have lost the capacity to remain healthy" (p. ix). Few businesses, professional associations, and policy makers take the time needed to reflect on the wider context for what they are doing. But, as writers across disciplines are emphasizing today, the deceptively simple idea of happiness is profoundly relevant to the ways people work and who they are, and become, at work (Cheney et al., 2008).

For us, addressing such questions is at the heart of ethics. All too often, we think of ethics as something linked with the rightness or wrongness of individual actions, rather than as connected to more holistic notions of personal and social well-being. So, above all, in this book we want to bring ethics out of the box in which we often find it and integrate its study and practice into a wide array of discussions and settings. These conversations about ethics and professional life are not new, but we wish to contribute something new to them. Ultimately, the discussion of professional ethics is not just for the classroom, the boardroom, or even the courtroom but also for the wider ways in which we conduct our lives and find meaning in the pursuits that command our passion, attention, and commitment.

How Did We Come to This Project?

George

George's specialty within the field of communication is the study of organizations—not only businesses but also governmental organizations, nonprofits, religious institutions, schools, and social movement groups. Over the course of his career, George has taught and researched topics such as identity, power, employee participation, consumerism, globalization, peace, and ethics. Ethics has been a strong interest throughout, and George has been teaching courses on communication and professional ethics since 1994.

When he first began teaching and writing about ethics, George took a largely traditional, deductive approach to the subject. Thus, in a semester-long undergraduate course, he would begin with major Western ethical theories (from Aristotle and Kant to Rawls and Nussbaum); next, the class would move into domains of application (such as interpersonal relationships at work or corporate policy on proprietary rights); finally, the discussion would move into contemporary cases and issues. While this approach was fine for graduate students, it left about four-fifths of the undergraduates behind and unmotivated to engage the material (or the rest of the semester). At the same time, this traditional course structure perpetuated an unnecessary bifurcation between academic material and discussions and popular material and discussions. This division didn't serve either the instructor or the students very well, and it left the impression that the scholarly treatments of ethics weren't relevant to "real life"— hardly the message George or any other teacher wants to convey.

Gradually, George adapted his course structure and content: mainly, by beginning with contemporary cases and issues, then by using those student-centered discussions to tease out theoretical points, allowing for a process of group discovery. Along the way, students actually became interested in what the theory of act utilitarianism had to say on a particular issue, such as the uses of wartime tribunals. Consistent with this course philosophy, George began to interweave readings from the news, popular culture, professional books, and academic research. This move allowed the class to see what role each genre of writing plays in a larger discussion and then to make informed comparisons between various treatments of the same issue, be it governmental deception or Internet privacy.

One more change occurred in the development of George's course that has a direct bearing on the present book: he introduced broad discussions of the framing of ethics and, by extension, encouraged students to examine the key, value-related symbols of our society. Students gravitated toward considering questions such as, When do we, in the course of our work, invoke the issue of ethics? What does it mean that practically every formal organization today has a code of ethics, a statement of values, and a mission statement? Why do we pay attention to certain ethical questions (e.g., corporate accounting scandals) or applications while ignoring others (e.g., possible limits on CEO compensation)? When does the talk of "corporate social responsibility" become so common as to become virtually meaningless?

Interestingly, these "meta" discussions led naturally into questions about the meaning of career, success, productivity, consumerism, and efficiency, that is, to some of the sacred symbols (or "god-terms") of contemporary U.S. society. These conversations prompted students to consider that some of the things they take for granted, such as the notion of a career as portable and as detached from others as a briefcase, have not always been seen that way. Nor was a particular framing of the matter inevitable. Students began writing reaction papers that probed deeply into the meanings of these master symbols and their applications to individuals and society. They recognized that a symbol as powerful as "success" is truly ambiguous, should both be explored historically and be evaluated in the moment, and ought to be defined with respect to cultural context. In truth, then, the idea for a more integrative treatment of professional ethics, via communication, came as much from George's students as from the research and his own reflections.

Dan

Dan came to the study of ethics, communication, and their relationship to work identity in the process of trying to make sense of his brief experience in the corporate world. After graduating from college, Dan, like many new graduates, worked a string of unrelated jobs while he tried (not always diligently) to answer the question, "What do I want to do with my life?" After several years working as a concrete-construction laborer, a college debate coach, and a bookseller at a large chain, Dan took a job as a marketing representative in the employee assistance program division of a regional managed-care corporation. Dan had never viewed himself as the corporate type but took the job because it because it provided well-paying, seemingly stable work in his hometown, where such opportunities were rare. For the first few months, everything was great. Dan found the work challenging and even began subtly but quickly adopting an increasingly corporate outlook.

All of that changed one October afternoon in 1999. With nearly all of the company's 250-plus employees called into the conference rooms of branch offices in several states, the company founders, who had tried to establish a "family feel" throughout the company's nearly twenty-year history, announced their decision to sell the company to a large corporation on the East Coast. In that conference call, the founders reassured everyone that this merger was a great opportunity not just for the company but for all of its employees. Within a month, however, an entire department had been eliminated. Dan was troubled by the ethical issues involved, but because he was in marketing, had to put on a positive face when representing the merger to the company's clients. Still, he saw the irony of the situation: a company that had made its money marketing the importance of employee well-being was deceiving its own employees.

Dan continued to work there for several months, witnessing a steady string of firings, despite the company repeatedly reassuring everyone that they should not fear for their jobs. One January morning, it was Dan's turn. The months after downsizing were particularly difficult, and Dan went through a period of depression. The next fall, he enrolled in graduate school, initially planning on working toward developing his own consultancy using his marketing contacts. But his studies quickly turned toward making sense of his brief corporate experience: Why had he been so emotionally affected by a job that he had worked for less than a year and that had never really touched him in the first place? How could his worldview and personality have shifted in such a short time and to such a degree that many of his friends later remarked (and not positively) on how the job seemed to have changed him? Why had he fallen so easily into a pattern of working seventy to eighty hour weeks, often without ever being asked to do so by his superiors, leaving him little time to do things he enjoyed, such as hiking, spending time with friends, or reading good books? In many ways, these questions have been at the heart of Dan's academic interests ever since, and they speak to ethics' relevance to broader questions of work and identity. It is here that rhetoric and ethics intersect in a manner that not only helps us understand how our work (and, specifically, professional) identities are formed but also helps us open up a desperately needed space for critical reflection on such issues, as well.

Dean

Dean's interest in ethics and communication arose from his working in the business world, particularly in Silicon Valley in the heady 1980s and 1990s. During that period the Valley culture was defined by both a drive to change the world with "insanely great products" (an enduring advertising blurb of Apple Computer) and a desire to generate large amounts of private wealth for shareholders and for employees. He noticed that products and wealth were considered ends in themselves and seemingly devoid of ethical dimensions. As he moved up the professional ladder, Dean observed that ethical considerations became even less noticeable, almost unpleasant topics of conversation. Silicon Valley's tremendous capital and human resources were (and remain) largely directed by the doctrine of Milton Friedman (1970), which stated that "the social responsibility of business is to increase its profits"—a narrow view, considering technology's awesome social impact. Personal computers, the Internet, biotechnology, the automobile, even the invention of the corporation—all have made transformative effects on the lives of billions of people. But two ethical questions arise when we consider technology and its implications. First, is radical social impact intended? Second, should those persons funding and creating these technologies be concerned with the implications of "insanely great products"? Except for high technology's few visionaries, those immersed in Valley culture promoted a limited view of professional actions and social consequences. Adam Smith's "invisible hand" and Voltaire's *Candide* ("This is the best of all possible worlds") were assumed to be culturally sufficient answers to inquiries about consequences.

Seeking to understand the apparent lack of connection between professional actions and social implications, Dean pursued a graduate degree in philosophy, emphasizing ethics. His pursuit of theoretical knowledge of ethics raised numerous questions concerning ethics, business, the professional life, and the law. What is the appropriate scope of a business decision and what distinguishes it from an inappropriately narrow perspective—for example, in terms of how wide a circle of stakeholders is brought into view? How do people explain (justify or excuse) certain behaviors at work with ethical principles they would reject in their personal lives? How can an organization truly promote ethics in the workplace? Enron, for instance, had an ethics officer, but that obviously had little effect (see D. Conrad, 2003). How does the language of the global economy and the market describe or imply an ethical system? Why are the ethics of the global economy not openly examined until there's a crisis?

Rhetoric was central to Dean's subsequent work producing ethics-focused pieces for radio and teaching workshops on rights-based political organizing. In this latter work the students, many of whom were involved in local conflicts concerning a "corporate assault" upon their community's environmental health and economic welfare, struggled with the language to express the problem. They found themselves needing to write book-length critiques of a proposed public policy (e.g., regarding zoning or land use). Meanwhile, defenders of those policies used well-known but loose concepts like "free market," "freedom," "democracy," and "property rights." In these cases, language directly affected community health and welfare because it led to certain policy conclusions and thus to certain tangible actions. The language of zoning and land-use processes thus "permitted" corporations the freedom to do what, in some cases, the majority of local citizens opposed. Once again, language matters: here it involves words that permit people to rationalize actions that are unquestionably destructive to the interest of specific others. On the other hand, we can use communication analysis to understand and invoke personal and social change. A critical awareness of language affords us the structure to bring into our workplace an ethical maturity that we would also be proud to take home.

Brenden

As a high school student, Brenden wanted to be a physician. He was fascinated by human anatomy and health issues. Also, he knew that medicine offered him a reliable, high-paying profession. His mother is a registered nurse and, now, a professor of nursing. He once asked her to summarize the difference between a doctor and a nurse. She paused and then said, "Well, I became a nurse partly because the conventional wisdom when I was getting my degree was that doctors treated *diseases* and nurses treated *patients.*"

Brenden didn't end up in the medical field. Instead, he majored in communication studies at the University of Montana. He complemented his studies in organizational communication with courses in the business school. One of those courses, Business and Society, explored the relationship between business organizations and social concerns. In one class session students were asked to imagine an "ideal business environment." The exercise revealed assumptions about who *is* and who *is not* a legitimate stakeholder. However, Brenden's group got a little off track—chatting about who liked the class, who disliked the professor, and so on. One of the group members sighed and said, "I just don't like her [the professor] shoving her *opinion* into the class. I mean, I'm here to learn *business.*" The student meant that discussions about right or just action were not appropriate in a business curriculum. This struck Brenden as odd. Stranger still was that each of his peers in the group nodded in agreement.

It's that sort of talk and thinking about society that continues to catch Brenden's interest. How do we deal with real people in our conversations and at work? What is that motivates us to obscure humanity in questions of ethics? Moreover, are there really conditions—such as, say, "business"—where responses are *just* an opinion? As a doctoral student, Brenden conducted several research projects, including two empirical studies that addressed those sorts of questions. One project examined how an office in a large university advocated for environmental change and structural transformation across the entire institution. Another project was designed to assist a nonprofit foundation in rural Utah that had initiated an alternative-currency program. Each of these endeavors represents his challenge to "business as usual" thinking. Brenden continues to ask, How might we think critically about our own perspectives, motivate just action, and enable personal and social transformation? This book is one response.

What Are We Trying to Accomplish?

Heightening Critical Awareness

Our first goal for the reader, as for students, is to heighten critical awareness. We do not mean that anyone will necessarily arrive at a particular ethical decision at the end of reading this book. Instead, we seek to move beyond taken-for-granted ways of thinking about ethics, considering them not only in abstract terms but as a way of life. For instance, when we probe the term *professionalism*, we find that this word also has negative connotations constraining behavior and, in some cases, preventing people from expressing moral outrage or exuberant support. "Acting like a professional" can therefore be code for not "rocking the boat" or not being fully human. Most of the time, these less attractive sides of professionalism go unnoticed, and so do their important implications for ethics. We can ask similar questions about other popular terms: "entrepreneur," "consumer," "knowledge worker," "wealth manager," and so on.

Getting Ethics out of the Closet

Our integrative perspective on ethics challenges the ways the subject has been contained in both everyday practice and in academic writings. On the street, ethics is usually treated as something to which one must *resort* to pressure others toward legal compliance or to claim the moral high ground. In this respect, the breakdown of trust—say, in a case of embezzlement within a university budget office—is seen as a problem to correct with closer oversight and more rigorous accounting procedures. On a good day, we see ethics as relevant to our relationships with family, friends, and close colleagues but perhaps not so much in the dog-eat-dog world that surrounds them. In the academic universe, especially in textbooks, ethics is presented almost as an afterthought, as the final chapter that "we'll get to if we have time at the end of the semester." In both academe and the so-called "real world," ethics is set aside as something to be dealt with only occasionally rather than as something central to the way we work and act in and on the world. We want to bring our everyday ethics into full view and to offer some useful tools for examining the ways we *do* ethics even we don't always realize it. For example, how do we regularly talk about people in their various roles at work as resources, competitors, collaborators, instruments of policy, stars, losers, and so on. Labels for people and roles have their implications in terms of *value*. So, how are we talking about ethics, at least implicitly, even when we think we're doing something else?

Ultimately, we hope that the reader will begin to notice ethics lurking in all sorts of news stories, bits of popular culture, and everyday interactions. *That is, we aim to show where ethics are and always have been in our lives, especially in our professional and other work activities.* This kind of shift in vision is important not just in the consumption of the messages surrounding us but also in helping realize one's own goals when faced with an array of choices about how to live a good life.

Inspiration over Regulation

As we already mentioned, every large organization and a lot of small ones have codes of ethics, and value or mission statements. These sorts of documents and messages are required if the organization wants to be part of "the crowd." Occasionally, the efforts to produce these documents are grounded in what grassroots participants— employees or members—think. More often than not, however, the codes or statements come from the top and either are a response to some crisis or challenge (perhaps legal) or are driven by concern for marketing or public relations. In such cases, the statements are often unrelated to members' daily concerns and are quite vague. When codes are specific, they usually have a strong regulatory and legalistic tone. Most ethical codes are oriented toward encouraging compliance with regulations far more than they are with elevating behavior. The U.S. Securities and Exchange Commission (SEC) announcement that it would enforcement Section 406 of the Sarbanes-Oxley Act of 2002 provides an interesting example at the "meta level" (U.S. SEC, 2003). Interestingly, the rule explicitly states that companies filing with the SEC must indicate if they have a formal code of ethics and are required to explain if they do not have one. However, they are not required to describe the ethics codes already in place. Their utility is simply taken for granted and not reexamined, per the law and an accompanying sense of compliance. In some ways, the *tone* of such documents provides an example for companies that have yet to construct codes of ethics: inspiration is missing from nearly all such documents, as are examples of outstanding ethical performance.

The larger society also has a hard time understanding ethics and what it means to be a virtuous person, let alone a virtuous corporation. Of course, we're not at all sure what it would mean for an organization to have a conscience. We identify certain paragons of virtue (e.g., in politics, sports, business, religion, or charity), who often fall from grace later. The revelation in 2008 of New York governor Eliot Spitzer's simultaneous solicitation and prosecution of prostitution is a good example of a recurring contradiction. Before the revelation of his transgressions, and his subsequent resignation, Spitzer had been called an ethics/ethical "enforcer," even a "crusader" (see, e.g., Ignatius, 2002; Tumulty, 2002). The stories we tell of the rise and fall of such people also serve to confirm an already cynical view of the world and to make goodness seem quaint, passé, naive, or simply unattainable. Consequently, we miss out on other ways to think and talk about virtue, happiness, and success and a good life.

Personally, we find that ethics is as enabling as it is constraining. As Aristotle (2002) observed, we are much more likely to achieve a visible end than an invisible one. Sheet music provides that structural end for musicians. Musical notations are technical instructions only. It is left to the musician to convert the notations into music, combining the wisdom and guidance of the composer, with his or her own technical skill, knowledge of musical styles, and expressiveness. Still, the end is visible in the beginning of that process. Reflection and conversation about the ethical dimensions of work (and life) can likewise guide professionals. By making ethics visible and legible, we begin to see that they are neither removed from life nor unrealistic. What *is* unrealistic is to ignore ethics, as when people claim that ethical discussions are secondary to the "progress of science" when it seeks to use biotechnology and bioengineering to create new life forms and genetically targeted "biological agents." So, are the origins of life and the creation of genetic weapons merely technical matters? We don't think so. It's above all a challenge to our notions of who we are, why we are here, what we are doing, and where we are going.

To answer these big questions, it is helpful to turn to Aristotle, who theorized that all actions are directed toward ends, even when they are not stated. For him, *eudaimonia*, traditionally understood as happiness, is the one good of human activity done for its own sake, not as a means to anything else. This concept, central to our arguments, is the ultimate good, directing our attention toward understanding how we flourish together with the world. We would be pleased if this book makes, for you, even a small contribution to that end.

Toward that end, we will explore all types of messages for the ways they can influence our understanding of ethics in the professional realm. Our point is neither to suggest that ethics is, at the bottom, *nothing but communication,* nor to suggest that our usual ways of speaking about ethics are entirely without merit. Rather, we point to the ways in which our everyday talk about ethics shapes our understanding of ethics itself. We do this hoping to encourage a fuller vision of ethics not as a space reluctantly entered when we encounter difficult dilemmas but rather as a perspective informing the totality of our professional and personal lives.

Chapter 1 explores the ways that we have limited our own understanding and application of ethics at work through the ways we commonly talk about it. The chapter begins by arguing that the ways we frame ethics are as important, and sometimes more so, than the specific ethical decisions we make. The chapter explains how a perspective on ethics grounded in communication and rhetoric can illuminate certain ways in which we unnecessarily restrain the influence of ethics at work. The chapter makes the case for examining popular culture and everyday talk, including aphorisms, for clues to the ways ethics is treated in our professional lives. Turning the maxim "talk is cheap" on its head, the chapter urges a serious consideration of what it means to say, for example, that one's work is "just a job" or "let the market decide." Thus, the reader is urged to find ethical implications in diverse messages and cases, ranging from codes and handbooks, to television shows and ads on websites, to everyday conversation, including sayings that become part of who we are.

Chapter 2 deeply explores how our common ways of speaking about ethics distract us from a more integrative vision of ethics in our lives. The chapter introduces three problems with the common ways we approach ethics, as revealed in our language: *compartmentalization,* or putting ethics in a box; *essentialization,* or trying to reduce or crystallize ethics in terms of one thing or simple answers; and *abstraction,* or creating distance (or alienation) between ethical concerns and everyday practices. The chapter then explains seven dimensions that cut across various understandings of ethics, in order to illustrate just what we mean by ethics when we speak about it in various contexts. These dimensions are agency and autonomy, discrimination and choice, motive and purpose, responsibility and relationship, rationality and emotionality, role and identity, and scene and situation. Along the way, we invoke traditional ethical theories to show how they tend to emphasize certain features over others. We conclude by arguing how Aristotle's idea of *eudaimonia* helps unite reframed notions of virtue and our most cherished life goals.

In the chapters that follow we explore how we communicate about ethics across several domains.

Chapter 3 addresses work as an important domain of ethical talk. The chapter argues that work and the talk about it are unavoidably ethical in nature and considers the multiple ways work is meaningful for people and the various roles it plays in their lives, taking into account historical and cross-cultural variations. Especially important in this regard are the ways "work" and "life" are commonly separated—but sometimes united—in contemporary (post)industrial society. How work is bounded and framed in everyday thought and talk has enormous implications for the ethical possibilities that any person, in any job, will see. We describe various ethical frames that apply to work, and their practical implications for making ethics more visible in everyday (work) life.

Chapter 4 addresses the domain of the professional, taking seriously the notion that the professional *is* personal—and social, political, and ethical. We trace the development of modern professional classes, particularly as they affect individual and collective moral practice. In certain ways, formal professions have the capacity to elevate moral practice and create barriers to ethical visions. We next consider the multiple sides of professional life, take a second look at the ethical claims associated with professionalism, and expose some of the problems with what we usually think of as an unmitigated positive force in society, that is, professionalism. As part of this evaluation, the chapter probes issues of professional style and categories for individuals and whole segments of society. We conclude the chapter with a call to reconsider the meaning of "career."

Chapter 5 focuses on the modern organization, showing how organizational culture shapes and sustains integrity (or doesn't). This chapter examines a unit of life experience that is taken for granted yet little understood. Considering a number of root metaphors for the organization, such as machine, organism, person, and family, we can see how ethics are cast in each case. The chapter reviews how organizations typically engage ethics, considering codes of ethics, ethics officers, and the movement toward corporate social responsibility, finding all of them valuable yet limited in scope. We then advance a wider perspective on virtue and culture in organizational life by showing how ethics can be woven into the totality of messages and interactions in an organization.

Chapter 6 focuses on ethics at the level of the market. There we argue that contrary to popular wisdom, the market is not amoral. Today the modern market is presumed to be both inherently good—the best way to do business and organize society—and yet amoral in terms of excluding or deferring ethical judgments. The chapter includes a detailed discussion of the meanings of the market in everyday talk and gives some historical and contemporary cases in which the presumed "super-agency" of the market leads people and societies astray. Also, we review relevant research on happiness, especially as it bears on the conceptions of economic productivity and success. The chapter concludes with a consideration of ethical reform in the market by making visible what is meant by "the market": how do we act with it, through it, and for it?

Chapter 7 returns to questions of happiness, *eudaimonia*, virtue, and the reframing of ethics in work and life, reviewing key points of previous chapters and explaining the value of looking beyond specific ethical decisions to the very ways ethics are typically approached and framed. Ethics, we learn, are relevant even in instances that are not readily identified as requiring ethical decisions. Our central argument is that, rather than thinking about ethics *as* work, as something over and above everyday work life, professionals would do well to embrace ethics as relevant to all their everyday practices. Ironically, as ethics becomes ordinary, applying it can lead to greater happiness. We turn to several contemporary cases to illustrate a new, non-heroic framing of virtue at work. This is where a revived and revised theory of "virtue ethics" can enhance conversation about ethics, especially now, when we are profoundly questioning how we do business.

1

(Re)Framing Ethics
at Work

Encounters with stories or people, in everyday life and in the imagination of drama, are sites for dialogue through which we can become clearer about the ethical views we or others already hold and through which our ethical positions can change.... [E]thical views are a facet of all the language and thought we use and encounter daily. (Edminston, 2000, p. 64)

"It's Just a Job" and Other Ways of Framing Work

"It's just a job" belongs to a family of sayings we use to talk about work, jobs, careers, productivity, money, and success. The first time George really noticed this saying, he was conducting his master's thesis research at a TRW plant in Lafayette, Indiana, in 1981–82 (Cheney, 1982). The Lafayette division produced truck engine parts. George's study focused on the link between workers' identification with the organization (e.g., "I have warm feelings toward this organization") and their day-to-day decision-making (i.e., what goals groups consider as they do their work). If a person really cares about the organization and what it stands for, perhaps investing a part of him or herself beyond the normal requirements of the job, the person will also *see* decisions in terms of what's best for the company. In other words, the "we" grows bigger in both the mind and the talk of the employee, and the employee becomes an increasingly trustworthy member of the group. This idea was posited by the Nobel laureate Herbert A. Simon (1997) in his landmark book *Administrative Behavior*, but the theory is more complex than that. For instance, one may still seek to identify with an employing organization long after it is psychologically satisfying to do so simply because of the powerful need to belong or because of past or imagined experiences with work (see, e.g., Patchen, 1970; Baumeister & Leary, 1995). In fact, one may identify with an organization or institution even when it departs from its initial goals or activities. Also, one may identify with an organization precisely because a negative attribute or behavior is what creates both camaraderie and common purpose (as with the immensely successful Alcoholics Anonymous; see J. Hedges, 2008). In yet another type of situation, people may identify with an organization as they remember it from their past association, regardless of its current situation. Given these bonds it's hard to admit that something in which we are deeply invested, both psychologically and economically, is on a path toward doing harm. This may partially explain the widespread failure of those in the know to blow the whistle on unethical organizational practices, such as accounting fraud in the early twenty-first century. So, loyalty and habit can be as influential as the desire for personal gain.

More broadly, the simple phrase "It's just a job" offers a taking-off point for a discussion of the role of ethics at work. We can see how the saying tends to divorce work from ethics just as it divorces work from meaning. On the one hand, this kind of containment protects the self from being overwhelmed by work. But such compartmentalization also prevents one from fully examining how the meanings of work, and the meanings constructed by individuals and organizations at work, can be tied to our personal aspirations. Further considering the impact of the phrase, if all of an organization's activities can be framed as "just" jobs, what difference does it make if the work of the organization is aimed at social betterment or not? A related form of devaluation can occur with children's activities, domestic labor, volunteer work, and so on, when we say that these are not "real jobs," that they aren't the tasks that run society (see Clair, 1996). "It's just a job" easily slides into "It's just business," which insulates work activity from ethical examination, and from responsibility. Then, we're back to "the market made me do it," which is tantamount to saying "the devil [boss, system, pressure, etc.] made me do it." Such rationalizations become a shield for an entire organization or industry. "It's just a job" and "It's just business" is followed by "The market made us do it" to logically conclude with "We're not responsible."

In contrast to cherished social bonds, one's work—and by extension, one's relationship with the organization—is often characterized as "just a job." In George's thesis project, he heard employees using that phrase for several reasons, emotional and practical. Some employees sounded rather matter of fact when explaining that their work had a clearly bounded and limited role in their lives, or at least in their sense of self. Others almost dismissed their work, taking pains to minimize its importance in their lives. In this latter case, it was almost as if they felt the need to assert that the job and the company didn't matter to them (i.e., "Please don't mistake me for someone who gives a damn!"). In still other cases, it seemed that interviewees were repeating something they heard from their peers, that putting the work "in its place" was the socially acceptable thing to do, lest they look like or become "company men or company women," or the much-maligned (and easily targeted) Organization Man of the 1950s (Whyte, 1956) or the One-Dimensional Man of the 1960s (Marcuse, 1964). Being conscious of the ways conformity can be either intentionally or unintentionally adopted helps us bring to the fore assumptions about what we do at work. Thus, the deceptively simple phrase "just a job" serves to articulate and reinforce a narrow vision of work's meaning.

Ethical Talk Isn't Cheap!

We're suggesting that ethics is both about ways of being and principles guiding moral behavior. If this is the case, though, isn't communication merely a secondary consideration? After all, if virtues are demonstrated or proven by action, isn't their *expression* mere ethical *discussion* rather than "the real stuff"? More broadly, shouldn't philosophy, which centers on principles, be privileged over rhetoric, which is mostly about pretty, seductive language or "spin"? As should be clear from the introduction and the examples that opened this chapter, we believe that talk about ethics is important in itself. Talk is not cheap; in fact, when we frame ethical values, issues, and goals too narrowly, we pay dearly, individually and collectively. For example, when we frame the subject of technology as "morally neutral," we are unlikely to notice how technology actually removes us from the idea of choice. For example, a search for new employment may involve little or no human interaction; email and online forms have replaced person-to-person communication, and software is used to "read" résumés, filtering out applicants who failed to satisfy certain keyword searches (Tugend, 2008). This process distances job applicants from potentially engaging conversations about work history, character, and the potential fit between the applicant and the organization. Framing a technology as morally neutral may speed us toward that moral conclusion, but the frame is not the picture: language is being used in such cases to obfuscate what we could and should know.

Talk about Work Really Matters

While it is easy to fall into the belief that organizations consist of mere bricks and mortar, industrial and electronic technologies, and even people, these images fail to come to grips with the fact that the lifeblood of any organization is *communication* (Hawes, 1974). The elusive idea of an organization is most easily attached to something immediately tangible; thus, we think of the university as the campus, the company as its offices, or the government agency as its personnel. Often we take the emphasis on "the person" so seriously that we see the organization *embodied* as a person (Christensen, Morsing, & Cheney, 2007), particularly in the legal creation of "the corporate person" (Ritz, 2007). This stress on *organizations as people* is both true and misleading. It's accurate in that personnel are terribly important. What's more, many organizations subscribe to an ethos or even promotes a personality based on the qualities of their leaders.

On the other hand, as Chester Barnard (1968), the CEO of New Jersey Bell in the 1930s, explained so well, by focusing on these tangibles, we miss the shape and dynamics of the organization as "a system of consciously coordinated activities or forces of two or more persons" (p. 72). The shift is not merely conceptual; nor should it be dismissed as word play. To understand the organization as a network of symbols, messages, interactions, and discourses is to realize how it is that individuals enter a stream of discussion, contribute to it, and ultimately step out of it. This is one way of getting beyond the image of an organization as something relatively static, like a machine, a pyramid, or even a body. However influential or authoritative any of us are, we never weave an organizational *culture* out of nothing; the fabric has its threads, its warp and woof. For now, though, we wish to stress that how people talk to one another at work is not something "added on" to the organization; in a very real sense, communication *is* the organization (Hawes, 1974). Talk in itself accomplishes things; although we regularly complain about meetings being "unproductive," what we really mean is that they're inefficient.

Of course, as mentioned in the introduction, we have a strong cultural preference for action over talk. At the same time, however, we know that this is a false dichotomy and that speaking is, in fact, a kind of action. Language *is* action, from the *performative* power of speech acts (Austin, 1975) such as the "fighting words" considered the equivalent of a physical provocation (see *Chaplinsky v. State of New Hampshire*, 315 U.S. 568 [1942]), the delivery of a verdict, or the pronunciation of "husband and wife" at the end of a wedding ceremony. Here, the action of talk is direct, but there's a more diffuse sense in which talk is seen as action. After all, the colloquialism "sticks and stones" is meant actually to deflect our attention from the power that words have to hurt us. Our symbols, messages, relationships, and networks have ethical and moral implications. To declare a part of the organization "dead wood," or to pronounce something "urgent," is to privilege one activity or person over another, to create a hierarchy of value, to suggest policy. Let's delve into this claim and consider how our professional ethics are implied by what we say.

What We Say about Ethics Makes Visible Our Professional Ethics

The contained view of ethics asserts that words matter only when we say they do. This is what literary and rhetorical critic Kenneth Burke (1950/1969) calls "word magic." We conjure the spirit of an idea and all its connections (or implications) when we name it. For example, talking about "democracy" heightens our awareness of issues of voting, citizen participation, and the distribution of political power. In this way, it's more than merely psychologically revealing to ask people about what they associate with particular terms. "Democracy" evokes all sorts of patriotic sentiments for many U.S. citizens, and simplistic notions of an unbroken lineage from ancient Athens to the contemporary United States (for much more on this point, see Sen, 2006). This is just one example of a value-laden and polysemous term evoking a rich and diverse set of meanings (See George Orwell's 1946 essay "Politics and the English Language," reprinted in Orwell, 1970). We could perform the same "word magic" exercise with "justice," "freedom," "equality," and so forth.

These are some of the value terms that dominate the national political culture of the United States and, indeed, that of many other nations. But organizations and professions have their own "god terms" as well; these include "excellence," "efficiency," "growth," "innovation," "entrepreneurship," "quality," and "change." While we typically think of these terms descriptively, we also should recognize their ethical implications. The strategic (or even mindless) uses of these terms are important examples where ethical judgments are communicated by framing. Consider, for example, contemporary uses of the term "entrepreneurship." In both management and academic circles, there is a lot of buzz these days about the implications for leadership that accompany the label "entrepreneur." Yet, there are certain gender, class, and even racial biases, when you consider the image most often promoted by the term and the examples frequently held up for emulation. The entrepreneur is innovative, ambitious, and willing to take risk; sees and capitalizes on opportunities; and is therefore an exceptional economic figure set apart from employees and even from small business owners. Speaking of entrepreneurship and calling oneself an entrepreneur invokes a whole set of contestable assumptions, in addition to preferences for certain right or appropriate behaviors and personal characteristics (Gill, forthcoming).

We tend to talk about ethics at work only in moments reserved for such conversation. These are times when ethics become explicit as when we *mention* ethics because the law requires it; speaking about ethics in this case is, ironically, a matter of compliance rather an ethical aspiration. At other moments, we raise ethical issues out of a profound concern; for example, we might urge our colleagues or coworkers to think about matters of value that we feel are being neglected. These issues may be connected to notions of respect, dignity, freedom, family, or society. We may call attention to a particular feature (or features) of an ethical system to persuade others to support our position, or to rationalize a particular moral position. In other instances, we use the ethical stance to trump another person's position or to dismiss that person altogether. By putting an (un)ethical or (im)moral frame around part of a discussion, a proposal, or even a colleague, we assert a superior position and try to win the day. So it is that someone might stand up at a meeting and proclaim, "This is the ethical thing to do; we must find the courage to do it. There is no other right course of action." In a strategic sense, making such a proclamation is a lot like saying, "We have to do the rational thing, and that is [my proposal]." Here we find both an emotional and a rational one-upmanship that can slide into a threat, as in, "If we don't do this, we'll be liable (indefensible, subject to condemnation)." But the same kinds of ethical declarations can be used to pacify a crowd or halt discussion, as when a manager insists, "We don't need diversity training here because we are all equal already and everybody knows that" (see Munshi, 2005). Thus, the "warm glow" of the rhetoric of value can be used to short circuit, sidestep, or forestall dialogue over important ethical matters (Sen, 1992).

In our work lives, why does it take a special occasion to think or talk about ethics, to bring it to the larger community? To us, this indicates a process problem. That is, the process should reflexively include an ethical component, but it fails to do so. Rather, it is a disaster resulting from mindless adherence to habits that often leads to the "discovery" of ethics. Ironically, these special ethical occasions serve to further contain ethics. For example, it wasn't until mid-2008, well after the U.S. housing bubble had begun to burst, that the U.S. Federal Reserve Board "put into effect rules barring a lender from making a loan without regard to the borrower's ability to repay it" (Morgenson, 2008, para. 23). Ethics are hauled out for inspection, the process is changed, and our thoughts move on to other things. How might these situations have been different if individuals had reflected on the larger process and streams of discourse, rather than just going along with them? What does the collective accession of "free market" professionals say about *collective* accountability? As we shall see in chapter 4, individual members of a profession have both individual and collective accountability. That is, they owe it to their profession to investigate and improve the profession's practices, and an individual's violation is an affront to the professional community. Are not ethics integral to every job, every profession?

How We Limit Our Ethical Horizons at Work

Our answer, of course, is that they are integrally related but that our ways of speaking about ethics have often prevented us from seeing them as such. When we talk about ethics, we typically cast them as relevant only to particular, passing, and problematic moments in our lives, moments presenting themselves as dilemmas. We can recall the stories we have told about ethics' place in our lives, stories that help us both recognize our encounters with ethics and discover what we ought to do in these encounters.

As we explain more fully later in this chapter, our predominant stories about ethics, particularly in the professional sphere, serve to limit ethics' scope and significance for us by prompting us to take three actions when encountering ethical dilemmas. First, we may *compartmentalize* ethics in our work lives and our professional interactions, holding ourselves to different ethical standards in other spheres of our lives. Second, we may *essentialize* ethics and morality in the embodiment of a person, particular institution, or country, thereby missing the point about how individuals, organizations, or a nation come to be as they are and to act in particular ways. Third and finally, in an effort to order our world both conceptually and practically, we may *abstract* ethical considerations and lose the sense of their relation to our situation and life. What these actions share in common is that they all place strict limitations on ethics' potential, diminishing the range of questions that ethics can ask us. These limitations are particularly powerful in the professional domain.

Now Professionally Speaking...

"Act like a professional" may not be an expression as recognizable as "time is money," but it is a commonly heard imperative, whether one is participating in discussions in boardrooms or observing the training customer-service "specialists" at fast-food restaurants. Still, how often do we reflect on what this command and all it entails mean in practice? As the sociologist Andrew Abbott (1988) explains in *The System of Professions*, the domains of knowledge and expertise that we identify with various professions also imply *social control*—an entire set of prescriptions and constraints that govern that person and through which that person governs others. "Acting professionally" is meant to elevate both one's activities and one's identity, and to place them within parameters that may not always be tied to ideas of human/personal betterment (cf., Cheney & Ashcraft, 2007). Such is the double-edged nature of professionalism that we explore in this book. Professionalism is rightly elevated in our society for the technical and moral standards it sets, yet it also fosters a culture of limiting moral horizons, and making handy justifications and excuses. Lawyers, for example, document agreement using contracts, thereby reducing confusion and conflicts; help citizens exercise their human and legal rights; and establish procedures and standards for the transparent operation of organizations. Why, then, are they often the butt of derisive and cynical jokes?

In Durkheim's fairly optimistic take on professionalism (1964, 1996), he contends that professional standards entail lofty goals, common reference points for practice, and collective responsibility for performance. However, the image of professionalism can become a habitual retreat for those who do not want to engage the question of whether their professional standards *really are serving the wider public*. For instance, can the supposedly objective method of reporting news actually conceal opinion and truth? The *New York Times* financial columnist Gretchen Morgenson, appearing on the September

19, 2008, broadcast of *Bill Moyers Journal*, commented on the present state of the global economy, saying, "This could be the biggest story since the Depression. And, I know that I'm not allowed to say the 'D' word because that makes everybody really afraid" (Moyers, 2008). Her informed opinion is opinion, and her subscription to journalistic standards of reporting to her suggests modesty in expressing it. A more extreme hypothetical case concerns news photographers. Arriving at the scene of a house fire, a news photographer sees a woman on the second floor desperately wanting to save her baby by throwing the infant into someone's arms. Is the reporter is supposed to decline because, as a professional photojournalist, he is there to photograph the news, not participate in it? The very institutionalization of professionalism can, in some cases, remove the individual sense of responsibility it is supposed to uphold. The potential moral "disconnect" implied by "it's just a job" likewise applies to "it's just a profession."

In any kind of work, people draw certain lines of responsibility around their activities and the products of their labor. In fact, this kind of boundary setting is necessary, lest we think of *everything* around us as our responsibility. Where one draws that line is an important professional consideration. It's also important to recognize that work circumstances can discourage us from engaging in ethical reflection on the job. Scott McClellan was the White House press secretary from 2003 to 2006 for President George W. Bush. In 2008 McClellan released a memoir on his tenure as press secretary, titled *What Happened*. McClellan describes his role in defending the Iraq War long after it was clear that Iraq had no hidden weapons of mass destruction, his account of the disastrous public revelation of Valerie Plame as a covert CIA operative, and his role in spinning the mistreatment of "detainees" and "enemy combatants." What is striking about the memoir is McClellan's admission that, in many instances, he was complicit in deceiving or misleading the press and public. What's also notable, though, is how McClellan characterizes himself as a youthful and idealistic professional eager to act as the president's spokesman. This appraisal of his own role, says McClellan, helped him defend the Bush administration unquestioningly and well beyond the point of believability. But McClellan stops short of characterizing members of the Bush administration as "liars." Instead, he paints a picture of *professional habit* in national politics, where politicians use omission, deception, and dogged advocacy to preserve their authority, amounting to a "permanent campaign" approach to governance. The take-home lesson, we think, is that McClellan was too quick to identify himself as a professional and attached his professionalism too closely to unreflectively defending the administration. Inhabiting the world of the professional, in any domain, need not mean abandoning constant and diligent ethical reflection.

Cultures Cultivating Ethics (or Lack Thereof)

The spectacularly disastrous case of Enron was still in the news years after its success was revealed to be mere financial trickery. "Enron" became synonymous with breaches of trust and greed gone wild, creating a gigantic illusion to which investors and employees succumbed. On September 26, 2006, Andrew Fastow, the cocky-then-repentant CFO of the giant energy corporation, wept in court as he was sentenced to prison. A big part of his own defense, supported by the testimony of even the prosecuting attorneys, was that he was "a changed man." Extraordinarily, even the prosecuting attorneys spoke of Fastow's character transformation at the time of his sentencing, arguing for leniency for this reason and because the defendant was cooperating with the investigation that helped secure convictions for Enron's chairman, Kenneth Lay, and its CEO, Jeffrey Skilling (Eichenwald, 2005).

While the tale of Fastow's redemption was heartwarming and encouraging, in terms of the possibility for human beings to redeem themselves, in this case the focus on the individual's change of heart distracted attention from larger questions of the structure, day-to-day operations, and culture of businesses like Enron, which foster, and sometimes even reward, behaviors like those of Enron's leaders (see J. A. Anderson & Englehardt, 2001). As the documentary *The Corporation* (2005) put it, in the United States we are given the "few bad apples" explanation when faced with wrongdoing, human-produced tragedy, and failure to succeed, whether the arena is professional or personal. All too often in public discussion, success and failure, goodness and badness are understood to be owned by individuals; as a result, we become preoccupied with laying praise or blame upon other individuals and forget to ask about the wider cultural and economic conditions that allow for or encourage certain behaviors. It was certainly the case with Enron that prior to its collapse, it was engaged in corruption and market rigging, even as its leaders were heralded as innovators and good managers (Lyon, 2008). As we discuss in chapters 5 and 6, even the provocative *The Corporation* ultimately employs an analysis relying on individual psychopathology.

This perspective fails to recognize the seductive and often dangerous combination of ideology and opportunity within a largely unregulated market economy in which the command to maximize private (personal) gain is persistently shouted at us (Newton, 2006).

As the global financial crisis began to be called a depression in early 2009, the inadequacy of focusing on individual cases became more evident. For the first time in well over thirty years, there were sustained calls from many quarters for the structural reform of a no-longer-trusted system. It's important that the word *trust* became so common to news reports and editorial commentaries on the crisis: that one word was linked to truth of information, professional integrity, the strength of relationships, the health of the market system, and faith in the future. An October 16, 2008, editorial column in the *Economist* highlights the crucial but tenuous nature of ethics in work and social relationships, in light of the global financial crisis:

> The main reason people place their trust in others is because it is less risky than the alternative.... Isolated people are often more vulnerable because they lack access to basic medical care and—when their harvests fail—to food. Integration with others massively reduces risk. Trust in strangers may be at odds with some of our instincts, but it is a price worth paying for a richer life. (para. 10)

"Richer," as it is used here, suggests an elevated life, one that is indeed *useful* but also *good in itself*. With the collapse of trust at many levels, from the workplace to the market, we find a call for rethinking and reframing professional ethics. The unprecedented declaration of bankruptcy of a nation, Iceland, in October 2008, laid bare the issues of faith, trust, and cooperation on which global commerce depends: the economy is as much symbolic as it is material (Pfanner, 2008). Interestingly, commentators have started to talk about "trust" almost as if it were the opposite of "greed" or "corruption."

Although the term has many definitions, we prefer the straight-forward explanation of trust at work as a strong sense of confidence that one's coworkers or colleagues will take others' welfare in addition to the welfare of the entire organization into account when making decisions. We might even extend that concern to the society as a whole—to the broadest public good. Today one finds both theoretical and empirical studies of trust in disciplines such as philosophy, psychology, sociology, political science, communication, anthropology, and economics. The business ethicist Michael Pritchard (2006) sees trust as the cornerstone of not only an ethical work culture but a society (see also Bruhn, 2002; Dirks & Ferrin, 2001).

Later we will examine entire ways of being, arguing for a renewal and adaptation of Aristotelian virtue ethics, with an eye to identifying the qualities and moral development required of individuals. We will also ask about the broader contexts for action that supports certain ways of being and acting. Messages matter. Organizations matter. Cultures matter. It is essential that they matter if we are ever to escape the tendency to reduce ethics and unethical behavior to individual choice, which is so often the case in this and other Western nations (Schmookler, 1993). Conflicts of interest in governmental and corporate contracts in the reconstruction of Iraq reveal systemic problems vis-à-vis ethics. Halliburton and other contractors accused of inappropriate links to Bush administration officials and cited for an inability to account for funds dispersed to them for reconstruction have been under scrutiny since 2003 (C. Johnson, 2008). The Department of Justice has declined to prosecute many such fraud claims because the contracts are between defense contractors and the Iraqi Coalition Provisional Authority (CPA) (established by the United States) and not the U.S. government: although the money comes from the U.S. government, the victim of the alleged crimes is the Iraqi CPA. With the CPA unwilling or unable to prosecute these cases on behalf of U.S. taxpayers, the contractors are not held to account, and the U.S. government, which allocated the funds and set up the CPA, becomes complicit in a culture of defense-contractor corruption.

There are *cultures* of organizations, industries, professions, communities, and nations that encourage or discourage certain ways of understanding ethics and particular ways of performing responsibilities. These cultures are always communicated to us and by us—and resisted through communication, as well (Mumby, 1997). The U.S. Air Force Academy sexual-harassment scandal of 2003 provides a prime example of how culture is communicated. Isolated cases (thought to be the work of a few "bad apples") multiplied, gradually revealing important facts about the conduct of many cadets, and even officers. The U.S. Department of Defense implemented new policies and created positions designed to monitor the treatment of cadets to prevent such abuse. Whether or not these structural changes have brought about observable changes in day-to-day practice is an important question that research has yet to answer (Shanker, 2005).

Now, we're not suggesting assigning formal responsibility to a *culture*, say, in a court of law. International law prohibits prosecuting entire populations. For example, the Geneva Convention disallows collective punishment (i.e., punishing a population for crimes committed by individual members). The illogic of blaming a society is neatly captured in the Monty Python sketch "Dead Bishop" (1972). Identified by God as the culprit in the mysterious appearance of a dead bishop, Klaus remarks to the Church police officer arresting him, "It's a fair cop, but society's to blame." The detective responds, "Agreed. We'll be charging them, too." Another memorable moment from popular culture reinforces the importance of maintaining individual responsibility: In the 1984 film *Repo Man* (Cox), the protagonist Otto's friend Duke lays dying after being shot while robbing a liquor store. Duke says, "I know a life of crime led me to this sorry fate, and yet I blame society. Society made me what I am." Otto's response is simple: "That's bullshit. You're a white suburban punk, just like me." In short, we have to be careful not to allow social conditions to wholly overwhelm individual responsibility.

The reverse is true as well, of course; we should be aware of tendencies to assign too much personal responsibility for certain actions. It is far too easy to assert that individuals make free choices, independent of their social conditions. Such arguments have long been a staple of the political Right's critique of the Left. But, claiming that "personal responsibility" trumps any social condition masks the ethical consequences of social deliberation and public policy, the very circumstances in which people live. Generally speaking, we are surprised when we hear of a wealthy person committing a violent crime; we are less surprised when the criminal is poor. It is illogical to believe that the difference lies solely in the "superior" personal responsibility of the rich as compared to that of the poor. That is, circumstances play a large role, and public policy and culture strongly influence circumstances. The complex relationships between personal responsibility and public policy are often dismissed in the way that we talk about peoples' ability or right to choose. This glossing over the role of public policy masks the ethical consequences of decisions that, for example, lead to the inadequate funding of schools, which may make crime seem like the only viable option. The failure to appreciate ethics on a collective, cultural level is a great loss for our society and for us as individuals. Similarly, organizations lose out when they see ethical behavior as simply a matter of adhering to rules and regulations rather than envisioning ethics as something to be cultivated throughout the organization and over time. How we do or don't talk about the role of ethics can therefore lead us to put ethics in a box to be opened only in crises.

This book is as much about professional ethics writ large as it is about specific issues of professional, organizational, or business ethics. From this broader perspective, what it means to be a professional, how we act in our professional roles, and even our emotional demeanor at work can be seen as ethical issues. We contrast this broader perspective with the traditional perspective, in which business ethics and our everyday lives are segregated, unintentionally discouraging the full integration of ethics into our lives. This segregated approach is partly a matter of convenience, but it leads us to question only those practices that most spectacularly violate the law, codes, or social norms. The effects of this compartmentalization for our society as a whole are not good, we believe. "We decided that having a separate ethics class was a lot like telling students that they could be bad during the week, but just had to go to church on Sunday," said Frederick W. Winter, the dean of the University of Pittsburgh's School of Business. "By taking out the one course, I think we'll be making every other course richer in the subject" (C. S. Stewart, 2004, p. 11).

Talking Ethics on Every Level

Our work, our professions, our organizations all function within a larger market context. Consider how professionalism became entwined with commercial interests, particularly in the computer software industry. Software companies such as Oracle and Microsoft promoted and sponsored and corporate-branded certification processes to credential product specialists as "Oracle Certified Professionals" and "Microsoft Certified Professionals." "Professional" was also included in product names, which can have ironic negative connotations when applied to software that isn't supposed to require expertise to use (e.g., "Windows Vista Professional Edition"). At the corporate level, professionalism is as much a way of branding and being, in and out of the workplace, as it is a certified world of knowledge and practice.

Our notions of professionalism and identity are just as much organizational and societal issues as they are about individual preference and choice. Rather, our work habits reinforce patterns of identity and relations of power (Ashcraft, 2007). The *speed* of work or life has implications for identity; for example, some people identify themselves as "very busy" people. While we do not often consider ethics dependent on the pace of life, it is important to realize how invocations of urgency or emergency are used to justify certain untoward behaviors, including some that go far beyond the depersonalization of interactions (D. I. Ballard, 2007). The elevation of time-pressure to a state of "emergency" is something we do *through communication*: we communicate the necessity of an action or insist on a particular outcome. The ethicist Kwame Anthony Appiah (2008) notes that our language suggests that "[when] the actor is securing his or her own survival, and, when the stakes are life and death, our moral common sense permits a special concern for oneself" (p. 100). It's easy, then, to see how fixating on ceaseless competition, rapidly approaching deadlines, or organizational survival might encourage a professional deeply identified with his or her company to lie, cheat, or steal in order to get through what is experienced as a crisis.

A broader consideration of work's meanings and moral dimensions is especially important when serious questions are being raised in industrialized economies about the value and values of much of what we consider productive activity (Cheney et al., 2008). Take, for instance, the production and consumption of food. The journalist Michael Pollan's book, *In Defense of Food* (2008), examines the changes in food, and in ideas about food, such as food's subjection to chemical processing, marketing, and so on. He points out that the question, "What should I eat?" would have been ludicrous not long ago and in many contexts outside the United States or what we call the global West or North. Pollan concludes that such confusion is the result of the near-complete replacement of food as a part of culture and ecology by what he calls "edible food-like substances," fare created with ingredients that many consumers would not consciously choose if the ingredients were seen separate from one another). And yet, science, government subsidies, and wholesale prices have driven down the retail price of "edible food-like substances" while increasing so-called externalities (e.g., obesity and related illnesses) and degrading social goods such as intact food cultures and communities. As Pollan's observations help illustrate, what we do for a living and what we do with our wages are never simply neutral. The market influences our behavior, but it doesn't usually invite us to attend to the ethical nature of the assumptions that underpin our work.

Today we find the rules of our economy being questioned at every level, from the global to the individual, and we regard that as a good sign. For instance, Adbusters, a progressive collective of former advertising agents and marketers, sponsors the production of a shoe called the Blackspot Unswoosher. The shoe is touted as the "world's most ethical shoe"; the manufacturer suggests using it for "kicking corporate ass" (see www.adbusters.org/cultureshop/blackspot/ unswoosher). Adbusters is exploiting the presumed *a*morality of the market, suggesting that the rules of production and consumption could be reorganized around ethical interests. Similarly, we see a growing market for global products certified as "fair trade." Also suggesting that money isn't everything, an increasing number of U.S. workers report that they would be willing to sacrifice salary to spend less time at work and more with their families (Olson, 2008). Such searching self-reflection about which activities count as "productive" and "profitable" may be necessary to sustain the planet as we know it, as a 2007 report of the Intergovernmental Panel on Climate Change suggests. What we do as professionals, then, is a matter not only of personal or private concern but perhaps also of material significance to one's community, one's nation, and the world.

Communicating Work, Meaning, and Morality

For us, the emergence of Herbert Marcuse's analysis (1964) of the one-dimensional man in the 1960s is particularly important, suggesting an expanded range of domains in which we might find the question of ethics. That is to say, the organization man of the 1950s demonstrates a kind of *intentional* conformity, an attitude that one "goes along to get along," even if the worker bridles inside. Marcuse would emerge as a philosophical hero of sorts for the 1960s counterculture partly because of his argument that the capacity for individual agency—the *choice* to conform—is constricted by cultural and ideological forces shaping a one-dimensional field of possibility. For our purposes, this contention suggests the importance of expanding ethics beyond simply the individual's actions. In order to fully engage the question of ethics, we need to better understand the broad social field of work in which individuals move. And while we have multiple roles in life, we inevitably find ourselves considering the overall, singular story that unfolds.

In order to see our lives this way, however, we have to first stop speaking about our lives as segmented, at least in terms of our ethical selves. We've already discussed the power that language and narrative have to shape our understanding of ethics and its role in our lives. But recognizing such power is not enough; we have to learn to hear how ethics is subtly framed by and for us, often limiting our ethical horizons.

Listening Carefully to "What's Really Going On"

At a more abstract level, communication and rhetorical theory help us understand the ethical dimensions of our object of study: in this case, the domains of work, professionalism, organizations, and the market. These domains have important material bases: professional classes concretely divide members of a society. Organizations have personnel, buildings, technology, and ecological footprints on the earth. And the market, including the world of finance, takes the form of transactions and networks that have enormous tangible consequences for people and the planet (Soros, 2000).

At the same time, communication and rhetoric are terribly undervalued in most discussions of what people do at work. With that lack of attention, we lose an important opportunity to examine how our own symbols shape our world. As previewed in the introduction, we have numerous maxims that tell us that what we say doesn't matter: "Talk is cheap"; "That's just rhetoric"; "Put your money where your mouth is." But, as titanic battles over the definitions of international friends and foes remind us, labels do matter, and can often mean life or death. Throughout this book we will show that labels, sayings, metaphors, stories, and discourses—broad conversational patterns— are very important to ethics. When we fully appreciate how much of what we *do* consists of words, images, and symbols, we'll find "it's like peering into an abyss" (Burke, 1966). When Kenneth Burke wrote this, he did not intend to be nihilistic or disheartening but to suggest that much of what we think of as solid is actually subject to the flow of symbols. His chief example of this process is "history," which, taken in a certain empirical sense must be understood as a story told from a particular point of view, with a stress on coherence and occasional breakpoints, and with victors whose views are privileged in the very writing of the tale. It's not that history lacks a certain truth but that it can never serve as the whole truth, from multiple standpoints, and with both chance and choice faithfully represented.

We will see and hear examples of the power of narrative throughout the book. In fact, Aristotle himself accorded "story" an important place alongside the quasi-logical *enthymeme* (an unspoken, but commonly understood premise) when he wrote of the power of the well-chosen example to win over an audience. Interest groups and politicians have employed the extended example with great success, so much so that the veracity of the stories and their applicability as a universalizing example are upstaged by their rhetorical power. Consider, for example, the appeal to certain portions of the U.S. electorate of John McCain's "Joe the Plumber" narrative in the 2008 presidential election, or the fictional story of "Harry and Louise," sponsored by the Health Insurance Association of America in 1993 and 1994; the latter undermined public support for President Bill Clinton's effort to "fix the broken system" of health insurance (R. L. Goldsteen et al., 2001). President Ronald Reagan used the narrative form so well that he earned the titles of Storyteller in Chief and the Great Communicator.

These and other means of persuading one another come into play, ethically speaking, when we are explicitly concerned with ethics: for example, in arguing for or against a troop buildup in Iraq (with proponents for the increase giving it the forceful, masculine label "surge"), as the U.S. Congress did in February 2007. In that case, values of security, human life, and investment (or sunk costs) all played roles in the debate. But there are far subtler manifestations of the interplay of communication and ethics as well. Take, for instance, the 2004 news coverage of presidential hopeful Dennis Kucinich.

On January 2, 2004, when the state primary and caucus season was just getting underway in the United States, the *New York Times* ran a story on the long-shot Democratic candidate and Ohio congressional representative Kucinich (Stolberg). In typical presidential-campaign fashion, the newspaper focused on certain personality characteristics, consumer preferences, and daily habits. In other words, the story about Kucinich featured his emotional demeanor, food likes and dislikes, and favorite brands. The *Times* noted he was a vegetarian, practiced yoga and meditation, and was looking (even in small towns) for products made and sold by socially responsible firms. None of this was especially noteworthy. But what caught our attention at the time, and what makes this case so important practically and ethically, is that the article about this candidate was in the *Style* section of the Sunday newspaper. Placing the "news" about Representative Kucinich there effectively framed his campaign in nonpolitical and consequently less serious terms. The logic was circular and self-confirming: A presumably minor candidate was covered in a way that minimized his importance a priori; even in an age where a political leader's style and lifestyle are taken to be serious subjects of concern, Kucinich's personal preferences were consciously labeled soft news by the *Times* to devalue his campaign and reinforce his marginal status in the race. Kucinich had been "framed."

This example shows the power of framing issues, situations, and people. But communication is relevant as well at the more immediate, personal level, where we make judgments within given situations. Consider this second case, related to us by a colleague. At a business conference in Salt Lake City some years ago, a female African American high-level manager gave a keynote address. After the applause subsided, several of those in attendance were heard to say, "She was *so* professional!" What does this mean? Why did they say that? Let's try to unpack their reaction to the speaker and the speech. It could be that the audience members were just paying the speaker a general compliment, the equivalent of "Wasn't that a great speech!" In this sense, lauding a person's professionalism is simply a way of saying that he or she has "made it" in our society. A professional speech is a good speech, an appropriate speech, an accomplished speech, a polished speech, and maybe even a distinguished speech. Of course, even with this apparently simple bit of praise, we are saying that someone "fits the mold" of what we understand to be professional and therefore probably isn't saying or doing anything outside the bounds of acceptable behavior.

But the comment could mean something else, different from or in addition to the first interpretation. It could reflect surprise that a person like the speaker—black and female—could actually pull it off! In this case, the reaction to the speech would reflect an intermingling of issues of race, gender, and perhaps class. This examination of ethics at work moves well beyond our typical notion of ethics as concerning crime, questionable action, and improper behavior. A case similar to the one just described emerged in February 2007 when U.S. senator Joseph Biden commented on his eventual running mate (and the future president) Barack Obama as being "the first mainstream African American who is articulate and bright and clean and a nice-looking guy." As the *New York Times* wrote, after the story torpedoed Biden's campaign: "For whites, the word ["articulate"] is a compliment to anyone. For blacks, it can be a toxic adjective" (Clemetson, 2007). It's striking how often African American leaders in the United States are either described as "very [surprisingly] articulate" or else dismissed as "inarticulate" in the mainstream media. Indeed, this discourse provides a backdrop for the absurd but instructive discussion of whether Barack Obama is "black enough." The question, then, is where do such notions come from?

Popular Culture as Revealing and Influential

It is immensely difficult to trace the origins of such deeply tacit knowledge about the work world, given our understanding that communication and rhetoric are not simply "add-ons" to human experience but are inextricably interwoven with how we understand what we do and how we engage one another. Accordingly, throughout this book we pay particular attention to representations of work, professionalism, and ethics in popular culture, including in our examination the growing presence of documentary film. Popular culture, because of its prominence and its frequent tendency to amplify subtler cultural currents, is particularly revealing, in that it directs our attention to understanding how various messages express and shape ethics. For instance, in the long-running CBS "reality" television program *Survivor*, participants address ethical dilemmas in all sorts of ways. Some of these are explicit, as when a character says, "I really don't want to do this, but I have to vote you off the island." But ethics are addressed in other, subtler ways, as various characters and the structure of the programs themselves frame issues of "teamwork" and collaboration (see Thackaberry, 2003). The *Survivor* series helps us see how the parameters of ethical discussions can influence both the choices and the thinking of persons operating within those boundaries. For example, most of the time the decision to vote someone "off the island" can be boiled down to one justification, "That's the way the game is played," and one excuse, "I had to do it."

As the several references to the *Survivor* series might suggest, how popular culture covers professional ethics is of central importance to the arguments we are developing here. While it might be tempting to simply dismiss popular culture as "fluff" or "mere" entertainment, a cursory treatment of Donald Trump's *Apprentice*, the program that Dan researched for his doctoral dissertation (Lair, 2007), suggests why we should take popular culture, in general, and its treatment of professional ethics, in particular, more seriously.

Programs such as *The Apprentice* are particularly revealing of how we speak about ethics. For example, *The Apprentice* consistently presents an overtly dismissive attitude toward ethical reflection. The phrase "it's not personal, it's business" is frequently heard, even appearing in the opening credits of every episode (we discuss its ethical implications in more detail in chapter 4). One episode has ethics as its theme, but the title, "Ethics, Schmethics," makes clear the disdain in which ethics is held (Burnett & Trump, 2004). *The Apprentice* (and similar popular representations of the work world) thus prominently display—albeit in an exaggerated form—ways of speaking about particular representations of ethics.

There's a second reason that we should take such popular representations seriously, though: they have some influence beyond merely offering us a mirror through which we can see how we speak. In the case of *The Apprentice*, at least during its first season, many colleges, universities, and even businesses explicitly used the program to teach students and employees lessons about the business world (e.g., Naughton & Peyser, 2004; Purdy, 2004). In some circles, *The Apprentice* was received as a popular management text. While this might be a unique occurrence (although, given Thackaberry's [2003] discussion of the treatment of *Survivor* in the business press, perhaps not), this interpretation suggests the increasingly blurred line between popular entertainment and popular management (Crainer, 1998). Here, Trump becomes a dispenser of both wisdom and favor (Huczynksi, 1993; Jackson, 1996, 2001), offering to an audience of millions a vision of how business should be done, with precious little space for ethical reflection.

Trump reflects popular beliefs about business leaders. Imagine a business show built around organizing a worker-owned cooperative. That business structure and its organizational model are so distant from common experience that it would likely be seen as a farce. As the *Pittsburgh Press* wrote many years ago about a worker takeover of a failing steel mill: "Why are the monkeys running the zoo?" (Boselovic, 1994, p. C-1). Such a show would likely get airtime only if the management team were dressed as hippies, confirming the triumph of style. Trump reflects what society already expects to see: an ambitious, confident, wealthy, decisive, and sometimes ruthless corporate leader. Popular cartoons in the United States satirized common representations of work, employers, and businesses: the imaginary human past of the Flintstones (featuring "Mr. Slate" as the stone-age Trump) and the imaginary future of the Jetsons (with "Mr. Spacely").

Of course, to track the influence of representations of the relationship between ethics and work would be quite challenging and is not our purpose here. So while our claims about the influence of popular representations of ethics are modest, we nevertheless suggest that it is important that we not simply write them off as "just" a window into ethical issues. After all, as the communication scholars Leah Vande Berg and Nick Trujillo (1989) argued in their study of decades of prime-time TV's popular images of organizational life, such representations inevitably serve as resources upon which viewers can draw to make sense of their own lives in organizations. Television is populated with fictional workplaces ranging from the frenetic (e.g., *E.R.*) to the mundane (e.g., Elaine's workplace in *Seinfeld*). Popular portrayals of professional ethics function as what Kenneth Burke (1966) terms "equipment for living," in other words, as modern-day proverbs audiences can use to think through their own dilemmas.

Limits on Ethics Talk

Compartmentalization: Ethics in a Box

First, we use communicative forms to compartmentalize ethics. Like a child who keeps different foods separated on his plate, we compartmentalize ethics to prevent it from touching our other activities or experiences. Consider that many of us minimally claim a private life as distinct from our public or professional one: the retort, "That's none of your business," or the policy of "Don't ask, don't tell," are examples of communicating the segregation of private from public life. More generally, though, modern life gives us almost as many roles as we have kinds of relationships. We might identify ourselves as a spouse, a parent, a child, a friend, a roommate, a teammate, or a coworker. Each of these roles reflects an interpersonal relationship. We also assume roles reflecting relationships with institutions. There is the role of a citizen of a country, consumer in a market, employee of a company, and professional within a profession. Each of these roles reflects an identity associated with a particular relationship to another, too, and each relationship creates an opportunity to compartmentalize ethics. This compartmentalization may also be conspicuous by its absence, as demonstrated by professionals whose personal moral positions take precedence over their professional duties. Examples include pharmacists who will not fill prescriptions for birth control, and soldiers who will not voluntarily harm the "enemy."

Relationships have a strong influence on whether or not compartmental boundaries are enforced or breached. Here, we refer not only to the obvious relationships between people or institutions but also those sometimes communicated within language; that is, "what goes with what" (Burke, 1966). We commonly say "sex and violence on television," thereby consistently linking them. In current U.S. political discourse, one hears about "blue states and red states," solidifying and perpetuating a dichotomy. The strength of compartmental boundaries reflects our relationship to the boundary itself. That is, it's less significant that we see a matter as public or private, and more significant that we perceive the distinctions and tensions between the two: public versus private, personal versus professional, secret versus shared. It is our belief in these boundaries that rationalizes ethical compartmentalization. This leads to the most important point about this treatment of ethics: compartmentalization may permit, in one role or relationship, behavior that undermines our having a unified ethical life.

Essentialization: Reducing Ethics to One Thing

Second, we often seek to essentialize ethics, trying to have everything reside in a single principle, place, or person. In the 2007 *Simpsons Movie* (Brooks et al.), Homer Simpson uses essentialism to explain the actions of another character: "Spider pig does what spider pigs do." Here, Homer's account serves to deflect attention from his own actions: spider pig is just a normal pig that happens to get hoof prints all over the ceiling when Homer physically holds him up to it. Such associations establish an "agent/act" ratio (Burke, 1945): good actions follow from a good person (the agent), and bad actions from a bad person. There is a similar logic to our employing arguments that essentialize ethics to the scene in which they occur. Think of easy allowances such as "You know how lawyers are," or "War is hell" (here, war becomes a kind of agent in addition to a situation). Thus, we essentialize ethics through a communicative technique like branding, such as when we identify a specific person as a hero or villain (Presidents George W. Bush and Bill Clinton have been made to fit the bill in both cases, depending on the perspective). The person comes to embody and represent a host of unspoken but comprehended characteristics.

Essentialism works in the opposite direction, too, as when an act is such a violation of a brand's perceived essence that the act alters the brand. The fictional Dr. Frankenstein, for instance, once possessed great self-respect but came to doubt himself because of the monster he created. Or, consider the precipitous falls of both Eliot Spitzer and Roger Clemens, two figures from widely divergent contexts (politics and baseball, respectively), both of whom fell deeply and quickly into disgrace partly because their actions (patronizing prostitutes, and taking performance-enhancing drugs) so cut against their previous public images. The expectation of perfection in our heroes, and our consequent disappointment when we finally discover they are all too human, offers compelling evidence of our tendency toward ethical essentialism.

We also essentialize ethics by reducing its scope. For example, we may apply the technique of reducing every issue or problem to one idea or root. In theory, we look for generative mechanisms. In everyday life, we seek root causes. It's appealing to simplify matters this way, and, of course, some factors do end up being more important than others. But it is rare for moral issues to arise from a single, isolated ethical root, though political elections generate many such claims: economic stagnation is caused by government regulations, teenage pregnancy is caused by sex education in schools, and "The terrorists are at war against us because they hate everything America stands for" (Bush, 2006b).

Over-individualizing ethical decisions is another version of essentialism. For example, we think of a particular event as the fault of "bad apples." Linking essentialism to individualism also points to how essentialized language like "bad apples" prevents us from questioning our culturally and historically accustomed assumptions. We avoid inspecting our usual assumptions until the number of bad apples overwhelms us, as happened in the 2008 U.S. subprime-mortgage crisis. At that point, the ethical inspection is de-essentialized and broadened to include examination of the cultural assumptions enabling the existence of so many "bad apples." Still, this unpacking of an essentialist claim shows how essentialism may also serve as a heuristic tool. First, such claims direct us to that which deserves further inspection; they may illuminate rather than obscure issues. Second, we also learn from an effort to essentialize, particularly when we distill the essence of a complex or nuanced situation. These beneficial uses of essentialism do not mean we should essentialize ethics, only that the customary ways we treat ethics when we talk about it may also be put into the beneficial service of expanding our understanding.

Abstraction: Ethics at Arms Length

Finally, in talking about ethics, we may abstract it, alienating it from its practical implications. The joke, "I know it works in practice, but will it work in theory?" plays on the pursuit of abstraction to the point of irrelevancy. Communicative devices often encourage this irrelevancy in several ways.

First, we may frame ethics as a kind of formalism, that is, ethics reduced to ethical theory and principles. The emphasis on principles is central to one classic contemporary debate about ethics, one that compares the ideas of Carol Gilligan (1982) and Lawrence Kohlberg (1981). Kohlberg advanced the idea that adherence to ethical principles is more morally mature than concern with specific relationships and situations. Gilligan responded with a reexamination of the same data on childhood development that Kohlberg had used. Her different conclusion led her to propose an ethics of care, that is, an ethics that values the particularities arising from relationships—the opposite of abstraction. Gilligan's theory does not necessarily reject Kohlberg's, but rather reminds us that moving up the ladder of abstraction when it comes to morality is only part of the big picture for judgment.

Moving toward ever-higher points of view of concrete situations or people may be necessary, or simply useful. However, when abstraction allows us to avoid realities, it likewise enables us to rationalize moral decisions with dire consequences (usually to others), as in, "I didn't fire 400 workers. In order to remain competitive, I had to let them go." Here, the reference to competitive principles obscures the human impact and management's culpability; the employees are no longer seen for their use value, only their exchange value. Statistics provide another excellent means of abstraction, directing attention away from the human. For example, economists speak of "gross domestic product" rather than the actual human benefits and costs of those products. Statistical measures of the economy have the effect of moving thought away from people and their experience. Statistics are the antithesis of the human-interest story, yet each has its place. We can't tell the stories of, say, 300 million people, but we can use non-economic measures to get a sense of collective circumstances (e.g., through data collected in a national census).

Absentee ownership is another kind of alienation, as is the limited-liability company. Both limit our liabilities (in the first case by limiting an owner's physical exposure to the effects of his or her factory, for example; in the second, by limiting the financial liabilities arising from business activities). Both structures create distance and facilitate a kind of abstraction called *commodification*. Generally speaking, commodification is associated with the following states: "the appropriation of the subject's life force or energy and the replacement of this by non-human technology; the colonization of use value by exchange value; the tendency for a veil to be drawn over the origins of products; and finally the pursuit of a fundamentally reductive logic, including processes of objectification, dissembling and reassembling" (Desmond, 1995, pp. 722–23). John Desmond observes that, through commodification, we learn to see the material as intangible and to reify the intangible as material. Thus, commodification represents one linguistic vehicle that moves across the terrain between what we call "reality" and what we call "ideas." As we commodify a forest, we no longer see forest or trees; we see board feet. We have human resources instead of employees. We want a healthy economy and feel love for inanimate objects like cars, phones, and software. Human-like relationships with things, and thing-like relationships between humans, allow us to rationalize behavior that has us do unto others what we would not wish done unto ourselves. In wartime, this tendency is taken to an extreme to allow for the complete dehumanization of the enemy, which many argue is essential for bureaucratized, mass killing (e.g., C. Hedges, 2002); derogatory group names are used to dehumanize and categorize group members (e.g., Japs, kikes, Krauts, Islamofascists) (see, e.g., Keen, 1988). Abstraction, like compartmentalization and essentialism, engenders a narrow view of ethics and limits our ethical aspirations because it depersonalizes and decontextualizes ethical situations.

Abstraction may also affect how we see ourselves acting ethically, commoditizing our very attempts to act ethically. For example, we have a class of professional observers to validate claims of "organic," "sweatshop-free labor," "fair trade," and so on. So, rather than having to change our behavior or that of the market (e.g., buy locally produced products, buy directly from the producer), we can work with the existing market framework and let the "professional" make the call. Even our ethics have, in some sense, become a commodity because now we buy an "ethical" product (the product has assumed the ethical properties of its production, essentializing the ethical product or brand), and we metaphorically incorporate these ethics into our being by "consuming" the ethical product (bringing new meaning to the aphorism, "You are what you eat").

Abstraction, though, can enable us to make tough decisions—especially decisions that may oppose our personal interests. As the ability to generalize across situations in order to infer or make guidelines and rules, abstraction is a defining characteristic of human beings with respect to morality (De Waal, 2005). It's not that homo sapiens alone possess the ability to perceive moral distinctions; rather, it's the human capacity for multiple levels of reflection about moral decisions that sets us apart from, say, chimpanzees. Abstraction allows us to move above a range or class of situations in order to make judgments about similar cases; otherwise, we might face each situation as if it were totally new, without any kind of repertoire of frames, principles, and strategies. The theory of the categorical imperative, as postulated by the eighteenth-century German philosopher Immanuel Kant, uses abstraction to achieve this end. In reflecting on a particular action, the categorical imperative advises us to reflect on the universality of our chosen action. We commonly apply to misbehaving children this aspect of the categorical imperative, asking, "What if everybody did that?" It is meant to remove "I" and our personal interests from the ethical equation. Abstraction, particularly when we talk to ourselves about ethics, may help us do just that.

Where Do We Go from Here?

This chapter has explored the ways we limit our own understanding and application of ethics at work through our everyday conversations about it. We began by arguing that the ways we *frame* ethics are as important, and sometimes more important, than the specific ethical decisions we make. We believe that a perspective on ethics grounded in communication and rhetoric can illuminate how we unnecessarily restrain the influence of ethics at work. Throughout our discussion, we've tried to make a case for examining popular culture and everyday talk for clues to the ways ethics is treated in our professional lives and have urged a serious consideration of what it means to say, for example, that one's work is "just a job" or that we should "let the market decide." Thus, we find ethical implications in diverse messages and cases, ranging from codes and handbooks, to television shows and ads on Web sites, to everyday conversation, including sayings whose message we unreflectively accept.

As we've explained, we're more interested in heightening awareness about the roles of and frames for ethics in our professional and work lives than we are with examining *specific* decisions or resolving particular dilemmas. We therefore close each chapter with three questions to help you consider how you think about, talk about, and act on ethics.

1. How do I use terms such as "morality" and "ethics" in the domains of my work, my profession, my organization, and the market?
2. What are some memorable messages I have received about ethics in each of these arenas?
3. What are some turning points in my experience of ethics in each domain?

2

Starting Conversations about Professional Ethics

Ethics in Surprising Places

Near the conclusion of the 2008 Oscar-winning film *No Country for Old Men* (Cohen & Cohen, 2007), Chigurh, a serial killer, talks with Carla Jean, his next victim. And while it appears to be a conversation determining her life or death, it is also, rather surprisingly, a conversation about professional ethics. In this scene, Carla Jean has just returned from her mother's funeral and entered the bedroom to find Chigurh waiting for her.

> CARLA JEAN: I knew this wasn't done with. [Chigurh sits at the far end of the room in the late-afternoon shadows.]
> CHIGURH: No.
> CARLA JEAN: I ain't got the money.
> CHIGURH: No.
> CARLA JEAN: What little I had is long gone and they's bills aplenty to pay yet. I buried my mother today. I ain't paid for that neither.
> CHIGURH: I wouldn't worry about it.
> CARLA JEAN: ...I need to sit down. [Chigurh nods at the bed and Carla Jean sits down, hugging her hat and veil.]
> CARLA JEAN (continued): ...You got no cause to hurt me.
> CHIGURH: No. But I gave my word.
> CARLA JEAN: You gave your word?
> CHIGURH: To your husband.
> CARLA JEAN: That don't make sense. You gave your word to my husband to kill me?
> CHIGURH: Your husband had the opportunity to remove you from harm's way. Instead, he used you to try to save himself.

CARLA JEAN: Not like that. Not like you say.
CHIGURH: What's done can't be undone.
CARLA JEAN: You don't have to do this.
CHIGURH: People always say the same thing.
CARLA JEAN: What do they say?
CHIGURH: They say "You don't have to do this."
CARLA JEAN: You don't... [Chigurh stares at her for a beat.]
CHIGURH: This is the best I can do... [He digs in his pocket for a coin.]
CHIGURH (continued):... Call it.
CARLA JEAN: I knowed you was crazy when I saw you settin' there.
    I knowed exactly what was in store for me.
CHIGURH: Call it.
CARLA JEAN: No. I ain't gonna call it.
CHIGURH: Call it.
CARLA JEAN: The coin don't have no say. It's just you.
CHIGURH: I got here the same way the coin did.

Chigurh is committed to his brand of professionalism absolutely and feels he must honor the threat he had delivered to Carla Jean's now-deceased husband. The killer has his own, admittedly twisted, set of rules, and he follows them unswervingly. Chigurh equates his sense of duty with proving himself a principled man, a real professional. Carla Jean, however, appeals to his *agency as a person* and not his profession as a killer: she insists he does have choice; he does not have to honor his threat, his profession, or his coin toss. Responding to her challenge, Chigurh likens himself to the coin: he believes he has arrived at this moment and this life—his life—as a consequence of the role he plays. He is tossed about like a coin. And while the specific conversation is extraordinary, the ethical implications are not. Most of us have, from time to time, pondered the relationship between our work, our profession, and our life. In this chapter, we show how ethics in our everyday talk relates not only to our professional goodness but also to our broader happiness.

How Communication Communicates Ethics

The end of chapter 1 describes how compartmentalization, essentialism, and abstraction serve to limit ethics in our work and lives. These three actions, sensitivity to which is essential for ethical understanding, arise from how we talk about ethics, aided by communication's native power of persuasion. Ethics has been both married to and divorced from considerations of persuasion throughout the history of rhetoric, that is, throughout the study of "the nature of human discourse in all areas of knowledge" (Grimaldi, 1998, p. 15). Communication, because of its ability to affect the choices we and others make, possesses an *inherency* of ethics: talk matters in terms of the opinions it can sway and the results it can cause (Johannessen, Valde, & Whedbee, 2008). The ancients recognized and respected this inherency, too. Not long after the formal study of rhetoric began, Plato used the essay *Gorgias* (1990a) to caution against the seductive power of language, especially in the spoken word, because of its presence and immediacy; he remained suspicious of rhetoric's power, even as he tried to elevate it (as is evident in *Phaedrus* [1990b]). By contrast, his student Aristotle (1991) grounded his rhetoric in explicit considerations of character, or *ethos,* and the need for balance between what he called the three main artistic proofs, or what we might terms *dynamics of persuasion:* the message dynamic, or *logos,* stressing rational content; the speaker dynamic, or *ethos,* best captured by the terms "credibility" or "character"; and the audience dynamic, or *pathos,* centered on emotion but by no means separated from reason. To the ancients, rhetoric was a carefully developed, necessary skill for those who wished to succeed in life.

Still, philosophy hasn't always viewed ethics and communication as bedfellows; the sixteenth-century rise of science first reduced rhetoric to an epiphenomenal concern, with rhetoric further marginalized as mere ornamentation (or "fluff") in the eighteenth and nineteenth centuries. Since the 1950s, however, philosophy has begun to reconnect persuasion and ethics. First came the rejection of a view of language that had treated it simply as a window on the "real world" or a "mirror of nature" (Rorty, 1979). For ordinary language philosophers, linguists, discourse analysts, and rhetoricians, language was again seen as an institution with its own dynamics. It is now all but impossible to conceive of language as simply a means of information transmission. As a result, what is sometimes called the *box car* model of communication, where what is loaded in the car is exactly what is delivered, has been replaced with a view that highlights the inventive use, ambiguous interpretations, and unpredictable results of language and other symbols. A nation's flag is a powerful symbol; the burning of the flag is seen by some as profane, by others as a protected means of expression, and by still others as a way to keep warm (and thus as not symbolic at all). Second, the study of dialogue (Bohm, 2003; Buber, 2004) has emphasized the importance of mutual understanding rather than supporting the idea that a one-way model of persuasion is central to an ethically grounded perspective on and practice of communication. This view, at least on the surface, is at odds with the traditionally adversarial, one-way model of debate and advocacy as exemplified in the legal systems of the United States and many other nations, and in the shouting matches portrayed as news analysis.

Acknowledge it or not, we enter into the realm of ethics every time we engage others, not just as salespersons or politicians but also as colleagues, friends, and family members. The German philosopher Jürgen Habermas (1979) of the Frankfurt School of Critical Theory has taken such ideas even further. He argues that the very nature of communication presumes issues of truthfulness and relational integrity because of how language and interaction shape the larger society, culminating in what he calls "an ideal speech community." Because the processes of persuasion and dialogue, by their very roles in human affairs, are bound up with ethics, interpersonal communication inherently implies ethical issues even when we do not overtly address them. Habermas is, in this way, concerned with the *formal* philosophical grounding of communication and ethics. Other philosophers, perhaps with an eye toward the implications of this idea, have written about how ethics are featured or suggested in everyday talk.

This broader perspective on rhetoric characterized its revival in the past century, when persuasion was seen as representing an imminent dimension of human interaction and symbol usage. This perspective aligns with the insights of British linguistic philosophers (Wittgenstein, 1999; Austin, 1975; and Searle, 1995) and is consistent with the movement to consider how broad discourses in society (e.g., the texts, artifacts, and trends associated with the construction of the modern individual) sometimes influence people in ways not immediately apparent to us (e.g., Foucault, 1984). In order to make apparent these influences we highlight three ways, or rhetorical dimensions, in which everyday talk is structured to communicate ethics.

The first rhetorical dimension, described in the groundbreaking book *Moralities of Everyday Life* (Sabini & Silver, 1982), is found in the seemingly simple act of naming traits. Warning a coworker that an officemate is "as sly as a fox," for instance, fuses morality and personality. This is a convenient conversational move by the person doing the naming, allowing them to order their world and chart their relations with others without acknowledging the real complexities of people or situations or the fluidity of life (e.g., that one might appear unscrupulous in certain situations but not in others). Thus, there is an ethical dimension even to the attribution of traits and virtues.

The second rhetorical dimension is how ethics is positioned in the very ways we frame or label situations, issues, and decisions, particularly how ethical considerations are included or excluded by such framings. For example, when corporate spokespersons talk of "change," do they treat those who question it as "resisters" or worse? Do they speak of "firings," "layoffs," "downsizing," or "trimming dead wood"? Consider how a government characterizes someone as a "terrorist," and what acts terrorism includes. Should the Icelandic teenager who made a crank call to the White House to request a phone conversation with President Bush be labeled a terrorist and be put on the U.S. no-fly list (Solnit, 2008)? Do we point to "the market" as if it were something "out there" and untouchable, or think of it as something a community organizes like a local farmers' market? What is the implication of the media's announcing that "we are in a recession" or a "depression," or something else? Even the timing of such pronouncements constructs a frame with ethical implications.

The third dimension relates to how every reference to an ethical theory or system, even a passing reference, suggests whole courses of action. Perspectives on ethics are therefore themselves persuasive. Sometimes we invoke formal ethical theories, such as utilitarianism, not only to defend a decision but also to support our own view of ourselves as ethical beings. At other times, we draw upon handy cultural resources such as "All's fair in love and war" to excuse potentially questionable behaviors. By influencing our plans and actions, ethically speaking, the persuasive power of talk implicitly links talk to action.

Although Aristotle could not have foreseen a society crowded with forms of expression and professional identities, his theories regarding the inextricable connections between rhetoric and ethics have increased in relevance as society has increased in complexity. His ancient work remains current, establishing connections that urge us to take a singular "big picture" view of ethics and persuasive practice in how we go about achieving our ends in life, particularly the end commonly called "happiness." As we'll explore at this chapter's end, happiness, in Aristotle's (2002) view, is produced by the sum total of our experiences and actions, captured by the notion of *eudaimonia*. Aristotle was also keenly aware of the role of language in social life, particularly its persuasive influence on belief and action, so we will invoke his *On Rhetoric* (1991) in addition to his *Nicomachean Ethics* (2002). In his view, life is both the subject and the object of ethical practice, and each of us is both a means and an end in the pursuit of a life successfully lived—in the fullest sense of success. Here again, the very framing of ethics in our lives must take center stage. There is simply no way around ethics—no sense that we can live without them, or that our ethics do not matter in our sense of self and life.

Given that we are by our very nature "symbol-using, symbol-making, and symbol-misusing animal[s]" (Burke, 1966, p. 6), it is natural that we use language to investigate ethics, not only at the level of specific decisions but also at the meta level. Indeed, humans have spoken at length and written reams on this matter, building a tower of Babel regarding right and wrong, desire and constraint, and means and ends. This Babel-building continues; so, while the number of business ethics–related articles has grown exponentially since the early 1990s (Tenbrunsel & Smith-Crow, 2008, p. 546), there has been little agreement as to the meaning of the terms "ethical" and "moral." That there is no single truth doesn't prevent "ethical" and "moral" from being used prescriptively and proscriptively; nor does it deter us from trying to make specific claims about these traits. In fact, the intertwining of rhetoric and ethics created the opportunity for this book and offers the opportunity for daily engagement with the subject. We have tried to define our terms clearly, while acknowledging that no one can legislate language and its meanings. Instead, we focus on how language influences our notions of the ethical and the moral, and how it, in turn, influences ethical decision-making. For us, "ethical" and "moral" are not interchangeable terms. For us, "ethics" describes systems of principles that guide and inspire what we recognize as "moral" behavior. Conversations are not possible without having a common language; that is, we must agree on the meaning of specific terms.

For our purposes, all of these insights are important, directing our attention to how, in the very talking about ethics or specific ethical issues, we create space for certain kinds of ethical, unethical, or presumably non-ethical actions to which ethics does not pertain. They also draw us to the creative power of labels, frames, categorization, metaphor, and narrative, in conversations about ethical pursuits. This emphasis represents something of a new twist on the ethics–persuasion relationship, we maintain, but it is holistic in the sense of looking at ethics as an enterprise, a domain of activity discussed in certain ways.

Making Conversation about Ethics and Professional Life

Everyday Talk

Reflecting on this chapter's title, we mean "conversation" on several levels. To begin, there is conversation at the level of everyday talk, including informal chat but also popular culture, with its advertising jingles and corporate slogans (e.g., the longstanding corporate slogan, "Like a good neighbor, State Farm is there"). These various conversations and messages are, of course, filled with words: words for things and relationships, words to describe ideologies and systems, and even words for things outside experience, such as in the metaphysical realm of religion (Burke, 1970).

Of course, the meanings of words are not permanently fixed, even when we try to *legislate* language, as in the field of law. Like magnets, meanings can become stuck and unstuck to one another (Mouffe, 1999); sometimes word pairs have an internal contradiction that we override through creative uses (e.g., "modern history," "deliberate mistake," and sometimes "business ethics"). We can plainly see such shifts in the changing nature of the terms "conservative" and "liberal" in political discourse, but they are just as visible with the ideas and images attached to and detached from other ideological terms, such as "capitalism," "democracy," and "socialism" (see, e.g., Almond, 1991). In fact, despite our cultural preference for precision, the power of language largely resides in its fundamental ambiguity. For air traffic controllers and surgeons, the preference for precision (or efficiency of expression) over poetry (and its celebration of ambiguity) is a life-and-death matter. But how we talk about the roles of doctors and nurses, for example, is a different matter because of how it implicates identity, relationships, and power; to hear a patient refer to his nurse as a "girl" and his doctor as "Doctor" reveals the patient's internalization of customary ways of positioning gender and authority. In many situations, language functions more like putty that is moldable in many, although not infinite, ways. Recognizing language's malleability, we often insist that it is important to "get beyond rhetoric," especially in politics. But how is this possible when so much of politics and life is experienced only through words?

Some consider the language of science as a different language realm, particularly because it should seem to be less malleable. Scientific discussions try to make language perfectly mirror reality, independent of symbolism. This was one of the main goals of the Vienna Circle of intellectuals in the early twentieth century: they tried to model all forms of inquiry, including the study of the human sciences, using a correspondence notion of language and truth (Ayer, 1946) that would have language line up perfectly with reality. But, as it turns out, language is not a mirror reflecting precise relationships. Language itself is inventive, creative, and generative of new ideas, not least because human language is marked by both *polyonomy* (the ability of one word to have many meanings) and *synonomy* (the ability of many words to share the same meaning), thus permitting both ambiguity and specificity in the expression and interpretation of experiences and ideas (Cassirer & Hendel, 1946, pp. 17–22). Spending time with an entry in the *Oxford English Dictionary*, such as the one for "run," reveals the malleable nature of language, how it may simultaneously reflect and propose realities. Accordingly, we must keep in mind that once language and other symbol systems enter the conversation (and they always do), we must consider the dynamics of the power of symbols themselves.

Talking about Right and Wrong

The second level of conversation pertains to ethical messages as embedded in conversations about right and wrong acts, that is, acts for which people may consider someone worthy of praise or blame. We account for these acts prospectively (before the act; e.g., in rehearsals of future conversations or encounters, we might say, "If she says this, then I'll respond with that"), concurrently (during the act, as when we say, "I'm doing this for your own good!"), and retrospectively (subsequent to the act, as when we say, "What did you expect?") (see Mills, 1940). The ethical content of accounts may be explicit exclamations of judgment (as in the claim "If that happens again, no one would blame me for quitting"), or obscured, as when a teacher makes a retrospective claim about a student's apparent ignorance by yelling, "Seven times seven equals forty-nine!" (MacIntyre, 1984, p. 13). In the latter statement, we note that the words themselves, while clearly pertaining to right and wrong, are morally neutral. What could be more morally neutral than the words, "Seven times seven equals forty-nine"?

In this level of conversation, we're also interested in the ethical implications of expressions that, on the surface, seem not to be about right and wrong at all. Slavoj Žižek notes how such seeming neutrality is often used to judge and manipulate. To illustrate, he describes a hypothetical father's effort to get his child to voluntarily visit his grandmother. The father says, "You know how much your grandmother loves you, but, of course, you should only visit her if you really want to." Right or wrong may not be explicit in the father's words, but the moral content and the intention to persuade are likely not lost on the child. Žižek emphasizes the child's dilemma: "Not only do you have to visit your grandmother, but you have to like it!" (in Taylor, 2006).

Discussing Ethical Theory

Conversations about ethical theory, usually of an academic nature, comprise the third level we address. Perhaps the reader feels perplexed by the word "theory." For some, the subjective association of ethics with dilemmas or with the complicated theoretical apparatuses we use to reason our way out of them stigmatizes ethical theory (Appiah, 2008), that is, ethics becomes a forced labor if we're conscious of it only when faced with a profound quandary or sometimes just an everyday challenging situation. Instead, one could take an explicitly communicative slant on this characterization of ethical dilemmas as *ethical discussions*, either in terms of merely private, didactic conversation or, in an even wider view, as part of a public conversation. The conversations themselves become a primary tool for examining the first principles of ethics. Along this line, the French philosopher Emanuel Levinas (1989) advocates ethics as the first principle of philosophy, with a particular emphasis on notions of relationship and responsibility. Our awareness of the world arises from encounters with the "Other," making ethics the ground of experience and knowledge, and thus of communication as well (see also Gibbs, 2000). The Other provides a context and contrast for recognizing our Self.

Talking about Professional Practice

Finally, we point to conversation at the level of professional practice; specifically, conversations regarding the institutions of work, one's profession, the organization, and the market. Here we refer both to the talk we do *at* work and the talk that *is* work. Take, for example, the words penned by Lawrence Summers when he was the chief World Bank economist and promoted the migration of dirty industries to less-developed countries: "I've always thought that underpopulated countries in Africa are vastly underpolluted, their air quality is probably vastly inefficiently low compared to Los Angeles or Mexico City" (in Lal, 2005, p. 1933) This comment is startling because, to most people, "underpolluted" is a ridiculous concept, especially in the way this statement uses it (as evidence of failure). But in Summers's economic context, it makes sense, and it shows how the formalized and semi-formalized language of experts shapes ethical thinking in an institutional context (e.g., economics) and in the larger society. If this language makes sense in an institutional context—that is, if it isn't questioned within that context—shouldn't the larger society be asking if that context makes sense?

This technical or instrumental approach underlies compliance. Every business is concerned with compliance, if only for the purpose of satisfying tax authorities' reporting requirements. Compliance requires adherence to the letter of the law, with the presumption that adherence minimizes legal liabilities. A large company may have a compliance officer to consolidate this knowledge and reconcile it with corporate activities, creating an opportunity for the company to "know itself." Like the CEO, the compliance officer should know the character and tenor of the company's practices. And while the CEO is supposed to use that knowledge to direct the company's "culture," the compliance officer has the limited scope of legality, not culture and not ethics in the grander sense. Typically placed in a company's legal department, compliance officers focus on satisfying the letter of the law and limiting the application of ethics to only the technical details of the situation or dilemma.

In this book, we advocate a critical and emancipatory view of ethics because we believe ethics is embedded in everyday interactions and in the web of symbols in which we operate. To be critical is merely to assess the merits and faults of an ethical system. To be emancipatory, we must seek to strengthen our ethics by examining how various ethical principles came about, how they work in practice, and how any given system encourages or discourages their use. We also advocate a holistic view of conversations, considering how language causes us to reflect upon, revise, or reinforce our beliefs. There are various ways of (re)vitalizing these conversations about ethics, by acknowledging the ethical context in conversations and understanding both how to extract ethical content from and how to insert ethical content into conversations. We aim to make visible some of these ways and, in doing so, draw attention to the manner in which we communicate ethics.

The Stories We Tell about Ethics

Communicative devices, such as narratives, call attention to particular ideas; they play a central role in our entire experience of communication and the world. The experienced rhetorician, like any skilled craftsman or artisan, draws on narratives as a tool for their craft. Stories are such effective modes of communication that we use fairy tales to teach ethics to children, sometimes blatantly ending a tale with, "The moral of the story is…" Since a story is simply an account of an event or experience, it's not surprising that stories are a prominent mechanism for communicating ethics, and for accounting for past, present, and future behavior, much as the ghosts of Christmas past, present, and future accounted for the life of Mr. Scrooge in Charles Dickens's *Christmas Carol* (1843/2006). Here, in exploring the communicative power of stories to shape ethical and moral messages, we first examine the power of stories to communicate ethics, and then the specific ways in which we usually treat the ethical content when we talk about ethics.

Some stories use value-laden language to intensify the ethical force and, perhaps, our connection to the story. Such language takes many forms: aphorisms, slogans, and vague but powerful value-based terms. These tools increase stories' power to communicate ethical content to reveal and promote a particular moral position and, often, a particular ethical principle. Value-laden terms promote ethical values, sometimes highlighting inconsistencies, as in the statement, "I believe in racial equality, but I wouldn't want my daughter to marry someone of different race." The ambiguities of language, especially with broad word–idea combinations such as found within the word "equality," enable this statement to make perfect sense to some but be nonsense to others. In everyday life, we stretch, bend, and sometimes constrain the meaning of terms such as "equality," but do so in ways that are difficult to accommodate in a single ethical system (see, e.g., Celeste Condit & John Lucaites [1990] for a nuanced rhetorical history of the term). Similarly, the "free market" is a particularly powerful value term, being used to rationalize all sorts of specific political and economic policies or to cast some of its "magic" upon the terms it modifies (e.g., suggesting that a "free-market solution" is superior to a solution outside the realm of market economics).

The power of the narrative form of communication was perhaps first explained in writing by Aristotle (1991) in *Rhetoric*, although the history of the story form is likely as long as that of human language itself. Aristotle saw vividly the roles of deductive forms of argument, including those employing quasi-logical expressions used in everyday speech (this he called the *enthymeme*), and those relying on anecdotes or episodes to support deductive claims. For this great thinker, both forms of communication—deductive logic and narratives—were essential to effective persuasion, and speakers who combined the two could become masterful orators. In other words, to interweave compelling stories in carefully crafted presentation enables the rhetorician to draw upon the two main features of communication: structure (the representation) and process (the means of sharing representation). To be sure, deductive logic and its derivatives have held sway in philosophy, communication theory, and other areas largely because scientific reasoning has been divorced from communication and rhetoric through the influences of Francis Bacon (whose contribution to the "scientific method"—the sequence of observation, hypothesis, and experimentation—privileges deductive, scientific reasoning), René Descartes (whose *cogito* privileges firsthand knowledge), and others.

However, the recognition that seemingly rational activities do not always elicit rational behavior has given rise to new fields, such as behavioral economics and neuro-marketing. Daniel Kahneman won the 2002 Nobel Prize in Economics for his work on how people make decisions among alternatives of risk. The basic revelation was that economic choice involves significant degrees of irrationality. The former U.S. Federal Reserve chairman Alan Greenspan, in a 2007 interview with Jon Stewart on *The Daily Show*, echoed this conclusion. "If I could figure out a way to determine whether or not people are more fearful or changing to euphoric...I don't need [complex mathematical models]; I could forecast the economy better than any way I know." In other words, deduction and analysis have their place, but so does belief (including anticipation). Just how are beliefs constituted, presented, and made memorable and actionable? One way is through the narrative form, including condensed economic stories such as those that tell us that, over time, holding on to stock is more lucrative than trying to time the market to make strategic sales; and longer stories, such as Aesop's fable, "The Tortoise and the Hare," which draws a similar conclusion: "slow and steady wins the race."

Myths as Big Stories with Ethical Implications

Human beings have always understood the power of the narrative form, but it took academics a while to catch up. Studies of narrative began flourishing in the social sciences and humanities in the 1960s and 1970s in such fields as anthropology, sociology, and psychology, and in the more expected fields of communication, literature, and linguistics. "Myth" (Lévi-Strauss, 1995), narrowly defined as narrative plus ideology (Frye, 1957), or more generally as a story meant to preserve and perpetuate a belief, becomes an important arena of intensive investigation for those seeking to understand the interrelations of language, consciousness, and social structure. Practically speaking, myths' ultimate importance is not so much their truth or falsity, but rather how they function in society, and the aspects of social life they either conceal or feature.

Take the myth of the self-made man, a myth well known to every aspiring entrepreneur. There are the rugged individualists embodied in Ayn Rand's (1996; 2000) mid-twentieth-century novels, and the fast-track successes, such as the conformist J. Pierrepont Finch, the average window-washer with grand dreams who was depicted in the 1961 Pulitzer Prize–winning musical, *How to Succeed in Business without Really Trying!* We recognize these as myths: not every entrepreneur is a rugged individualist; nor does hard work ensure business success. Still, these stories (and the stories of successful real-life entrepreneurs such as Steve Jobs of Apple Computer and Sam Walton of Wal-Mart) advise us, perhaps even resonate with us. This resonance can be at odds with our reasoning. We know that the stories are, at best, approximations of what happened. We know they lack important details such as the innumerable micro-decisions and serendipities that contributed to each entrepreneur's success (Gladwell, 2008). Still, despite those rational recognitions, these stories resonate with us.

In his book *The Myth of the State*, the Swedish philosopher Ernst Cassirer (Cassirer & Hendel, 1946) unravels the reason behind this resonance, describing the function that myth serves in society. In brief, "myth gives us a unity of feeling" (p. 37) and, as such, lets us identify (with) a community. The stories of successful entrepreneurs in fact and fiction lend emotional assistance to aspiring ones. Through the narrative form, these feelings—of encouragement, of the "can do" attitude, of how it feels (or should feel) to pursue a dream—become objects to us; the story of Apple Computer, the story of LEGO, and the story of *Atlas Shrugged* or *The Fountainhead* each triggers a feeling in those with whom the story resonates. Cassirer suggests that we objectify both the story and its evoked feeling when we use that story in order to trigger that feeling (p. 45). No longer a reflection of us, the story and the feeling are instead outside of us, out there in the world; they have become "an objective empirical reality" (p. 45). Feeling unity with this imaginary story, we give the story and its accompanying feeling meaning, incorporating them into our experience. Ironically, Descartes's conclusion that we must begin with firsthand experience is misapplied to these stories because their resonance makes us feel as if they—these myths—are firsthand experiences. By turning symbols into apparent realities, narratives and myths have tremendous power to selectively promote or downplay particular beliefs. This persuasive power also applies to ethical beliefs. Take, as an example, how the catchphrase "What would Jesus do?" gets its force from the strength of the image that the life of Christ evokes. The Christ story is powerful enough to evoke identification and inspiration, even among nonbelievers, in Jesus's divinity or status as a prophet.

The field of organizational communication rediscovered this power of narratives late in the twentieth-century. The communication scholar Mary Helen Brown (1990) and others pioneered the study of narratives in organizations, thereby inverting the accustomed order of formal communication over informal. Brown showed how the characters, plot lines, and climaxes of stories frequently told at work were far more than side conversations, more than epiphenomenal to the primary business tasks. As she and others (e.g., Mumby, 1987) demonstrated, even seemingly offhand or tangentially relevant stories can both indicate profound aspects of organizational culture and help shape it. Stories that employees tell or are told about a company's founder are most revealing in this respect. Wal-Mart employees are quick to recount the folksy, affable style of Sam Walton, who was known to routinely visit stores and distribution centers. Patagonia's marketing efforts are rich with mention of its founder Yvon Chouinard's authentic "dirtbag" climbing past and his ongoing outdoor adventures. Consider all of the interactions at your past or present workplace that led to one person being labeled the "gossip" (Hafen, 2004), another identified as the "closer," and yet another person identified to new hires as "someone to avoid, if you can." Larry Browning (1992), another communication scholar, took a page from Aristotle's *Rhetoric* (1991) by showing the difference that *lists* (as implicitly deductive forms) and *stories* (as inductive ones) make in shaping organizational life. Various professions have gravitated toward codes of ethics and lists of do's and (mostly) don'ts, yet it is in the stories of professional triumph and, sometimes, goodness that we find inspiration.

Accounting for What We Do (or Don't Do)

Related to the study of narrative is research exploring *accounts* (or justificatory narratives), first developed in sociology and then applied in other fields. The basic idea underlying this research is that if we are interested in why people do things, one logical point of inquiry is to ask them (Harré & Secord, 1972). Accounts research offers an important distinction between excuses and justifications, especially in terms of their implications for practical ethics. Excuses acknowledge the harmful, perhaps even shameful, nature of an event and may well call it "a mistake," yet they appeal to some external force (which can be an internal condition, like insanity). A classic excuse in the educational domain is "My dog ate my paper"; an updated version might be "My hard drive crashed." Think of all the signs in offices or on highways that begin with "Pardon our mess..." and "Please excuse..." These messages anticipate questions from clients or drivers and try to forestall them with a ready excuse.

By contrast, justifications acknowledge no mistake, although they may well recognize harm. The defining feature of a justification is the affirmation of the act as a "good thing," even if only as something made necessary by factors not immediately apparent. So, a justification for killing might be self-defense; a frequently cited justification for war is "the greater good" or "winning the peace." Consider here the reasons given for actions such as mass layoffs, outsourcing, plant shutdowns, mergers, and takeovers. In many cases, as we will see, the common reason given is "market forces." Importantly, this reason can be used as either an excuse, acknowledging the badness of the act, or as a justification that elevates the act. As we will discuss in chapter 6, the market, as a symbol, provides a handy linguistic agent for all sorts of attributions, although we don't deny the material power of market pressures.

Explicit and Implicit Ethical Systems

Earlier we defined the term "ethics" as systems of principles that guide and inspire moral behavior. Ethics concerns right living, as in, "How shall I live?" whereas morality involves distinguishing right from wrong, as in, "What should I do?" In everyday usage, however, we often blur these concepts; consequently, the narrow regulatory applications of ethics causes us to lose sight of ethics as advising us on right living writ large. The great myth of ethics is that it is something to consult only in special situations; it is set aside from daily life and made irrelevant or unreachable most of the time.

Characteristically ethical questions reflect the broader applicability for an ethical system: How can I tell right from wrong? How do I conform to society? How can I be a good person (and still get ahead)? How shall I live? How are we to live? How shall I live in a way that gives meaning to my life? How can I be happy? It is the means of right living that is the object of these questions, a life rich in relationships with other people either directly or through common institutions. A life aspiring toward this end is what is classically called a "good life." An ethical system is one that informs our agency so that we may direct ourselves toward living a good life.

We all have lay theories of ethics just as we do for important things like power, money, love, family, friendship, and death. That is, we have a lay theory for how we are supposed to live and the kind of person we are or aspire to be. Maybe your ethical system isn't so consciously constructed that you would call it a theory, but it is there, whatever you call it. It may be a disjointed collection of guidelines for our own behavior: why some sex is immoral and other sex is sacred, or when it is OK to tell a lie. And in describing behavior this way, we reveal the presence of an implicit ethical theory. For each of us, there are "moralities of everyday life" (Sabini & Silver, 1982) composed of our personal collection of accounts. Take as an example the effort invested by the ethicist Peter Singer in his attempt to chart the ethical system of President George W. Bush in his book, *The President of Good and Evil* (2004). Singer concludes, "Bush's views do not fit with a coherent ethical framework, because he reacts instinctively to specific situations. He feels that he knows what to do on any given occasion, but because he is not a reflective kind of person, he makes no attempt to put his judgments on specific issues together and see how coherently they fit with each other" (p. 210). In other words, Bush is not theorizing about ethics, even at the level of connecting various personal standards and experiences. We believe that his system would be more accurately portrayed as one that happens at a gut level, where decisions about behavior are categorically unreflective (e.g., "because killing is wrong") or vague (e.g., "it feels like the right thing to do"). But even in such a case, where gut-level spontaneity ("seat-of-the pants" judgment) is prized (even electable), we find that it falls short in some crucial, practical matters. First, intuitive reasoning discourages reflection, hampering moral development. Second, it cannot be explained to others. While it may be an acceptable approach for private decisions (e.g., "I feel like wearing the blue suit and flag lapel pin today"), it's antithetical to informed decision-making, the process assumed for cooperative activities. We're instead left with a decision settled by authority, as in, "I'm the decider, and I decide what's best" (Bush, 2006a). To be sure, given the time pressures of professional life (Virilio, 1977) and the insignificance of most decisions, the gut-level approach can enable us to navigate smooth seas and to do so with relatively consistent behavior (Gladwell, 2005). After all, we bring a lifetime of experience and habit to our gut-level approach, so consistent behavior isn't that surprising. Perhaps, though, we should consider the quality of our performance and the character of our behavior.

This requires going beyond—or we might say, outside—the gut. The opportunity for us, personally, is to reflect on our moral positions, allowing the gut, the head, and the heart to inform us as we discover and inspect our present ethical system and decide if it fits and wears as well as we'd like.

Ethical Systems: Highlighting Distinctive Features

So far, in this chapter, we have alluded to various features found in ethical systems, terms like agency, identity, and responsibility. In this section, we attend to seven different dimensions of ethics. Each of these dimensions is reflected in our talk and in ethical theory. Over the course of the discussion, we consult prominent theorists in the Western tradition to show how various theories illuminate specific features of ethical situations, issues, and decisions. In this way, we offer a creative, interpretive account of the central impulses and practical implications of theories. But instead of treating the theories as complete systems unto themselves, we apply them as lenses through which to examine ethical life, as heuristic devices for advancing reflection and conversation.

Agency and Autonomy: Putting the Person in Ethics

"All the world's a stage, and all the men and women merely players" (Shakespeare, 1998, pp. 150–51). We all act in the world. An *agent* is a particular kind of actor, one who has and expresses motives and makes choices—within roles, over time—using both emotional and rational resources, to achieve broad fulfillment. Let's unpack some of that broad description's implicit assumptions. First, an agent should be able to comprehend the circumstances and consequences of his or her choices. For some populations, specifically children or adults with mental impairments, the choices are limited. For example, we may grant agency to young children, allowing them to choose between but not to conceive the choices: "Do you want to brush your teeth before or after you put on your pajamas?" While the child may be an agent of choice, there is no doubt that the teeth will be brushed. A more fully realized agent conceives of possible choices. Immanuel Kant's theory of the categorical imperative may advise us on how to make a choice—"act upon a maxim that can also hold as a universal law" (1996, p. 17)—but it doesn't increase our capacity to identify the range of possible choices.

This limit leads us to the second assumption, that agency is voluntary. The comedian Jack Benny famously joked about being held up at gunpoint. The robber gives him a choice, "Your money or your life." After a long pause, the robber demands an answer, to which Benny replies with frustration, "I'm thinking it over!" Ethically speaking, it's funny because Benny responds as though he has a voluntary choice to make, whereas most people immediately see the answer as both obvious and coerced. Benny's joke recalls Aristotle, who distinguished between voluntary, involuntary, and counter-voluntary actions (2002, p. 224). Benny's reaction might be an involuntary action if it is based on his ignorance about the situation. Maybe he's pondering the nature of heaven, and thinking that this might be preferable to life. For most of us, the response "Take my money!" is an involuntary one. Counter-voluntary actions differ from involuntary actions in that they cause regret or pain, as expressed in the hypothetical dying words, "On second thought, take my money."

We can find many accounts affirming agency, or the lack of it. The market is sometimes claimed to satisfy consumer desire for agency because the choosing belongs to the consumer; however, determining the set of available choices does not belong to the consumer, and thus consumer agency is limited. The U.S. comedian Flip Wilson made famous this account for a lack of agency: "The devil make me do it!" Appeals to agency are sometimes used to provoke action. For example, in saying "act like a professional," or "grow up and act like an adult," we assume the listener both realizes what characterizes a professional or adult, and has the agency and is in a position to choose to do so. That's why it's absurd to ask such a thing of a small child, a pet, or an algorithm. In our focus on agency and choice, we don't mean to imply that choice requires consciousness—even life-changing choices may be made without thought. A reader's response to an article about the *Twenty-One* television game show scandal of 1957, made famous in the 1994 film, *Quiz Show*, skillfully highlights the fuzzy edges of agency: "If a soldier can fall on a grenade to save his buddies' lives, and later truthfully claim that he did it without thinking and does not feel like a hero, can we not find ourselves cheating at a game show without really having thought about it?" (Fish, 2008). Sometimes, agency just happens.

Consider the possibility that there are styles of agents. We can loosely describe three types: the decider, the refiner, and the absolutist. We define a "decider," as George Bush once characterized himself (Bush, 2006a), as a person who practices an implicit ethical system and whose accounts are categorically unreflective or vague. Simply, deciders intuit or "feel" what's right. Perhaps such claims are part and parcel of the political profession, as we can find other politicians telling voters that same story. The U.S. senator John McCain, for example, proclaimed, "I know what's right, and I'm going to do what's right, and at the end of the day, I'm going to sleep well at night, because I know what's right for America" (McCain: "I Know What's Right For America," 2007). "Deciders" tell themselves stories about their moral development, tout the moral rectitude of "their gut," and eschew ethical and moral reflection. In these cases, as in so many like them, the assertion of right and wrong and one's ability to tell the difference between them serves as a comforting reminder to an audience that believes morality is a fundamental concern for a leader—even though the leader's ethical system may not be explained in any depth.

An *absolutist* sticks to ethical principles regardless of their applicability or the absolutist's experience. This is an extreme position, as it demands that situational particulars be ignored if the principles do not recognize them. For example, architectural constructivists assert that buildings should be used for their designed purpose only; similarly, judicial constructivists assert that judges apply the laws as written, without interpretation. By favoring principles over particulars, absolutists have a tendency to abstract the real lives at stake. Citing market forces when deciding to offshore and outsource previously internal business activities suggests this type of agency. But constructivism provides for interesting options to change the principles, as it only requires that we decide to construct different principles. Assuming that the principles are a construction, the option remains to reconstruct or, perhaps, remodel the construction. For example, we had only to construct and commit to the ethical principle of moral equality to arrive at the moral conclusion that human beings can never be classified as property and slavery is thus immoral.

A *refiner* engages in moral and ethical reflection in order to understand and, sometimes, refine his or her moral positions or underlying ethical system. Susan Flader's 1974 book on the environmental writer Aldo Leopold documents the emergence and evolution of the man's environmental philosophy. Leopold's remarkably varied career enabled the ongoing refinement of his thinking. For this early ecological philosopher,

> thinking was shaped by the land itself, and by his changing perception of it.... It was his conviction that ecological perception was a matter of careful observation and critical thinking.... When one looks for critical junctures in his

thinking, one finds them as often as not associated with some new field of experience. He was extraordinarily willing to look and to see and to alter the contours of his thinking about a problem if what he saw warranted it. Yet he maintained a broad perspective on means and ends, grounded in the basic values of integrity, stability, and beauty, a perspective that enabled his ideas to grow and change naturally during the course of his life, and in the process impart greater depth, breadth, and clarity to his philosophy. (Flader, 1974, p. 35)

Our own book asks you, the reader, to act as a sort of refiner. It would be a wasted effort for us to present these ideas on the communication of ethics, identifying how we use communication to shape our ethical practices and *live* a good life, if you, the reader, did not engage in refinement.

Whatever type of agent we may be, we sometimes find ourselves in a position to act for others. Agency may be delegated. For example, if we know in advance that we will be unavailable or unable to execute important duties (e.g., because we're undergoing surgery), we may temporarily delegate our legal agency to another person to act on our behalf. One may also delegate responsibility to a group of persons. For example, the shareholders in a publicly traded company delegate authority to the board of directors, who then delegate more specific authority to officers of the company, and so on. As employees, some of us are delegated authority to act as agents of our employer, making binding commitments ultimately on the shareholders' behalf. Agency has a way of getting around, both individually and collectively. Delegation by shareholders to a corporate board retains a line of authority in that delegation. The delegated powers are well documented and under the authority of the shareholders. But what about agency not so much delegated as it is abdicated, particularly to a machine or system rather than an accountable agent? The journalist William Greider (1998) describes the market as a headless machine programmed in many languages and with many conflicting instructions. And while we may delegate a chess match to a computer program, what about delegating decisions to the market, that is, using a market "program" that is set to run on its own without a clear line of ultimate authority or accountability? What agency can it ultimately have, and what does it say about us as agents if we delegate decisions to it, or acquiesce to its authority?

Discrimination and Choice: Telling the "Difference"

Agency necessarily involves making choices, committing to decisions, struggling with dilemmas. *Discrimination* lies at the heart of an ethical practice, as it is the method of distinguishing between the actions one should do and those one should not, usually embodied in the principles that comprise an ethical system. Many ethical systems have explicit mechanisms for discrimination, offering specific rules or principles. We've already noted that part of the discrimination advanced by the categorical imperative is that we should choose the option that we would advise others to make if similarly situated. Sometimes we ask for advice from others, framing a question reflective of the categorical imperative "What would you do if you were in my situation?" Similarly, others often support our choices by stating, "That's what I'd do, if I were you." The categorical imperative privileges the right action *in all possible cases*; as Kant advised, "Act only according to that maxim whereby you can at the same time will that it should become universal law" (1993). Here, discrimination takes on a deontological cast, where motive arises from *duty*.

Consequentialism, on the other hand, is a category of ethical theories distinguished by their focus on ends. "The end justifies the means" summarizes the most extreme version of consequentialism. The best-known implementation of this theory, primarily due to its use by "free market" proponents, is utilitarianism, readily recognized as articulated by John Stuart Mill in the nineteenth century (1863/2002). For Mill, ethical acts are those that maximize aggregate happiness for everyone, with happiness understood as "pleasure or the absence of pain," and unhappiness as "pain or the privation of pleasure" (Mill, 1863/2002, p. 239). The concept of utility recognizes that different people value pleasure and pain differently, meaning that things *themselves* aren't compared, but rather their respective value to those affected by the consequences. It's easy to see why free-market proponents are so enamored of this method of discrimination; it may be interpreted as affirming the universality of money as the representation of value. In an economic utilitarian calculus, profit is good, and more profit is better; the ultimate good is a difference in quantity not kind.

Utilitarianism's method of discrimination has some shortcomings. First, it fails to deal with the distribution of happiness. Superficial application of utilitarianism can justify the loss of rights for a minority in order to bring greater happiness to the majority ("the greatest good for the greatest number"). Another issue is the quantification problem. While we may have a formula to assist in the selection of a moral position (do that which maximizes aggregate happiness), what exactly are we aggregating—what is a unit of pleasure or pain?

Mary Wollstonecraft Shelley's novel *Frankenstein* provides an example of this calculus in action. Pleading for a compassionate favor from his creator, the monster declares, "Every where I see bliss, from which I alone am irrevocably excluded. I was benevolent and good; misery made me a fiend. Make me happy, and again I shall be virtuous" (Shelley, 1818/1994, p. 128). He wants Dr. Victor Frankenstein to create for him a companion (a wife who loves him—a monster—as he is). Dr. Frankenstein wrestles with the request, aided by the utilitarian formula. Viewed in this scope Dr. Frankenstein believes the world would suffer greatly from the creation of a second monster, perhaps a race of monsters, should they beget monster children. The suffering brought to the world by a race of monsters, he calculates, would be greater in its aggregate than his own suffering, if he refused the monster's request. Dr. Frankenstein concludes, "I shuddered to think that future ages might curse me as their pest, whose selfishness had not hesitated to buy its own peace at the price perhaps of the existence of the whole human race" (Shelley, 1818/1994, p. 193).

Well-stated principles of discrimination, however, can falsely convince us that we're being rational. For if we cannot rationally explain our principles, then the conclusion that stems from them is likewise irrational (MacIntyre, 1984, p. 8). We may find ourselves believing in our rationality, but no one else does (certainly not those who disagree with our conclusions). The contemporary philosopher Alasdair MacIntyre notes that without agreement on principles we will have "interminable" conversations on moral issues. Consider how some who oppose abortion, citing a principle sanctifying life, may simultaneously hold a belief affirming the death penalty. On the other hand, supporters of physician-assisted suicide may simultaneously argue strongly against the death penalty because of the belief that, in principle, the state should not impose limitations on one's control of the end of one's life. Without rising to ethical principles, debates on moral particulars likely remain interminable. And yet, debates over principles may be as interminable as those pertaining to particulars. Perhaps what we need is a method for *defining* principles. This is the social contract theory approach of John Rawls. Considered a classic of the twentieth century, his *Theory of Justice* (1971/1999) proposes a hypothetical circumstance wherein rational people engage in a deliberative process that concludes with a theory of justice, that is, a system of discrimination. While his objective is to generate a theory on the distribution of rights and liberties, not ethics, his approach may be applied to creating a theory of ethics. He invests a great deal in affirming that fairness would result from the circumstance and process because, he believes, if we agree on the process, then, implicitly, we agree on its conclusion(s). Consider it a system of discrimination for creating a terminable system of discrimination, that is, a method of distinguishing between the actions one should undertake and those one should not. Rawls's approach introduces us to the idea of committing to a method of discrimination, and more generally, to committing to performing right action. This commitment is reflected in the next ethical feature, *motive*.

Motive and Purpose: Compelled to the Good

A *motive* is what compels us to right action, driving us to be agents seeking ethical fulfillment. It would be ironic if an ethical system provided means for discrimination but no motive for doing so. Exploring the "possibility of altruism," the contemporary philosopher Thomas Nagel (1978) characterizes rational motivation as either internal or external. With internal motivation we are obligated by the truth of an ethical proposition; that is, the proposition's truth dispenses with any need to look outside the proposition for motivation. Immanuel Kant calls this "acting from duty," the duty being to the apparent truth of the ethical proposition. Internalism makes several assumptions. First, it assumes that duty implies motivation. Second, it presupposes that humans are rational and thus able to recognize the truthfulness of a proposition (a moral agent complies with such a proposition). Consequently, to an internalist, it is irrational to recognize that you ought to do something and not want to do it. The caveat with internalism is that this does not depend on the proposition being proven true or objectively true, but only on the person believing in an ostensibly objective conclusion about a proposition. Until the fall of 2008, the former chairman of the U.S. Federal Reserve, Alan Greenspan, believed in this apparently self-evident truth: actors in a free market have an interest in the survival of their respective business organizations, and this interest moderates impulses to reckless action. Because he believed this to be self-evident, he engaged in a method of economic discrimination that considers minimally regulated economic activity to be good public policy. This internal truth failed to reward his commitment to it.

Internalism is a feature of *deontological* ethical systems, that is, systems whose motive arises from duty. Again, we turn to the categorical imperative for an example that binds reason and duty. Reason tells us what must be done (categorical), and its method of discrimination is so self-evident that duty binds us to it (imperative). It values the right action over the right consequence, a prioritization that Bok (1988) explains is emphasized most clearly by Kant's maxim, "Do what is right, though the world shall perish." Therein we might prove the internal motive: that one sacrifices self and subverts self-interest in compliance with right action.

With externalism, we have personal reasons compelling us to action—reasons external to the truthfulness or certainty of the proposition itself. Self-interest is key to securing external motivation. It is perhaps the original motivation, as the renaissance political philosopher Thomas Hobbes noted in his treatise, *The Leviathan* (1651/1997, p. 72), that we possess an instinct for self-preservation. We can deduce that the good life minimally includes remaining alive. This motivating power of self-preservation is further reinforced by World War II concentration camp prisoners forced to "work" assisting in the killing and cremation of fellow prisoners: "We feel that we should kill ourselves and not work for the Germans. But even to kill yourself is not so easy" (Reese, 2005, p. 232). Externalism, in such extreme situations, may be an irresistible motive. As to conventional ethical theories, utilitarianism relies on externalist motives: who could possibly reason to the conclusion that life must always be pleasure and no pain? The philosopher Zygmunt Bauman (2008) noted that utilitarianism represents a turn to modernity because it attempts to replace internal motivation with external motivation (p. 113), heteronomy with autonomy, or Kant's duty with personal desire. For this position on motive, too, we can see why free-market proponents have an affinity for utilitarianism.

It is interesting to note that we can find ourselves motivated to have a motive, compelled to be compelled. Even with seemingly irresolvable dilemmas or issues for which no decision or action is required, we can feel compelled to make a stand. Burke's theory of "frames of acceptance and rejection" (1937) reveals how we have a hard time staying on the fence about any one person, issue, or situation. We want to evaluate, good or bad, feeling some way or the other about taxes, politicians, brands, unions, and Wal-Mart. We want to sort things out to conclusions, often after the fact, in our accounts of beliefs and actions. Language is integral to this: stories we tell have morals to them; we use value terms; we make motive-based appeals when advocating a moral position; we appeal to the internal motive of logic and to the external motive of interest, and sometimes we cite one motive but claim that it's really the other, as in, "this is how business works," or "I'm much better informed than you are, so just trust what I have to say." These latter examples express external motives masquerading as internal ones, or statements of preference masquerading as self-evident truths. We're so compelled to account for our motives that we're willing to lie— sometimes even to ourselves.

Responsibility and Relationship: Beyond the Immediate Situation

Responsibility reflects a duty toward someone or something. Responsibility presumes *relationship*; it also assumes a degree of truthfulness of messages and trustworthiness of the person expressing them. Generally speaking, you don't have a responsibility to do someone else's job or to care for an imaginary child. If you do have one of these responsibilities, there must be a relationship somewhere in the mix (though not necessarily to the job or the imaginary child). Yet, relationship does not automatically confer responsibility. Further, because some situations of responsibility are unidirectional, we can also distinguish between responsibility and blame (Gibbs, 2000). Imagine a doctor saying, "Hey, I didn't cause that car accident (or that pregnancy); treating this patient is not my responsibility." Responsibility to care for the patient, in that case, minimally arises from the doctor's relationship with the medical profession that conferred professional standing upon him in exchange for his commitment to honor the tenets of the profession. Other examples of unidirectional responsibilities include those a caregiver has to a newborn, or a "caregiver" to his Tomagotchi toy. Over time and with frequency of interaction, some of these relationships evolve and a bidirectional responsibility develops. An ethical system features principles of responsibility, and we would likely see them reflect relationship, including whether or not a particular relationship is possible. For example, an ethical system may ignore or preclude an ethical relationship with plants, animals, or nature in general, or value it less than the relationships we have with other persons or institutions. If we work on a factory fishing boat, we may hold our relationship to our family (earning income to support them) as superior to our relationship to the fish we catch. This would be reflected in a diminished degree of responsibility and, ultimately, moral concern.

The willingness to fulfill one's responsibilities comes from many sources. We highlight shame. Shame is a consequence of failing to act responsibly. Aristotle is one philosopher who advocated a place for shame as an appropriate and motivating response to a voluntary action that sullies our reputation and character, and argued that we do have a responsibility for our character (2002, pp. 135, 158). Now, it is one matter to ascribe shame to an individual, but what about *groups* of people? This brings up the situation of collective responsibility, an important consideration given the high visibility and claims of corporate social responsibility (S. May, Cheney, & Roper, 2007). The philosopher Elizabeth Wolgast summarizes the situation: "The ability to speak for others that makes artificial persons both useful and attractive also frustrates the conditions of responsibility" (1992, p. 144). It is shame's reliance on conscience that is the source of frustration. Shame requires agents to possess a conscience; to think that a corporation (as a collective agent) has a conscience confuses the metaphor of the artificial person with the reality that a corporation is merely a legal fiction (Ritz, 2003). So, while a corporation may "speak" with one voice, it has no conscience, and cannot experience shame, remorse, or an emotional motive toward responsibility. When a CEO or political leader says, "the buck stops here," it is an admission of the ultimate individual human responsibility, even when that human person is only a participant in collective action.

Individuality, though, can be taken too far, causing us to lose sight of the forest because we're myopically focused on the trees. For a short period in 2008, amid the global economic upheavals, Anderson Cooper's television show, *360*, featured a segment titled, "Culprits of the Collapse." The title indicates the myopia of these segments: it all comes down to greedy individuals. While that is strictly true—in the sense that people are the creators, owners, managers, and agents of every corporation—there are systemic influences upon individual behavior, too. There is, of course, pushback on this myopic blaming of individuals: "This was not an intentioned plan to destroy the world. Wall Street was designed to make money" (Copetas & Harper, 2009, para. 23). Or, paraphrasing *The Simpsons Movie* (Silverman, 2007): "A market does what markets do." As we shall see in succeeding chapters, these systems often culturally or contractually demand specific behavior in order to participate, that is, in order to be in explicit relationship with them: we have a relationship with our work, with our profession, with our organization, and with the market. Yet, those responsible for creating and maintaining systems that encourage undesirable individual behavior may be complicit in that behavior and thus should reasonably bear some of the responsibility.

Our recognition of responsibility diminishes when we abstract relationships, or the other with whom we have a relationship. Adam

Smith (1759/1976a, 1776/1976b) noted that a factory owner should live in the same town in which his factory operated; such co-location facilitates relationship and thus responsibility, and encourages action that respects these relationships. Exposure to this Other may bring about the transformation of personal values. Consider the very public transformation experienced in 1995 by the television actress and talk show host Kathie Lee Gifford, when she met some of the women producing her branded clothing in Latin American factories. The activists who arranged the meeting trusted that real faces and their personal stories might overcome or disrupt Gifford's prioritizing the monetary exchange value of these workers over their use value as human beings—and might realign American consumers' expectations for the Gifford brand (Kendall, Gill, & Cheney, 2007). In other words, refusing to abstract relationships maintains an appropriate place for shame, promotes responsibility, and brings the Other back from the edges of moral concern.

Utilitarianism abstracts relationships, but it does account for them in that our calculations of aggregate happiness are supposed to include everyone. That's a generous though impractical scope. John Stuart Mill (2002), writing in 1863, apparently understood this. The foundation for his argument against a self-centered calculus, in which we throw up our hands to the impossibility of accounting for everyone's happiness, is his appeal to the "noble character" (p. 244), a reflection of the "sense of dignity...which is so essential a part of happiness" (p. 242). Mill argues that if everyone acted only for the betterment of others and never for the direct benefit of himself, they would still be happy, though he does not advise us to such an extreme position.

We can see the importance of relationship in the ethical theory best known as *ethics of care*, brought clearly into view by the social psychologist Carol Gilligan (1982), and sometimes characterized as feminist ethics (though not by her). Rather than the abstraction and impartiality of other ethical systems, an ethics of care contextualizes ethical principles by recognizing relationship and particularities. We can see this in the contrasting approaches of affirmative-action programs and equal-opportunity programs. The former adjusts standards to be relative to an applicant's background, whereas the latter seeks to overcome the limited visibility of opportunities in certain communities and populations. With affirmative action, the applicant and his particularities are real, not abstract. With equal opportunity the applicant is abstract but the applicant's community is real. These are different relationships, with consequent different responsibilities leading to different moral positions on hiring practices. Sometimes, who you know makes all the difference.

Rationality and Emotionality: Two Worlds or One?

Passions for justice and other social ideals are as important as calculations of it. The tension between *rationality* and *emotionality* (or passion) is a central theme of the television series *Star Trek*, with the characters of Spock and Captain Kirk representing logic and passion in the original series, and Data and Captain Picard representing the same in a reprisal series. A common moral lesson of these shows is that moral questions are best resolved through a blend of rationality and passion rather than by logic alone—and not just here on Earth. The captains are agents of ultimate authority on their respective ships. Both are at ease expressing their emotions and are astute observers of others' emotions. They repeatedly prove their mastery at blending rationality and passion, portraying this mastery as an essential characteristic of leadership. Spock, as the epitome of logic, attempts to counterbalance Captain Kirk. And yet, Spock's background—he has a Vulcan father (a humanlike species without emotion) and a human mother—feeds a personal struggle between rationality and emotionality, the same struggle that's writ large in most episodes. The series featuring Data and Picard also includes this subplot. Data is an android, not an animal. And though equipped with a computer brain, he eventually experiences the same internal struggle as Spock. One of Data's recognitions of this struggle derives from his participation in a chamber music ensemble (Snodgrass & Bole, 1989). He notes the musical contributions of both rationality and emotionality, recognizing their co-residence within his android brain and the necessity of balancing their contributions to life in general. Aristotle calls the ability to balance rationality and emotionality *phronesis*, or practical wisdom; those who have earned this practical wisdom have the resources they need for right living.

Emotionality and rationality each finds favor or disfavor in respective ethical systems and with regard to different ethical features. Regarding rationality, utilitarianism appeals to the higher capacities of people, "Better to be Aristotle dissatisfied than a pig satisfied," and recognizes that many people are compelled to the "lower forms of pleasure" (Mill, 2002, p. 242). But this emotional proclivity should be counterbalanced by reason. To the person of intelligence and reason, lower forms of happiness become little more than momentary distractions. Aristotle affirms that bodily pleasures have their place in life, but self-control and moderation are virtues. The fictional *Star Trek* starship captains, James T. Kirk, and Jean-Luc Picard, follow in Aristotle's tradition, at least on this point.

This is not to claim the severability of rationality and emotionality. Rather, each contributes to the effective capacity of the other, particularly in the skills required for social functioning (Planalp, 1999) and even ordinary decision-making (Damasio, 1994). We commonly criticize those who lack balance, saying they "act like a robot" or else are "hysterical." Rationality's contributions to this relationship are obvious to Westerners. After all, Western culture prizes logical thinking, and this logical thinking has led to this conclusion: emotionality is an essential ingredient of moral development (Planalp, 1999, pp. 181–83). Carl Jung provides an anecdotal note of this, writing:

> Observance of customs and laws can very easily be a cloak
> for a lie so subtle that our fellow human beings are unable
> to detect it. It may help us escape all criticism; we may even
> be able to deceive ourselves in the belief of our obvious
> righteousness. But deep down, below the surface of the
> average man's conscience, he hears a voice whispering,
> "There is something not right," no matter how much
> his rightness is supported by public opinion or by the moral
> code. (1953, p. 40)

Emotions provide this sense of fairness, "orient[ing] us to the *good* and the *should:* to things that we value and to things that we feel we ought to do" (Planalp, 1999, p. 161). As many a fourth-grade teacher will tell you, children have a sense of fairness. Of course, given their limited ability to balance reason and emotion, their recognition of fairness doesn't mean they will act fairly. The emotion of empathy begins to be demonstrated by children between the ages of two and three. Empathy contributes to moral development because this emotion initially connects us to the ethical features of relationship and agency, and secondarily to the features of role and identity (detailed, below). An empath does more than feel for the other's emotional state, he or she feels the emotions and resonates with that state. While we logically know the emotional state isn't truly ours, or even rational (e.g., a person who literally weeps over spilled milk), empathy gives us more clues about the moral situation we're in. Knowing exactly what should be done, and having the discipline to act according to that knowledge, comes later. This combination of emotionality and rationality comprises practical reflection. *Phronesis*, though, encompasses much more than reflection by an individual person: it involves successive considerations of an issue or a question that arise out of interaction with others. Aristotle's practical wisdom, then, is intimately bound up with relationships, so that no one is thinking alone.

Role and Identity: Finding Our Place

As detailed in chapter 1, ethical compartmentalization (putting ethics in a box) and essentialism (reducing ethics to one thing) may be encouraged when we see ourselves bound by roles or identities. Similarly, ethical systems may prescribe the assumption of an identity—a psychological uniform, if you will—especially if the ethical system is role-related (e.g., related to a profession, an economic class, a tribe). And the stories we tell ourselves about an identity reinforce that sphere's boundaries. Phrases such as, "I'm one of the guys," or "I want to be a great trial attorney, like Perry Mason," have ethical implications because they are strongly identity-related, packing assumptions about right living. It's crucial to explore not just what such phrases mean in the critical sense, but also how they got their meaning for us in the emancipatory sense. Part of the ethical power of identities isn't just how we respond to a specific identity (e.g., guy, attorney); there also is a compelling power in the idea of identity itself. Asking children, "What do you want to be when you grow up?" promotes the idea of identity even as it implicitly tells them that they should want to be something other than what they already are. When we weave a story around a particular identity, we also weave a story around the idea of identity itself.

Examples of identity-based generalities (reflecting an essentialized view of an ethical system) is the Christian query, "What would Jesus do?" (sometimes expressed in the WWJD bracelet fad), and the mocking reactions embodied in the bumper sticker reading "Who would Jesus bomb?" and the 2007 film *What Would Jesus Buy?* Identifying with the character of a god or, in these examples, his son, is meant to encourage a particular set of behaviors as described in the stories told about him. Packaging an ethical context as an identity is an especially useful device when its advisory principles consist of generalities. It deflects questions about specifics by appealing to an essentialist view of the identity. The Jesus examples encourage us to metaphorically assume the role of Jesus, enter the ethical context as we believe he would, make moral assessments about the particular situation, and, finally, act as we believe he would.

Identities may turn into common expressions, as in "Don't be a Scrooge," a direct reference to Dickens's avaricious Ebenezer Scrooge

(1843/2006). Letting the ethics of his profession dominate the ethics of his person, Scrooge devalues human relationships if they require that he spend money (or take a hiatus from earning it) to maintain them. Identities may also become part of a slogan, as in the U.S. military recruiting campaign touting "An Army of One." The images from that campaign elevate the role of a soldier to that of a mythological hero; that is, a person who ventures into the unknown, engages in adventure, and then returns home with experience that contributes to both the community and the self. In the unexpected use of the word "Army" to represent an individual person lies the metaphorical power of this slogan, which serves in turn to aggrandize the individual person.

How we each see ourselves—or our potential selves—steers us on the course of ethical practice. If only we could hear the words of ethical principles and moral propositions without hearing in them our identity or that of the speaker. This elimination of our particular situation and interests finds expression in debate societies. Competing teams are assigned moral issues such as forced sterilization or capital punishment (another dead metaphor, originally meaning decapitation). Teams do not know whether they will advocate permitting or prohibiting the action. Their preparation must ignore their predispositions and instead focus on the facts and reason, not who they are or wish to be (see Greene & Hicks, 2005). The "I" is irrelevant. Imagine being able to negate the influence of our identity. Would we have a different understanding? Would we be less prone to compartmentalize ethics, that is, confine ethical considerations? Would we be less accepting of ethical generalities and instead demand specifics? This is not to say that we should ignore our identity. After all, we do things in order to achieve a particular end. We play the flute to make music. We work extra hours because we're trying to distinguish ourselves at work. And we live in order to be in the world and to be a particular person through this life. The goal of a holistic identity provides a useful point of orientation, and helps us recognize and reconcile life's roles. These ethical reflections and musings become part of who we are just as they are part of who we would like to be.

Scene, Situation, and Scenario: Where the World Comes In

In a way it seems odd to include the entire *scene* or *situation* for our ethical pursuits as a feature of analysis. After all, aren't ethical dilemmas and decisions just various situations? When we take a closer look, however, we realize that the scene or situation becomes an important grounding for ethical decisions and actions in how we think and talk about ethics. We also imagine how situations might arise or influence us, and this is why we include *scenario*. In general, we know that scenes are places we step into, like actors stepping on stage. The stage gives us certain things to work with, but it also constrains us. The same is true for situations. So, we speak of being born into certain circumstances (e.g., "born with a silver spoon/foot in his mouth"), being in places at the wrong time, or having good fortune. All of these are references to the scene or situation. So are excuses like "I got caught in traffic" and "He hit me first!" These are attributions to forces external to us and presumably out of our control. Above all, they are claims regarding the influences upon us in that situation, whether temporary insanity or a moment of selfless clarity. And in each case, it is important to bear in mind that all such attributions are communicative acts: the way we invoke situation or scenario profoundly influences how it affects us. To take the stage metaphor seriously, we should always remember that plays are written by human authors.

It is tempting to divide references to the scene into "real" and "perceived," in that some constraints and opportunities may have an objective, material presence in our lives. If you are stopped by a police officer for speeding while rushing to an appointment, you will likely be late for the meeting. If you lose your job and have no other source of funds, you will certainly have less income. If diagnosed with a terminal illness and given just months to live, then there is a real and known time limitation on everything that you do. Seeing a terminally ill friend outside a sweets shop, deeply engaged with a frozen treat, the writer Sy Safransky noted, "So that's how you eat a popsicle when you know you're dying" (2006, p. 47). But even in these cases, where the world seemingly intervenes in the flow of our lives, there are or were choices. We could have headed off to work a little earlier. Stressed over a loss of income, we can decide to live much more simply. Knowing when the ultimate end will come, we might choose to shift attention to spending time with loved ones, or showing greater gratitude for simple pleasures like a popsicle on a hot summer day. Reality and perception blend together in important but not always well-understood ways.

In listening to people talk about ethics, we can observe how people reference the scene as grounds for behavior. In TV's *Survivor*, "the game" is a common point of reference for the characters, who downplay their loyalties to one another while at the same time professing their friendship and even love. When we speak about "how the game is played" as an excuse or even a justification for a ruthless strategy, we are, in effect, saying, "My actions are determined by the context in which I live and work." This is tantamount to saying that you have no real agency under these circumstances, as in, "I had no choice but to fire you."

Putting aside the question of power and external forces, we can still notice patterns in how people make such attributions. And this applies to collective agents, such as corporations, as well. Isn't it curious that corporate annual reports tend to make internal attributions when describing successes (e.g., "Thanks to our innovation and foresight"), whereas poor performance is assigned to external attributions (e.g., "The higher prices of certain commodities held back our product development") (see Conrad, 1993)? While performance in this sense may be considered to be more "factual" than ethical, we find similar patterns for cases that are more squarely in the domain of the moral.

The ethical systems already noted share an interest in the agent's accurate assessment of his or her situation. Making a moral decision based on the wrong problem; well, that's hard to label a success. Consider the other features. Can any of them operate if we lack the skill and sensitivity of accurate assessment? Aristotle's virtue ethics describes *phronesis* as this ability to make sound judgments based on rational assessment and thinking. A wise person, lacking accurate assessments, is barely better off in his moral decision-making than an unwise one.

A Narrative, in Principle

Willa Cather's 1912 novel *Alexander's Bridge* (2002) illustrates many of the features of an ethical system, and also supports a central theme of this book: that the professional is the personal. This novel, Cather's first, attempted to deal with ethics both in a highly personal way and across spheres of activity. Outwardly, Bartley Alexander is the model of personal and professional success. He designs bridges, tremendous spans that literally and metaphorically demonstrate the reach of his success. From modest beginnings he developed himself to a place of professional success. He is personally fortunate, too, blessed with a beautiful, intelligent, and devoted wife, and a fine home in turn-of-the-century Boston. It is the personal life we would expect of a successful man; and it is the professional success we would expect of one who is living so well.

Cather takes this complementary relationship between the professional and the personal into an ethical space. She portrays the ethical unity of Alexander by connecting his ethical failings person-

ally (adultery) and professionally (consciously permitting the construction of a bridge whose design stays within legal requirements
but overreaches the tolerance of his engineering intuition and experience). He knows he is doing wrong personally—he is a reflective
moral agent—and despite the support of his mathematical analysis,
he suspects he is doing wrong in his design of this bridge, which was
to be the crowning achievement of his career. Alexander unquestionably and consciously invites the actions that culminate in his personal
and professional failure. Yes, his bridge does fall down. But of greater
tragedy to the man is his realization of *personal* failure: that he isn't
the man he thought he was. And although his wife would never discover his adultery, *he knows*. With that self-discovery, he recognizes
his life as something that does not distinguish between the personal
and the professional: "'I am not a man who can live two lives,' he
went on feverishly. 'Each life spoils the other'" (Cather, 2002, p. 82).
He is a unitary ethical being who has learned his values by his conscious choices and habits, and thus crafted his character.

This novel touches upon a number of the features of an ethical
system, a balancing act along the dimensional axis of each feature.
The novel presents Alexander's system of discrimination as permitting multiple identity-based ethical contexts (e.g., husband, bridge
engineer, lover). It illustrates the struggle over boundaries of ethical
contexts, how we manage them as distinct or blended, and reconcile conflicts between them. It also illustrates his moral maturation
as he grapples between reasoned conclusions and emotional urges,
culminating in his ultimate assumption of agency and responsibility
in his marital and professional roles in order to recraft himself as the
particular kind of man he wishes to be. Of particular interest is how
the novel pressages Alexander's struggle with the kind of person he
is versus the kind of person he could have been, and the challenges
that this struggle places upon his practice of discrimination. A trusted
friend raises this issue with him:

> "No, I'm serious, Alexander. You've changed. You have
> decided to leave some birds in the bushes. You used to want
> them all."
>   Alexander's chair creaked. "I still want a good many,"
> he said rather gloomily. "After all, life doesn't offer a man
> much. You work like the devil and think you're getting on,
> and suddenly you discover that you've only been getting
> yourself tied up. A million details drink you dry. Your life
> keeps going for things you don't want, and all the while

you are being built alive into a social structure you don't care a rap about. I sometimes wonder what sort of chap I'd have been if I hadn't been this sort; I want to go and live out his potentialities, too. I haven't forgotten that there are birds in the bushes." (Cather, 2002, pp. 12–13)

How he sees himself motivates his powers and practices of discrimination; that is, the story he tells himself or the beliefs he has about his own character motivate particular life choices, with his bridge symbolizing (among other things) the connection between who he is and the "chap" he might have been. But he also knows that by making different choices, particularly ones contrary to the dominant story of his life, he will alter his character and thus his motivation.

Clearly, a life of moral awareness requires a lot of work, and we may find meaning in everything, including our suffering (Frankl, 2006). In the novel's conclusion, Alexander's widow is described by another character as expressing "the most beautiful sorrow [he has] ever known" (Cather, 2002, p. 136). Her sorrow preserves Alexander's presence so effectively that, though dead, in his house "[Alexander] really is there" (p. 136). His preservation has becomes her purpose. This is reinforced by her name; she is referred to by everyone *except* her husband as "Mrs. Alexander," a title that declares her identity and her life's purpose. It has become her greatest good. But does it become her greatest happiness? In the eyes of her peers, Mrs. Alexander may be a successful widow, but what of her life beyond that role? Does her success as a widow bring about her happiness as a person?

Ethics, Communication, and Happiness

Sift through your memories of happiness. Is there one that stands out so powerfully that you would want to remain in that moment for eternity (Akieda, Sato, & Koreeda, 1998)? What made that moment stand out? Likely, it was a combination of who you were at that moment and the circumstances. Did you consciously prepare for the moment, as an athlete prepares for the moment of Olympic competition? For athletic champions, would they choose the moment when the gold medal was hung on their neck? When they heard their national anthem? Or when they were making the medal-winning dive, tumbling through the air in the culmination of years of effort? If ethics advises us about right living, shouldn't it advise us on achieving happiness, whatever that is?

Happiness is a topic that not long ago would have elicited giggles but now gets the serious attention both of our students and of scholars. What's happened? For one thing, it is now a concentrated area of research in academic disciplines, including psychology, philosophy, economics, sociology, political science, management, and communication. The positive psychology movement, led by Ed Diener at the University of Illinois, Martin Seligman of the University of Pennsylvania (see, e.g., Diener & Seligman, 2002), and others, is built on the study of reported life satisfaction and paths to higher quality relationships and experiences, including work.

Among the more provocative results of this research are: comparative studies of national-level indicators since the 1950s; reports on exactly what makes people happy; and connections to the roles of work, consumption, and the market in our society. In general terms, cross-national comparisons show that while most nations fall upon a relatively predictable regression line (picture a forward slash) for the relationship between material affluence and life satisfaction, there have been some surprises. Latin American countries consistently score somewhat higher on happiness than their comparative levels of income and material possessions would suggest. Further, material affluence has its limits in terms of happiness. Some of the most advanced economies of the world, notably those the United States, Germany, and Japan, seem to have gained very little or not at all in terms of happiness, even as their economies grew. The graph of the relationship of the gross national product, the most common indicator of societal economic standing, and reports of happiness as found in the World Values Survey (cited in Diener & Suh, 2000) indicate that not much of anything is too far from the regression line. Still, for the United States, the evidence from surveys taken over a fifty-year period suggests that happiness peaked in about 1957 and has plateaued since then (see the winter 2009 issue of *Yes!* magazine). These facts come as a surprise to many people.

Studies of what makes people happy are fascinating, especially because so many assumptions turn out to be misguided; for example, we believe that as we get richer beyond a certain point, we will continue to experience additional "increments" in happiness; that the most memorable events in our lives are ones involving great achievements or accolades; and that success is defined in the ways advertising typically presents it. In fact, happiness is a lot more complicated *and rich* in ways other than popular notions would suggest. Very happy people say that "high happiness seems to be like beautiful symphonic music—necessitating many instruments, without any one being sufficient for the beautiful quality" (Diener & Seligman, 2002, p. 83). The findings show that satisfying close relationships with friends, family, and coworkers are a necessary but insufficient condition. Extraversion, along with low neuroticism and psychopathology can also play important roles in determining who is consistently happy. Myers and Diener (1995) also find a sense of personal control, optimism, high self-esteem, interesting work (flow), and high spiritual commitment among people who report high levels of happiness. Overall, they conclude, "happiness grows less from the passive experience of desirable circumstances than from involvement in valued activities and progress toward one's goals" (p. 17).

This sounds so simple, and in a way it is. But we are led to wonder about the extent to which we really organize our lives this way. How do we spend our time? Which goals do we elevate? How much do we consider life satisfaction to be an indicator of "success"? And what do our notions of personal happiness reveal about the way we see our dealings with others, at work and elsewhere? Part of the issue is that people tend to think they know what makes them happy, even when they don't.

Such misunderstandings are tied up with advertising and broad cultural expectations. Some psychologists, extending the line of research that has questioned our rational models of our own decision-making, have decided to test whether people always know what is best for themselves. Examining these empirical studies, Timothy Gilbert and Daniel Wilson (2000) have coined the clever term "miswanting" to suggest that we are often misled by certain biases into thinking X or Y will make us very happy. A good example is what they call "focalism," best expressed as, "When I win the lottery (or attain something else), I'll be very happy." The problem here is that people tend to overestimate the impact of achieving something because they assume its effects will be purely positive, that the good feelings produced by it will last longer than they really will, and that the same pleasure cannot be found with other things (in other words, they misread the distinctiveness of the focal objective).

Diener and Oishi (2000) summarize the practical and ethical implications of all we've learned about happiness this way:

> If wealthy societies are reaching the postmaterialistic point where added goods and services enhance [subjective well-being] very little, we may be at a critical crossroads in terms of public policy and individual choices. People in wealthy nations feel an increasing time shortage, and yet many are

working even longer hours than before. People seek a level of material wealth undreamed of by earlier generations, and they make sacrifices in time and personal relationships to attain it....As long as people want more goods and services, they will tend to be somewhat dissatisfied if they do not get them. Thus the educational challenge is to convince people that other pursuits may sometimes lead to greater fulfillment than does the pursuit of more money. (p. 215)

Happiness and Virtue

The research suggests that the source of happiness comes from how we interact with the world, not how the world is independent of us. This is why worldly goods go only so far to facilitate happiness. The onus is on us, as it is our agency and autonomy that grant us the possibilities for life choices. This brings us back to Aristotle and ethics. As earlier noted, ethics advises us on right living, and the objective of right living would seem to be happiness, well-being, success, human flourishing, that is, *eudaimonia*. To understand what that means, we should lightly walk along his logical path and prepare ourselves for his conclusions. His landmark of Western philosophy, *Nicomachean Ethics* (2002) serves as the primary source of his ideas on this subject. His thoughts remain of enduring relevance to the human species, to our understanding of what we do and what we should do, and to thinkers who have, over the centuries, produced many thousands of pages exploring and expanding his recorded thoughts.

Aristotle begins with the observation that all "expert knowledge and every inquiry, and similarly every action and undertaking, seems to seek some good" (2002, p. 95). That is, it functions for the sake of an objective. Musicians function to make music. A luthier functions to construct stringed musical instruments. A politician functions to draft legislation. Functions arise from roles; roles implicate relationships. The musician has a relationship to the audience, the politician to the citizens and the nation, and the luthier to the musician and, perhaps, to the tree that provided the wood and the cat that provided the gut strings. Each of these Others, as the complement to the relationship, also has a function. The challenges we experience with the compartmentalization of ethics may also be seen as a battle of dominance between one domain of activity—one relationship and thus one ethic—and all others. But what of the human relationship to life itself, its function in total? Hypothesizing this function as the greatest good, Aristotle concludes that we would want to consciously direct ourselves to it and seek an ethical system that helps guide us to this greatest good.

Two primary characteristics help identify this greatest good. First, it should result from actions that only humans are capable of. Second, it should be desirable for its own sake. Consequently, all other goods ultimately are sought for the sake of it; it is not done for the sake of any other good. Useful advice, but we still have the question of how to define "good." Aristotle did not believe that there was a property of "goodness" that can be found in all "good" things or actions. That is, Aristotle recognized the *naturalistic fallacy* (G. E. Moore, 1903/2004, pp. 10–11), as did Plato before him (Plato, 1987). The naturalistic fallacy is the false belief in an objective property of "good." Such a claim inevitably leads to an infinite regression of asking and attempting to answer why those properties are good, and then asking the same of the properties of those properties, ad infinitum. A more Aristotelian argument against "good" as an objective property is that such a property isn't related to a function of a human being. Rather, the core function of a human being is to live a kind of life (Aristotle, 2002, p. 102). The good, then, varies in *kind* not quantity, and the highest function of a human is to live the kind of life that achieves that still-to-be-determined greatest good.

Answering the broadest ethical question "How shall I live?" has led us to "How may I experience the greatest good?" We use the word "experience" because living is an ongoing venture, at least until death. So, although it isn't possible to *achieve* the greatest good, by living a particular kind of life we may be able to experience its presence. For Aristotle, the chief good is *eudaimonia*. This is the motive and purpose of virtue ethics. He summarizes the kind of life we should seek to live in order to experience *eudaimonia* "as being activity of soul and actions accompanied by reason...in accordance with excellence" (2002, p. 102). As a kind of life, it is a life being lived, a happiness that is not an achievement but rather an active state, and thus there is no conclusion until death: "A single swallow does not make spring, nor does a single day; in the same way, neither does a single day, or a short time, make a man blessed and happy" (p. 102).

Here we must distinguish the way activities are done from the measure of their excellence. Excellence is expressed as virtue, hence the name, *virtue ethics*. The virtues, or "excellences of character," include: courage, moderation, open-handedness, munificence, greatness of soul, a nameless excellence to do with honor, mildness, three social excellences, and justice. Each exists along an axis where one end denotes an excess of the virtue and the other a deficiency. It is incumbent on each of us to express the correct balance between the two, a balance appropriate to who we are and the circumstances we are in. For example, what is courageous for a twelve-year-old child in a given situation likely is different from what is courageous for a thirty-five-year-old person similarly situated. For that child to act like the adult expresses an excess of courage, that is, recklessness. Conversely, for that adult to respond like a child expresses a deficiency of courage, or timidity. Such differences reflect different ethical sensibilities, acknowledging the particularities of the situation, not asserting that one approach is right and the other is wrong (see also Gilligan, 1982).

Aristotle's set of characteristic virtues raises questions about their appropriateness for today. Some virtues, such as courage, transcend time. Others, like munificence, may be appreciated differently, depending on the times and situations. It isn't that virtues are purely a reflection of culture, relativistic. Rather, the names for certain qualities may change over time. And new situations may well require a different mix of characteristics, not just for the individual but also for the society as a whole. For example, Aristotle recommended a different set of virtues for slaves, holding that what is just for the master isn't necessarily just for the slave. It's not so much that times change, but rather that our ideals do. This lack of specificity about the ideal expression of an excellence, particularly its apparently loose advice on discrimination and choice, has caused some to dismiss virtue ethics as impractical. Conversely, Aristotle's extensive and thoughtful treatment of the resources required for *eudaimonia* challenges us to reflect on the kind of people we are, our capabilities (assessing the present) and our capacities (estimating our potential). The basic resources are voluntary agency and decision-making ability. The premier resources we bring to bear as we strive for excellence of character are intellectual virtue, moral virtue, and practical wisdom. *Intellectual virtue* is composed of *scientific knowledge*, an active reflection on those "things whose principles cannot be otherwise"; and *calculative knowledge*, an active reflection on those "things that can be otherwise" (Aristotle, 2002, p. 177). *Moral virtue* reflects a proper balance between the non-rational and rational parts of the soul (p. 109), the ethical features we previously introduced as rationality and emotionality. With excellence of moral virtue, we act with the proper motive, that is, "in accordance with excellence."

Practical wisdom, or *phronesis*, is the only virtue that is both intellectual and moral. D. S. Hutchinson summarizes its many traits as "an appreciation of what is good and bad for us at the highest level, together with a correct apprehension of the facts of experiences, together with the skill to make the correct inferences about how to apply our general moral knowledge of our particular situation,...quickly and reliably" (1995, p. 207). An imbalance toward a deficiency of moral virtue causes us to be clever but to act unwisely (Aristotle, 2002, pp. 187–88). A deficiency of intellectual virtue has us correctly motivated to act with excellence but incapable of doing so (moral awkwardness). As Aristotle notes, happiness "is brought to completion by virtue of a person's having [practical] wisdom and excellence of character; for excellence make the goal correct, while wisdom makes what leads to it correct" (p. 187).

In the above treatment of virtue ethics we present it as just another ethical system. That was a choice of writing style, desiring to keep it consistent with other treatments. That virtue ethics also may be described in terms of the features of ethical systems suggests that there may be overlap. In fact, virtue ethics shares with utilitarianism and deontology an interest in motives, the tension between emotionality and rationality, and the importance of character overall (Nussbaum, 1999). Further overlap may be seen with other ethical systems in their similar recognition of scene and scenario, responsibility and relationship, and agency and autonomy. The critique about virtue ethics' lack of specificity in its process of discrimination and choice may be viewed as a benefit in how it opens up the possibilities for application of other ethical systems. With its focus on reflection and contemplation (essential to intellectual virtue, agency, and decision-making), virtue ethics compels us to understand various ethical systems in order to assist the development of our practical wisdom. The twentieth-century virtue-ethics revival isn't a matter of fashion; rather, it is a matter of recognizing ethics writ large as a way of actively living and flourishing in this temporal and limited life.

A big tent for virtue ethics includes the ways in which we strive for excellence of character and *eudaimonia*. Given a clearer idea of how to live—that is, an ethic—wouldn't a society of excellence facilitate its members' achievement of *eudaimonia*? This isn't a theoretical speculation; it is a foundation for the modern conception of human rights and, particularly, the groundbreaking 1948 Universal Declaration of Human Rights. Consider human rights as a collective excellence, just as the virtues represent human excellence. If individuals have an ultimate good, then it seems that, for the benefit of us individually and collectively, the ultimate good of an association of persons (e.g., organization, profession, government, market) should facilitate human achievement of individual ultimate good. This raises profound questions as to the function of the domains of the professional life with regard to the flourishing of individuals and the collective. Perhaps most importantly, both are active views of ideals: the ideal human life, and the ideal collective life. To the extent that we actively aspire to *eudaimonia*, we are human, and to the extent that a society seeks to secure and distribute rights, we are a humane society.

The solitary life constrains our opportunity to develop the virtues and excellence of character. For example, you cannot practice munificence without there being other people; being good to others requires that there are others to be good to. The *eudaimonia* of the individual requires the person to live in a society, to be part of the collective. Given how much we learn from and rely on the collective, we owe it to the collective to help maintain and improve its efficient support for the *eudaimonia* of its members. The successful functioning of the collective and the individual are interdependent. Our happiness grows through interdependence.

Ethics and Communication: Toward Happiness

The study of rhetoric reminds us that ethics are not simply given. This applies even to principles we may think of as universal, or nearly so. Ethics are wrapped up in the communication process in the sense that we always have the capacity to persuade one another and affect others' choices, even when we don't notice it. Think, for example, of how employees often try to anticipate "what the boss wants" even though the boss has said nothing explicit about direction. Similarly, to engage one another in conversation, debate, or deliberation is to exercise the potential to influence the "oughts" of life even when we may be focused on what "is." To tell someone else that "these are merely the facts, and I'm not suggesting what you should do" is still to direct their attention to parts of an issue or a problem, however earnest or truthful that framing of the situation may be. As earlier noted, ethics has an inherency in rhetoric. Ethics then, just like rhetoric, concerns situations of uncertainty where decisions can and sometimes must be made. Attending to certain facts is one kind of decision, though it is seldom recognized as such; deciding on a policy is, of course, another kind of decision, one that announces itself as such.

In certain cases our ethical decisions are, or ought to be, obvious; they don't really count as dilemmas. But, more often than not, there are choices to be made *between* various principles, duties, loyalties, and groups of people. That is, we must make tradeoffs, even if we refuse to accept them. Whether we like it or not, we are compelled to decide how to conceive and pursue ambitions, how much time to spend with family versus at our work, whether to challenge (or even chastise) a close colleague for a presumed violation of professional standards, or how far to go in damaging "the competition" to acquire a greater market share for our company. All of these are situations of judgment, of choice, where our interactions with others, ideas gleaned from a lifetime of socialization and experience, formal theories and tacit knowledge can all affect what we actually do. Both formal and informal theories of ethics remind us to pay attention to certain features of the situation and may convince us that the best measure of ethical success or progress can be summed up with a standard.

Yet, when we step back from ethics and consider not only specific decisions or issues but also the big picture, we realize that there is a meta- or overarching decision to make: how will we see and talk about ethics as related to our life's path and to the larger society in which we make our way? The relationship of ethics to rhetoric and communication is important, for if we think of ethics simply in legalistic or regulatory terms, as relevant mainly when scandals erupt, we're not going to be very inspiring for ourselves or for others. That constrained view frames ethics as something abstract and removed from most of everyday life, invoked or triggered only by troublesome events. When viewed expansively, ethics become a dimension of life that is interwoven with our individual and collective pursuits, a means to individual and collective success. This latter perspective actually privileges ethics by no longer setting it aside in a "special place." There is a new myth, a new story we can tell about ethics.

This is exactly why a revived and expanded form of virtue ethics combined with notions of the pursuit of happiness—or flourishing—is crucially important. We've become so accustomed to compartmentalizing, essentializing, and abstracting ethics that we have lost sight of its larger role in our lives. At the same time, we've been constrained by such limited notions of happiness, achievement, and success that we continue to employ narrow measures of those goals and remain unsatisfied with the results (as we discuss much more in the chapters that follow).

What precisely Aristotle meant by virtue ethics and *eudaimonia* makes for an interesting academic conversation, but it is hardly the point (Nussbaum, 1999). From our standpoint, Artistotle offered us

certain tools for understanding ethics and rhetoric (or communication) writ large, and we can take those tools and build a perspective
that fits contemporary lives and aspirations (Appiah, 2005). Thus,
we would reframe virtue just as we would reframe ethics, at least
in terms of how both have been understood typically in Western
thought. A renewed focus on virtue ethics isn't about devising a
checklist or finding and emulating the "best" people. Rather, with
new light on virtue ethics, we can see better how our ongoing ways
of talking about and relating within situations foster or limit ethical
horizons, including our flourishing.

Virtue and *eudaimonia* apply just as much to the collective as to the
individual. In fact, we need to liberate ourselves from thinking of ethical decisions, and lapses, as matters for personal or professional choice
by persons, or as egotistical personal development. From removing
"bad apples," then, we move to cultivating "the good orchard." A
revived and enriched version of virtue ethics can help us reflect on
what the very things we hold as values are and how they come to be
points of orientation for our activities rather than mere slogans.

Each of the next four chapters revolves around a term, which
may also be thought of as a domain of practice in our lives. This book
is about ethics related to work, and "work" is the key term for chapter 3. Rather than taking certain assumptions about work, meaning,
and ethics for granted, however, we try to begin with questions of
how "work" functions as a point of reference in everyday life and
what difference those formulations make in terms of ethics. In chapter 4 we probe the various meanings of "professional," including the
less appealing ones, before offering some answers about what professionalism could mean with an expanded view of professional ethical
practice. In chapter 5 we turn to the organization as a basis for inquir-
ing about ethics. Here, the very metaphors we use to represent organizations carry with them subtle distinctions about what it means for
us to be part of a machine, a body, a system, or a culture. From talking
about the ethical culture of organization, we move to the level of the
"market," which is now commonly used to represent what our society is and is about. Various expressions of the market have their own
ethical implications, and this is just as true when we treat the market
as amoral. These four terms—work, profession, organization, and
market—have their value-related implications, just as they invoke
certain kinds of activities and decisions. By discussing each one in
turn, and along the way applying the ethical theories outlined in this
chapter, we are better able to see the larger landscape of ethics in both

our personal and our professional lives, and especially to consider how ethics and ethical goals are framed in each case.

Three Questions about Virtue, Ethics, and Stories

In this chapter, and throughout the book, we emphasize Aristotle's virtue ethics. His list of virtues regarding excellence of character can be opaque (e.g., "a nameless excellence to do with honor"). Such ambiguity can be useful. It prevents us from jumping to conclusions just because the virtue's name already means something to us. Instead, we have to consider both the extremes of each virtue and the vast middle ground in which virtues reside. Accepting and working with uncertainty can help us avoid unreflective self-assuredness and prompt us to actively open up conversations about ethics. These questions are intended to center your reflection on the communication of virtues and ethics.

1. What are the virtues proposed by Aristotle and others that have the greatest resonance with your own sense of excellence? Why? What are the virtues you want to cultivate over the next five years? How could these change over the course of your lifetime?

2. Describe the memorable moments in which you learned about a virtue or virtuousness. What stood out about that situation, including any messages you heard? Did this lesson have to do with work? If not, how could it relate to professional life?

3. Think of an instance in which you made a decision or took an action that you now think of as virtuous. How did you display virtuousness? How would or do you tell the story of that turning point? How might *another person involved* tell the story of the same situation? To use bodily metaphors, was this a decision made or act taken from your heart, your head, your gut, your spirit, or, perhaps, the whole of your being?

3

Working for a Good Life

What we do all day habituates and orients us in profound ways that over time impress a pattern on our emotional and intellectual life.... This is why, for many, work cannot merely be another of life's routines but is rather a key source of their identity. (Muirhead, 2004, p. 28)

What's Ethical about Work?

Usually, when we talk about ethics in the work world, we have something in mind quite different than the approach to ethics just outlined in chapter 2. We typically consider ethics at work when facing a dilemma that prompts us to ask ourselves questions: How will we react when pressured to lie? When is it time to blow the whistle? Can I call in sick to take care of personal business? While such dilemmas, grand and small, do represent ethical moments at work, the problem, we've argued, is that we reduce ethics itself to such moments. What gets left out when we do so is *character*. Character is not an abstract quality possessed only by extraordinary people, nor is it determined strictly by good deeds. As explained in the preceding chapter, this book treats character as embodying and giving voice to integrity—for an institution or collective and for a person. Integrity involves all the elements that come together to make a person, message, or institution credible, though not necessary fixed or unchanging, over time.

Our position on ethics is also distinguished by its connection to how we frame it. For example, the explicitly and implicitly ethical questions we ask guide our ethical reflection. Further, the connections between work and ethics go far beyond the decisions we might commonly think of when we hear the term "business ethics." Instead, how we frame and do work relates to our ideals of the good life in both individual and social terms, though the dominance of work in an adult's life makes it easy to treat work as a sphere distinct from the rest of his or her life. Our workplace is, after all, where we spend the bulk of our waking hours. And yet, one could see this dominance as evidence of its connectedness to *all* parts of life, individually and collectively.

Consider the contemporary "Take Back Your Time Day" movement in the United States. "Take Back Your Time Day" ("Time Day") is sponsored by a group of scholars, activists, and practitioners involved in the Voluntary Simplicity movement (www.timeday.org; de Graaf, 2003), which since the 1970s has promoted the idea that individuals can choose to reject consumerism, de-clutter their lives, and connect with nature. Time Day, occurring annually on October 24, was created to unite people, using the issue of "work time" to bring together activists on a variety of contemporary issues such as health, family, and the environment.

At first glance, you might think there is nothing particularly noteworthy about Time Day. Where Time Day is remarkable, however, is in its emphasis on the individual and social problems resulting from people spending too many hours at work. It offers a window onto just how intertwined our work is with the rest of our individual and collective lives. For example, Time Day activists seek to link both the devastation of the rainforest and the obesity-related health problems that excessive fast food production and consumption have contributed to what we is called *time poverty*: because we don't have the time to cook healthy meals at home, we often eat foods that are damaging to our health, and whose production has environmentally devastating effects. In making these connections, Time Day encourages people to rethink their relationship with their work based on its effects on other elements of their personal and social life. It is instructive for the way it highlights the ethical dimensions affected by the very way in which we work, particularly how we shape the relationship between our work and the rest of our lives.

The problem of time revealed some of the most telling lessons learned from a yearlong honors seminar at the University of Utah on quality of life in 2006–07. As students began to research pace of life, they identified both the ethical and the practical implications of rushing through one's day (and one's life). One implication manifests itself in the spectacle of road rage, but rushing through life has equally insidious effects on relationships at work and at home, and on the fabric of the wider community. Rhetoric plays a role, too. Consider how expressions such as "I just don't have the time" serve to rationalize these effects of busy-ness on a wide range of relationships. Remarkably, very little has been written about the ethics of pace, in any discipline (for a notable exception, see D. I. Ballard, 2007).

Time Day also suggests to us that we need to view work as a context for other social relations, as opposed to an independent domain disconnected from the "rest" of our lives. We are so accustomed to compartmentalizing our lives and society that this kind of integrative thinking takes some effort. Kenneth Burke (1974), in his essay "Art under Capitalism," vividly illustrates the connections among the spheres of life, showing that "work-patterns and ethical patterns are integrally related" (p. 314). Burke observed that, across many cultures, conformity with religious, spiritual, and/or otherworldly moral expectations is often expressed in terms of practical work duties in the secular world. For a prime example, Burke points to the great monastic orders of the European Middle Ages and their organization of everyday practical duties; this tradition of organizing and performing work persists today in many contemporary monasteries still devoted to the practice of a craft, such as the Belgian Trappist monasteries' breweries, or the hospitality of the Benedictines. At least in the Judeo-Christian tradition, the ethical and spiritual dimension of work has its roots in the Genesis story, with work emerging from The Fall as both a curse and a blessing—but mostly a curse.

The ethical face of work has a strong secular tradition as well. The psychoanalyst and social critic Erich Fromm (1961) noted an often-misunderstood philosophical pillar of the economic criticism advanced by Karl Marx (1961) was that individuals' characters are fundamentally shaped by *the manner in which they produce*, that is, how they work. Marx, Fromm argues, meant that the drives and passions of humans are actually *shaped* by their work: "Certain economic conditions, like those of capitalism, produce as a chief incentive the desire for money and property; other economic conditions can produce exactly the opposite desires, like those of asceticism and contempt for earthly riches" (Fromm, p. 12). In short, our economic activity, our work, shapes our desires and hence the way we live our lives.

The materialism (in the contemporary sense, connoting unrestrained consumerism, as in Madonna's 1985 song "Material Girl") common among contemporary consumers can be seen as stemming from a quite different relationship between the individual and work than Burke's monks. Consider the persuasive description penned by the economist Juliet Schor (1992, 1997), of the "overworked" and "overspent" American, caught in the "insidious cycle of work and spend" (1992, p. 107). Here we find people working longer and longer hours at jobs (often ones they don't enjoy) to pay off debt, spending the money they make to try to satisfy their desires, thus going even further into debt. And, as Stephen Greenhouse (2008) has observed in his book, *The Big Squeeze: Tough Times for the American Worker*, things have not improved. The average U.S. worker logs just over 1,800 hours of work a year, which is three to nine more weeks than their European counterparts. The upshot is that the very manner in which they work ties them ever more tightly to their identities as consumers. Regardless of the reason for overwork, however, we often attempt to obscure its effects by claiming it as a badge of honor, giving us "bragging rights," both individually ("I'm *so* busy") and culturally ("Those lazy Europeans and their long vacations").

The worker–consumer relationship is just one highly visible illustration of how work shapes who we are, or at least how we see ourselves and are seen by others. Paraphrasing the British prime minister Winston Churchill's famous remarks on the rebuilding of the House of Commons, the business ethicist Al Gini (2001) writes, "First we choose and shape our work, and then it shapes us—forever" (p. 2). Given the overwhelming influence of work on our identities, we should pause to think seriously about the role work plays in our lives. Unfortunately, few of us seem to do so (perhaps because we're too busy). In this regard, one of the most penetrating insights about our contemporary relationship with work comes not from a quotable luminary like Churchill, but rather from an anonymous reviewer of Joanne Ciulla's *The Working Life* (2000) on Amazon.com: "Work is, for most of us, something we do, not something we think about" ("The Working Life," n.d., para. 1). A logical extension would be to say that work is not something that we *talk* about much, either; or at least we don't pay careful attention to how we do talk about it. We may talk a great deal about what happens to us *as* we work, but on the subject of work in general, we remain relatively mute. As a result, deep reflection on these matters often gets delayed until retirement (see the 2002 film *About Schmidt* for a good example) or some kind of emergency or tragedy (e.g., a terminal illness), if ever. The utter failure to enter into such an ethical conversation is on display in the 1992 film about real estate agents, *Glengarry Glen Ross*.

The artificial division between work and life has important ethical implications. After all, if work and life are viewed as largely separate domains, then there is little space to consider work's role in answering the question, "How may I live in a way that achieves the greatest good?" Here, again, we can see the connections between ethics and happiness. Work is squarely in the domain of ethics not only because of its consequences but also because of its intrinsic connection to human flourishing. To explore these ideas further, we continue examining colloquial ways of speaking about the world of work and our relationship to it. We then offer a brief review of key moments in the development of modern, industrial society's attitudes toward work, which have contributed to this split, before finally turning to a reflection on the ethical implications of this split.

What Is Work, Anyway?

"Work" is a common word in the English language, with many uses. We use the term to cover a dizzying array of activities and situations. For instance, in a given day we may go to work at our place of paid employment, go to the gym to work out on our lunch break, come home and do some housework or help a child with homework, squeeze in some time to work on a hobby, and sit down to read a great literary work. We work up an appetite, and then the waiter at the local restaurant asks us, "Are you still working on your dinner?" Each of these uses of "work" may seem, at first glance, quite different from one another, but as the political theorist Russell Muirhead (2004) observes, what they share is a sense of *compulsion*. In each instance, the worker is compelled or expected to work: whether to get a paycheck, maintain health, complete a teacher's assignment, fulfill a drive for artistic expression, or finish a meal.

Here, then, compulsion can be internally or externally motivated, beneficial or detrimental. Further, the term "compulsion" is divided into two colloquial distinctions. Many describe their "work" as personally compelling when doing it allows them to express themselves through their labor. But others describe their "job" as something they are compelled to do against their will. Two friends of George, who are involved in green construction, speak about loving their work but not wanting to feel like they have "jobs." At the end of this chapter we'll reflect more fully on the difference between the compelling and the compelled, but what's important here is to capture the essential duality of work framed as compulsion.

If we site compulsion at the center of work, we see a wide range of activities within its rubric. Work might be seen as what some educators (e.g., Papert, 2002) have termed "hard fun": something that challenges us but affords us enjoyment in its challenge. Of course, not all work is fun or, for that matter, hard. The difficulty of defining work is illustrated in a game that Dan plays with his first-year college students. During orientation week, Dan asks his students to write down whom they see working and what they see those people doing when the students take a tour of downtown Denver. On the first day of class, the students bring in their lists and play a "Scattergories"-type game to figure out who identified the most unique "jobs." The point of the game lies in the arguments students inevitably get into over what counts as work. Is the person soliciting signatures for a petition working? Are they paid? Does it matter? Is the street performer soliciting donations working? Is the homeless person asking for spare change? (Dan's class once got into an extended debate over whether guide and police dogs are "working," delving into the question of whether work is a uniquely human experience.) Many students make compelling arguments as to why these various activities should be considered work. The attractiveness of these arguments fades quickly, however, when Dan asks them, "What would your parents say if you told them this is what you want to do for work?" Faced with this question, it's easy to imagine their parents replying, in a manner essentializing work, "Is *this* really what you want to make of your life?"

We seem to operate under the assumption that we know what work is when we see it, yet this assumption is as incorrect as it is necessary if we are to maintain a distinction between jobs and work. But let us not forget that there are clear ethical implications in what we take to be work or not work. Those implications, we argue in the section below, stem as much from how we talk about work as from what we take to be work.

The Surprisingly Ethical Dimensions of Work Colloquialisms

The general cultural preference for "action" rather than "talk" shows up regularly in the business world. IBM's 2007 television advertising campaign, with its slogan "Stop talking; start doing," is indicative of this kind of conventional common sense. The understanding of "communication" that such notions imply is that it is a relatively transparent process in which ideas can be more or less directly transmitted from sender to receiver. And while this transparency is assumed in all communication, it is particularly prominent in terms of our use of everyday, colloquial expressions. As with dead metaphors (e.g., "skyscrapers," "branches" of government, and "windfall" profits), we tend to look through such expressions as if their meaning were obvious. But overlooking their figurative meaning doesn't mean it's not there. In fact, the seeming transparency of these sayings may serve to heighten their ideological ability to frame the world in a subtle but powerful manner (Billig & Macmillan, 2005). Many of our popular sayings are more than just clever word play, and our colloquial expressions about work may have strong ethical implications because they suggest a variety of behaviors outside the worker's domain, casting them in largely technical terms that obscure their ethical dimensions. In other words, and quite contrary to the message of the IBM ads, whenever we talk, we are inevitably doing quite a bit. Consider the significance of two colloquialisms used to explain the relationship between ethics and work: "I'm just doing my job" and "It's not personal. It's just business."

"I'm Just Doing My Job"

As a colloquialism, the phrase "just doing my job" is often invoked as an ethical defense against the negative ramifications of the acts one performs in doing his or her work. It attempts to cleanly separate agency from some of its consequences. Speaking of the violent nature of his boxing career, Muhammad Ali once remarked, "It's just a job. Grass grows, birds fly, waves pound the sand. I beat people up." While Ali's observation primarily draws attention to the inherent—and thus expected—violence in boxing as a profession, the "just a job" dismissal, and the deferral of ethics it implies, is especially apparent when his remarks are juxtaposed with the lyrics of Bob Dylan's same-era song, "Who Killed Davey Moore?" The verses consist of a series of abdications of responsibility for the titular fighter's death in the ring. The song culminates with the verse answering the song's central question:

> "Not me," says the man whose fists
> Laid him low in a cloud of mist,
> Who came here from Cuba's door
> Where boxing ain't allowed no more.
> "I hit him, yes, it's true,
> But that's what I am paid to do.
> Don't say 'murder,' don't say 'kill.'
> It was destiny, it was God's will." (Dylan, 1991)

In each of these cases, the explicit and implicit invocations of the "just doing my job" defense amount to an abdication of agency, placing the locus of control outside of the worker and suggesting that the worker ought not be held accountable for the consequences of his work.

A few brief examples from a range of contexts help illustrate the enduring vitality of the "just doing my job" defense. For instance, Dr. Leslie Cohen (2001) used it to title her *Journal of General Internal Medicine* column reflecting on the ethical dilemmas she faced as an insurance company medical reviewer under pressure to deny as many claims as reasonably possible to protect the bottom line, making explicit the tensions that would emerge several years later in the stories of other workers in the managed-care industry presented in Michael Moore's 2007 film *Sicko*. Another example comes from a Los Angeles tow truck driver, caught in a television news hidden-camera exposé on a rash of illegal towings, who explained to the reporter interviewing him while he was being arrested, "I was just doing my job, sir. That's about it" ("Life & Times Transcript," 2005, para. 33). And, in January 2007, ABC's newsmagazine show *Primetime* revisited Stanley Milgram's famous 1961 experiments on authority—experiments conducted at the same time that Adolf Eichmann was famously invoking the phrase at his war crimes trial. When one participant was asked why he did not stop administering electroshocks, in light of the obvious suffering of the person being shocked, the participant explained, "I was just doing my job" (Borge, 2007); that is, he was just following the orders given to him by the researcher. In each of these cases, "just doing my job" is invoked as a ready-made excuse, a cultural resource people can use to evade responsibility for their actions, at least in the short term.

Here, the ease of invoking this colloquialism seems particularly important: it allows people to focus on what they "have to do" to receive their paycheck and affords some solace in its being a cultural convention. The phrase serves as much as self-persuasion as it does as a public justification. This self-persuasion is evident in the actor–director Tim Robbins's reflections on his research both for the 1996 death penalty film *Dead Man Walking* and for his role as a South African detective who committed brutalities in the 2000 film *Catch a Fire*. Both films portrayed characters who face moral quandaries as an "occupational hazard" of sorts, leading Robbins to remark, "Oftentimes what happens is you take that compromise, you take that moral weight on your shoulder. You take that soul-deadening act that you're doing. And you take it upon yourself out of duty, out of service, out of love for your family. You know it, you know you're doing wrong, but you do it because that's your job and your duty" (cited in Jacobs, 2006, para. 40). Here, Robbins attempts to understand and sympathize with those whose work lies in the service of power, and he shows us how very different people divorce themselves from the ethical implications of their work in their day-to-day struggles simply to "get by" given their situation and responsibilities. Moreover, Robbins's insight reveals the extent to which questions of ethics don't easily fall into one category or another; what Robbins discovers is a blending of consequentialist ("I have to do this to get paid") and deontological ("It's my duty") reasoning.

Although we want to be careful here not to diminish the struggles of those who find themselves making difficult ethical choices as they work to "get by," we call attention to how colloquialisms such as "just doing my job" can suppress questions in the first place, foreclosing space for ethical reflection. That the phrase "just doing my job" is culturally accepted doesn't actually relieve one from ethical responsibility. As Ralph Waldo Emerson (1983) observed in his 1841 essay "Spiritual Laws": "We must hold a man amenable to reason for the choice of his daily craft or profession. It is not an excuse any longer for his deeds that they are the custom of his trade. What business has he with an evil trade?" (p. 114). Here, Emerson argues against the compartmentalization that makes work/business a sphere with different ethical standards, arguing instead for an ethics across all spheres of our lives. Our argument, then, is that we are responsible for the work we do, and that responsibility should be foremost in our minds when we ask ourselves how we can live in a manner that fulfills our life's meaning.

"It's Not Personal. It's Just Business"

While the saying "just doing my job" may have found its single most famous expression in the voices of Oppenheimer and Eichmann, the expression "it's not personal; it's just business" likely has its origin in Francis Ford Coppola's 1970 film *The Godfather*. Michael Corleone, after deciding to get involved in the family business after the attempt on their father's life, explains to his brother, "It's not personal, Sonny. It's strictly business." Whereas "just doing my job" renders ethical concerns as outside the narrowly technical demands of a particular job, "it's not personal" instead places emotionality and ethics outside the demands of the business arena in general. We are left with the assumed rationality of business.

The phrase "it's not personal" was prominently featured in Donald Trump's reality TV series *The Apprentice* and can be read as establishing the show's core ethos. Not only is it the last piece of text to flash across the screen during the opening credits, it is also frequently evoked in conversations among the show's contestants. For example, a contestant named Chris confronted his dysfunctional team as he prepared to assume leadership for their weekly task, saying, "All right. First of all, on a personal level, obviously I have to prove that I can be a leader. So, let's get all the [bullshit] out of the way. We're not here to be friends. There's nothing personal here. This is [fucking] business. At the end of the day, we're all fighting for the same job" ("Runaway Pride," November 11, 2004). For Chris, the phrase served to justify an authoritarian leadership style that silenced his followers. In this, and similar usages, the "it's not personal" theme serves to discharge contestants of ethical obligations to one another, allows leaders to assert a strong dominance over the led, and reinforces the highly individualistic, self-oriented ethic at the heart of *The Apprentice* and, at least in terms of the program's central conceit, business itself.

Perhaps even more easily than in the case of "just doing my job," the legitimacy of "it's not personal, it's business" dissolves under scrutiny. Keith Hart (2005) describes the colloquialism as the "Hitman's Dilemma," highlighting the fact that, despite our disavowals, all business is always immensely personal: killing the victim may be the professional killer's job, role, and identity, but once the killer's duty is executed, it is the victim who pays the ultimate and very personal price. While a hypothetical extreme, the Hitman's Dilemma nevertheless illustrates the problem with arguing that an ethical duty exists only in one domain, as such compartmentalization readily draws our attention away from our fundamental duty to others.

But, considering how the way we work shapes who we are, determining just who the "victim" is turns out to be more difficult than it may first seem. As marketing consultant Seth Godin (2006, para. 3–4) has observed, "Anyone who is willing to lie to you, cheat you or treat you with disrespect because it's just business is doing more damage to herself than to you. Work takes too much time and too much emotion for it to be just work." That is, because such unethical action is voluntary and the agent has more autonomy regarding the action than does the victim, it harms the unethical actor in addition to his or her victim. In short, despite protestations to the contrary, business is *always* intensely personal, both for the person harmed by behaviors excused and for the excuser. Still, we try hard to separate ourselves from this personal dimension of work and from other people because it makes doing our job more comfortable. Consequently, there's more than a hint of a magical wish behind the phrase. Much like the expression "sticks and stones," we invoke "it's not personal" as if it were a spell that could ward off unwanted damage. We say "sticks and stones" because we know just how much words can and do hurt; we say "it's not personal" because we know just how deeply personal business always is.

The Power of Colloquial Expressions

We know, then, that these ways of speaking about work are anything but "just words." The anthropologist Howard Stein (2001) likens the implicit logic behind phrases such as "it's not personal, it's just business" to the euphemistic language used to justify, or at least defer responsibility for, the Holocaust. (Here, again, we should remember Eichmann's invocation of the "just doing my job" defense.) Such euphemisms allow us to "couch brutality in languages of expediency, of practicality, of necessity, even of survival...We terrorize with our words and with their intentions" (2001, p. xvi). At first glance, comparing modern-day business to the Holocaust might seem outlandish, exaggerated, and dangerously excessive, but as Stein is careful to explain, the parallel is not one of magnitude, but of a certain essential logic.

It is easy to see how we use colloquial expressions to dismiss, excuse, or hide the damage that our work does to others and to ourselves (Godin, 2006). On that score, we seldom hear "dysphemisms"—words that make something sound worse or make profane something usually deemed sacred. We prefer euphemisms, as in the expression for death, "pushing up daises." Each of these colloquial ways of speaking about work, in their own way, serves to compartmentalize ethics, first by bracketing work as a sphere separate from life, and second by treating work as a place where a separate set of ethical standards apply, particularly a special sense of duty and responsibility. Together, they offer workers ready-made, culturally approved justifications for behaviors that they would not condone in their "private" lives. Ethics is cast largely as lying outside the purview of work. When the subject of work and ethics is broached, it is most often from a perspective considering only how we *do* our work, rather than the *work* we do, holistically speaking. Imagine, for instance, an assassins' conference, where the work done (killing) is left unquestioned, and instead the participants attend how-to seminars: "Strangulation Made Easy—and Humane!" While outlandish, the logic of this joke is similar to that of attempts to draw an ethical "line" around marketing mortgages to marginally qualified (or unqualified) buyers, whose

lives promise to be devastated by a financial failure more or less professionally anticipated. Here, the ethical imperatives engendered by
the social implications of how we work are clear.

The stories we tell about ethics at work seldom deal with the
ethical character of work in general. It is as if the Protestant Work
Ethic has been cut in half: its injunctions to work hard, be frugal and
the like remain, but the notion of a calling, an ethical dimension to
choosing one's work, has been displaced. We retreat from the ethical
through our ways of speaking about work, especially when we draw
on artificial distinctions between work and the rest of our lives. For
instance, if we think back to Time Day, we can see that the popular
notion of *work–life balance* is not simply a matter of individual concern, a matter of each person making the proper choice about the
proper fit between these two spheres of their lives. Rather, the notion
of time itself is a social and ethical issue, not simply a personal one.
In asking ourselves questions about the life we lead or wish to lead,
we would benefit greatly from seeing work as woven into the total
fabric of our lives.

The Ethics of Separating—and
Integrating—Work and Life

While we may not know it, we all operate with certain folk theories
about the nature and meaning of work. Take, for example, the colloquial expression "a real job" (Clair, 1996). This expression is remarkable in terms of both its cultural malleability and its reach. While it
is hard to imagine someone unfamiliar with the expression and its
general meaning, its specific meaning varies greatly according to context. For example, in Dan's undergraduate classes, it never fails that
at least one student tells of having offended a coworker by describing
his or her (usually short-term, college) job as somehow "not real,"
whereas it is very real for an older coworker doing the same job. In a
related vein, while we were meeting to work on this book together, as
we walked to a Seattle café, Dean remarked how great it was to not
be working that day, but for George, Dan, and Brenden, writing this
book is directly related to their work. In short, we all have implicit
notions of what counts and does not count as work, in addition to
what makes work "real" or somehow valuable.

One of the clear implications of how we speak about work is that
we tend to divide our life into spheres: work and home, work and
family, work and life. This tendency to make divisions extends beyond

the United States. For example, ICIC Prudential, India's largest life-insurance policy carrier, markets its retirement and other insurance plans with the slogan "Retire from work, not life." Colloquially, the "work, not life" distinction is more diffuse than "just doing my job" and "it's not personal, it's business." The colloquialism seems to capture a general sentiment that is relatively independent of its particular form of expression. In this regard, "work, not life" might be considered a general trope, a resource for sense making rather than a ready colloquialism to be invoked.

This symbolic division between work and life is most evident in the increasingly popular notion of work–life balance. Over the last thirty or so years, the notion of work–life balance has received a great deal of academic and popular attention as society strives to prevent overwork, despite high-profile academic research showing that the idea that separation is possible is essentially a myth promoting organizational interests over individual ones (Hochschild, 1989, 1997; Kanter, 1977a, 1977b). Also, the idea of "balance" suggests some sort of realizable end state to be achieved and maintained (Golden, Kirby, & Jorgenson, 2006), an impossible goal likely to produce only greater feelings of frustration and failure. Our argument is that this myth is ethically problematic as well because it obscures the way work tends to bleed into life, and life into work.

When Work and Life Blur Together

No matter how much we speak of a separation between work and life, our lived experience questions that these boundaries exist. We can clearly see the impossibility of maintaining the boundaries between work and life when we find ourselves bringing work home with us—grading papers, responding to emails, reading reports, preparing presentations and the like. Some of us even set up a home office. While, at first glance, bringing home work may seem innocuous, natural, and inevitable (at least for many of us), our earlier discussion of the ethical dimension of work time suggests this is not the case.

Similarly, the work–life division dissolves when we consider that we increasingly bring our work with us when we try to escape home, as well. In 2005 USA Today ran a feature on the "Top Five Destinations for a Working Vacation" (Pascarella, 2005), offering advice on how to plan vacations around working efficiently. Similarly, in 1997 AT&T ran an ad for its cell-phone service portraying a mother dealing with her daughters, who are begging her for time as she prepares for work in the morning:

OLDER DAUGHTER: Mom, why do you always have to work?
MOTHER: It's called videos, food, skates...
OLDER DAUGHTER: Can't we go to the beach?
MOTHER: Not today, honey, I've got a meeting with a very important
    client.
YOUNGER DAUGHTER: Mom, when can I be a client? (in
    "Telecommuting and the Working Mom," n.d.)

Feeling guilty, the mother informs her children that they have five minutes to get ready for the beach. The ad ends with the mother loung-
ing on the beach, answering her cell phone to talk with her important
client. Similarly, in Dan's seminar on the meaning of work, one of
the most persistent complaints from his students about their parents'
attitudes toward work is that on vacations one (or both) of their parents always carves out time away from the family in order to work.

We bring our work home (and everywhere else) in a less literal
sense as well. That is, given the important ways in which our work
shapes our identities, it can often be difficult for us to escape our work
at home, even if we are not immediately and obviously working. The
very performance of work itself threatens to spill over into the private sphere of the home, not in the sense of "bringing work home"
but rather in the sense that we may not ultimately be able to detach
our working selves from our private selves. Take, for example, the
1979 film *The Great Santini*. The film tells the story of Robert Duvall's
character Lt. Col. "Bull" Meecham, whose relationship with his family is strained because he can never fully shed his work persona. This
theme is echoed in a short story from David Foster Wallace's *Brief
Interviews with Hideous Men* (1999). One of Wallace's "hideous men"
speaks of his traumatic relationship with his father, a man who has
spent his career as a bathroom attendant in a posh hotel. The behavior expected of an attendant—to present himself as existing only
for the service of his "clients," and only when they need his services—slowly took over his entire identity. Like Lieutenant Colonel
Meecham, Wallace's character could not shed his work persona, and
that persona wormed deeply into every aspect of his life.

Arthur Miller's *Death of a Salesman* (1998) portrays perhaps the
most famous example of work being ingrained in one's identity. The
play's protagonist, Willy Loman, is an aging, once-successful traveling
salesman unable to live up to his earlier success. Nevertheless, Willy
remains wrapped up in his version of the American Dream, which
exacts a heavy financial and psychic toll, eventually leading to his
suicide. At his funeral, Charley, his only friend, offers a famous
defense of Willy's life: "Nobody dast blame this man. A salesman is

got to dream. It comes with the territory" (p. 111). That last sentence, "It comes with the territory," is now commonly invoked to excuse the undesirable aspects of our work. Here, we can see the dangers of artificially separating work and life; we are either torn between two aspects of the false dichotomy, or lost when one consumes the other. Willy Loman's son, Biff, responds, plainly: "Charley, the man didn't know who he was" (p. 111).

When Life Slides into Work

Of course, the boundaries between work and life, or work and home, can disappear in another way as well. In fact, the admonition "leave your personal life at home" has long been standard advice on how to act professionally, albeit a piece of advice that has increasingly come under scrutiny. The underlying assumption is that one's private affairs—sick children, troubled relationships, financial difficulties, and so on—distract from the *official business* of the organization one works for and so should be left "at home." Of course, the idea that one can effectively forget one's personal circumstances is a fiction, and an often counterproductive one at that. In Missoula, Montana, one locally well-known café owner used to go so far as to tell her employees, "If you think your personal stuff will keep you from being 100% present on the job, I'd rather you stay home that day." Her point was not not to be punitive, as one might infer, but rather as an expression of genuine care for her employees and their personal lives. But the issue with this generous view is that it begs the question of who can maintain the line that cleanly, or know when it's going to get blurry? Nevertheless, our tendency to compartmentalize ethics says that such a clean division is indeed possible and even desirable.

Life and work can resist such compartmentalization on other fronts as well, however. As noted in chapter 2, a person's life can bleed into their work insofar as one's personal values take precedent over the values one is expected to uphold in the workplace. Consider, for example, the recent controversy surrounding the filling of prescriptions for drugs, most notably birth control and the morning-after pill. Some pharmacists refused to fill these prescriptions because they felt that doing so was a violation of their religious beliefs. In one high-profile case in April 2005, the State of Wisconsin Pharmacy Examining Board reprimanded and limited the license of Neil Noesen, who had not only refused to fill a birth-control prescription for a local college student but also refused to transfer that prescription to another pharmacy. As a result, the woman had to wait until another pharmacist was working at that pharmacy, causing her to miss a dose (Epstein, 2005).

Noesen's case was one of many in 2005 and 2006 that provoked legislative activity from representatives of both sides of the issue, at the state and federal levels. For example, Wisconsin Republicans proposed legislation that would allow pharmacists to opt out of filling prescriptions that violate their conscience without being sanctioned. In support of this legislation, the Pro-Life Wisconsin director Peggy Hamill argued, "No pharmacist should be forced to daily check his or her conscience at the workplace door" (in Forster, 2005, p. B1). Similarly, Steven Aden, a lawyer for the Health Care Right of Conscience Project at the Center for Law and Religious Freedom, argued that to require pharmacists to dispense drugs that do not take into account their "professional judgment to decide how to heal without doing harm" is to reduce pharmacists to "automated medicine dispensers" (2005, p. 14A). Such arguments suggest that one should be able to bring the personal to the professional, something we will discuss further in chapter 4.

Opponents in this case argued that professional responsibility to patients ought to trump one's personal morality. This principle is reflected in the emergency order that the State of Illinois governor Rod Blagojevic made in April of 2005 to require pharmacists to fill prescriptions for legal birth control regardless of their own personal, moral objections; Blagojevic's public injunction was "No delays. No hassles. No lectures" (Epstein, 2005, p. A1). The California senator Barbara Boxer introduced federal legislation that would require pharmacies fill these prescriptions or transfer them to a pharmacy that would (Epstein, 2005). Capturing the spirit behind such policies, the University of Wisconsin bioethicist R. Alta Charo argued, "As soon as you become a licensed professional, you take on certain obligations to act like a professional, which means your patients come first. You are not supposed to use your professional status as a vehicle for cultural conquest" (in Stein, 2006, p. A1). This is a clear expression of social contract theory in the practice of a profession and in its application to an individual practitioner. What's important to note is that the individual who joins a profession, with its agreed-upon standards of behavior and performance, voluntarily assumes these responsibilities by the very taking up of the profession.

The prescription controversy highlights the role of agency as well. Pharmacists, through a state-licensing procedure, are granted the privilege of dispensing medicines. When a patient requests that a pharmacist use his or her exclusive authority to fill a prescription, must we assume that the patient also is granting the pharmacist the authority to withhold the medicine? Does the exclusive authority granted to the pharmacist cause the patient to lose authority over her medical decisions? Does pharmacists' monopoly privilege also grant them authority over the doctor?

Our purpose in this discussion of pharmaceutical ethics is not to take a position on the issue itself, partly because it is one tied up in relatively complex interpretations of the professional codes of ethics and in U.S. constitutional law, and partly because, as one commentator observed, the issue seems to be something of a "new front" in the ongoing abortion debate (Stein, 2005, p. A1). Clearly, there is something more at stake in this issue than the ethics of dispensing prescriptions. Nevertheless, the issue does offer a particularly interesting window into how we speak about work, professionalism, and ethics. As Elizabeth Nash of the Guttmacher Institute, an organization dedicated to researching reproductive-health issues, has observed, the rash of legislation on the ethics of issuing prescriptions "represent[s] a major expansion of this notion of right of refusal. You're seeing it broadening to many types of workers—even into the world of social workers—and for any service for which you have a moral or religious belief" (as quoted in Stein, 2006, p. A1).

Debates over such "right(s) of refusal" find parallels in other arenas as well. Imagine bank loan officers whose moral opposition to usury causes them to reject every loan application. Or, more concretely, the controversy over David Horowitz's *Professors: The 101 Most Dangerous Academics in America* (2006). He claims that college professors, as members of a profession, inappropriately bring their own personal, radical views into college classrooms, particularly in state institutions. The accusations Horowitz makes are rife with misunderstandings both about the nature of academic freedom in general and about what actually occurs in the classrooms of these "most dangerous academics." Still, his argument, like the one about pharmaceutical prescriptions, brings into public view the ethical tensions surrounding how much one's life—in this case, a professor's own moral and political convictions—ought to affect one's work. It is ironic that the conservative voices condemning professors for importing their personal "liberal" views into their work are often those loudest in defending the rights of pharmacists to import their personal "conservative" views into theirs. The high profile of this controversy is likely due in large part to the heightened sense of political divisions in the United States today, yet it reminds us of how the work–life division is an ethical flashpoint.

As we have already argued, focusing on ethical decision-making in the day-to-day performance of work is a necessary but only partially sufficient approach to professional ethics. We must begin to recognize that work is not its own domain but rather intersects with others, posing ethical dilemmas in the process. Therefore, it's important to question not only the mythical notion of a work–life balance but also the very separation of work and life as distinct spheres. Here, the insights of feminist scholars who have critiqued the work–life dichotomy over the past several decades are particularly useful. They note that the work–life dichotomy rests on a broader distinction between the public and private spheres, which have been coded, respectively, as masculine and feminine domains (Ashcraft, 2000). This dichotomy posits that the spheres remain distinct from each other, but it is soon apparent that this is an illusion because, inevitably, "the tasks of one domain continually intrude into the other" (Kirby et al., 2003, p. 8). Accordingly, women often face increased burdens as they attempt to compete in the public sphere of work while still facing a primary responsibility for the care of the private sphere of home. Obviously, how we conceptualize work's role in relation to the "rest" of our lives has far-ranging effects. To help us find ways to think and speak about work without compartmentalizing, we will briefly examine just how the work–life division arose in the first place.

Separating "Work" from "Life": A Brief History

The seemingly universal desire to bracket work as a sphere in which a completely different set of ethical principles applies is deeply seated in the cultural history of Western attitudes toward work, which have framed work as both curse and blessing. Euro-American attitudes toward work have been marked by a consistent duality allowing and even encouraging us to separate our selves from our work and our work from our selves. While a comprehensive description of this development is well beyond the scope of our argument here (for exemplary historical treatments, see Joanne Ciulla's *The Working Life* [2000] and Richard Donkin's *Blood, Sweat, and Tears* [2001]), a summary of key moments in this development provides insight in this regard. Let's start, quite literally, at "the beginning."

The Biblical Genesis

If Western views toward work are marked by a deep ambivalence, then certainly one of the earliest expressions (if not one of the primary origins) of that ambivalence can be found in the Book of Genesis.

In its very first chapter, Genesis presents God at work in the act of Creation, resting from his work on the seventh day. The fact that the Creation is explicitly described as "work" (Gen. 2:1) is particularly significant. As the theologian Arthur Geoghegan observed, "Surely, if the Most High is described as the Divine Laborer, it cannot be dishonorable for a man to work" (in Applebaum, 1992, p. 180). Indeed, after the Creation but before the Fall, Adam worked in the Garden of Eden, charged by God "to dress and to keep it" (Gen. 2:15). What's important to note, though, is that this work is not the *toil* that follows the Fall. When God banishes Adam and Eve from Eden for partaking of the fruit of the tree of knowledge of good and evil, he does so in part by cursing the nature of work: "Cursed is the ground because of you; in toil you shall eat of it all the days of your life...In the sweat of your face you shall eat bread till you return to the ground" (Gen. 3:17–19). What emerges, then, is a fundamental dualism in the nature of work, conceived as both blessing and curse. While this dualism is different from the split between work and life as separate spheres, it sets the stage for the conflicted attitudes toward work that make such a split possible.

The Ancient Greeks

The proper split between work and life seems to have its origins in the views of the ancient Athenian aristocracy toward work. These Greeks did not share the early Judaic ambivalence for work, preferring instead the *curse* side of the dualism. As Hannah Arendt (1998) observed, work was one sphere of activity, distinct from politics and the life of the mind (Arendt uses the terms "labor," "work," and "activity" to describe each of these spheres). Aristotle has something to say here, too, according to the anthropologist Herbert Applebaum (1995): "The mechanical arts had a degrading effect on the body and mind. To perfect a skill...was to be stricken with a bent of mind that made one unfit for contemplation and philosophy" (p. 49). Here, we can see something of Burke's (1935/1984, p. 7) notion of a "trained incapacity": performing work, for Aristotle, makes the worker unable to fully develop his capacities as a human. This view of work as diminishing the capacity to be human suggests a wholly different value being attributed to work. So, for example, whereas unemployment is one of our most despised vices, for Aristotle (1996; 2002), unemployment was, at a minimum, necessary to self-development; if it was not a virtue itself, at least it led to virtue. Accordingly, for the Greeks, the separation of work and life, or at least a meaningful life, was not simply a matter of different spheres of life for individuals but for altogether different segments of society as well.

The Medieval European Monastic Orders

We've already mentioned how the monastic orders of Europe's Middle Ages developed a more integrated view of the work–life relationship. Specifically, we looked at them through Burke's (1973) discussion of the integration of work patterns and ethical patterns. Benedictine monasteries considered work one of the three integral parts of life, the others being prayer and sleep; consequently, the monastic vision saw work as central to the moral development of the whole person and can thus be productively read as revealing one of the earliest positive views of work (Applebaum, 1995). Monasteries were the "employing elite" of their era. Unlike modern corporations, the elite employers of today, "the monasteries did not offer individual wealth, but spiritual wealth to those who were willing to combine learning and worship within a strictly disciplined pattern of living" (Donkin, 2001, p. 34). Of course, the monasteries were elite "employers," largely isolated from the rest of the social fabric and offering work to only a few. So while a more integrative view of work and ethics may have existed within the orders, the fact that monks were sequestered leaves them, at best, to represent a counterpoint to how popular discourses of work build and maintain the work–life boundary.

The Protestant Work Ethic

Most famously discussed by Max Weber (1905/2002), the Protestant Work Ethic comes close to an integration of work and life, at least in its theoretical and theological underpinnings. The ethic encouraged people to think of their work as an essential part of their life with God. Work then, was not only designed by God to be an activity that would keep busy otherwise "idle hands," but also a vehicle through which one could demonstrate that he was a member of the "elect," destined for heaven. In this regard, work began to be seen less as a curse or a blessing, and more as virtuous in its own right. One is called by God to particular work and finds virtue in the fulfillment of that calling. So while the view of work as a curse and blessing distinguishes between work and religion, the notion of a calling, as developed in the work ethic, drew no distinction, instead presenting the two as a seamless whole: work as worship. In this way, the work ethic, at least in its pure form, suggests that there is no sharp division between work and life—at least a moral–ethical life.

At the same time, however, elements of the work ethic have stood in the way of the kinds of broader ethical reflections about work that we are advocating here. First, the Protestant Work Ethic does not encourage a *questioning* attitude toward work—your calling is what it is, it's not for you to ask; it is God's will. Here, it is interesting to note that the notion of a "calling" did not originate with Martin Luther and John Calvin but rather traces its theoretical roots to ancient Greece and the thinking of the post-Aristotelian Stoics (Edelstein, 1966), who taught that morality was to be found in conformity with the laws of nature. In this regard, the Protestant Work Ethic has served the interests of the powerful as a deeply religious grounding for the status quo divisions of labor.

Second, the Protestant Work Ethic has been remarkably susceptible to a sort of split, stemming from the loss of religious notions of the calling and the celebration of secular values. It is important to note that one of Luther's key departures from the earlier, monastic view of work was his criticism of this older approach as essentially selfish because it withdrew work from the public realm into the confines of monastery walls. Luther believed that work should be dedicated to the service of some broader public good (Applebaum, 1995). In short, the calling has a distinctly *social* function, as God's way of ensuring a proper division of labor leading to a well-functioning society. Perhaps beginning with the aphorisms of Benjamin Franklin's *Poor Richard's Almanack* (1986), serialized in the mid-eighteenth century, we can begin to see the secularization of the work ethic as work is transformed from being *virtuous* into being a *virtue* itself. Ironically, when work becomes a virtue in itself, it loses its social purpose: it is no longer hard work in a calling that matters but rather the mere fact of work itself. Work here is stripped of any inherent sense of ethics, as ethics becomes something that you locate *in* work. It is no longer *of* work. In other words, work no longer occupies a central place in the question, "How do I live a meaningful life?" Rather, work is relegated, at best, to a purely instrumental role, one leaving questions of the "good life" for other domains.

In both its secular and spiritual senses, however, the (Protestant) work ethic acts to compartmentalize questions about work: work is something to be done, to be borne, but not to be thought or talked about. In the first sense of the term, a calling is deeply religious, such that whatever work one finds oneself doing is God's will and, as such, should remain unquestioned. While this attitude toward work may seem somewhat old-fashioned, it remains with us today in people's tacit (and often grudging) acceptance of their station in life. Few people feel themselves realized through work, though they often admit to being merely utilized. The sense of calling is more common today, with a culture obsessed with work as a virtue, stripped of a religious nature that might open up space for ethical reflection. This lack of a deeper purpose, in turn, serves to support the division between work and life by encouraging people to find meaning in other arenas.

The European and North American Industrial Revolution

There can be little doubt that the Industrial Revolution in Europe and North America ushered in profound changes not only in the social organization of work but also in our cultural understandings of work of it (Ciulla, 2000; Donkin, 2001). One of most profound changes stems from the separation of the public and private spheres. Before the advent of the Industrial Revolution, the bulk of work in Euro-American societies was performed by the family unit: "The family was a community of work in its own right and the home space was a site in which family members, male and female, young and old, labored together" (Kirby et al., 2003, p. 5). This began to change with the advent of industrial, factory-based labor, which increasingly segregated work along gender lines, as men were seen as generally more fitted for the dangers of factory work, and women more suited for work at home (Beder, 2000). (Still, this division was by no means hard and fast, and industrial employers were certainly ready to exploit the labor of young, unmarried, and poor women when that was deemed appropriate [Donkin, 2001]). Work at this time became increasingly regulated by the clock, resulting in the advent of shift work and the creation of a clear division between "work" (public) and "family" (private) time (E. P. Thompson, 1967).

Along with time, gender, race, and class all became convenient— though often unstated—excuses for arranging and dividing work in particular ways. In this regard, the etymology of the word "job" is revelatory (see Ciulla, 2000). Beginning with the fourteenth-century term "gob", job originally meant a "lump" or "piece," and by the seventeenth century, just before the earliest stages of the Industrial Revolution, was being to used to refer to hired, but not permanent, bits of labor. It wasn't until the nineteenth century in the United States that "job" took on its contemporary meaning of "steady, paid employment." As the leadership scholar Joanne Ciulla (2000) observes, however, the word "job" is unable to entirely overcome its linguistic history. Ciulla captures the word's residue, arguing that it "doesn't imply that there is a relationship between workers and their product. It also doesn't say anything about the quality of work—whether the work is physical or mental, creative or dull, painful or purposeless— but it does say something about the quantity. What matters is that the work is a finite amount of things that a person gets paid to do" (p. 33). Here we can see how notions of "job" color our understandings of work as something finite that we can relegate to a particular sphere, a slice of life. Accordingly, to the extent that job colors work, the temptation is great to dismiss this piece of our lives as "just a job," as a place that isn't central to our selves and, consequently, as one place where we can tolerate a greater ethical ambiguity, if not outright dismiss the importance of ethical reflection.

Karl Marx

As one of the earliest critical observers of the Industrial Revolution, Karl Marx (1844/1961) was centrally concerned with the ethical questions surrounding the evolution of work in this new cultural form. Let's focus on his penetrating insights into the relationship between work and human nature. One profitable way for us to examine Marx today is to draw a distinction between an early, more sociological Marx, and a later, more economic Marx. The latter Marx was concerned with the economic processes through which workers are exploited, but it is the early Marx that is of the most interest to us here. This Marx was deeply concerned about the relationship between humans and their work, and it is during this phase that Marx first developed his ideas about alienation, the manner in which the form of work can separate the worker from his or her human dignity. As Erich Fromm (1961) has observed, "Marx's aim was that of the spiritual emancipation of man, of his liberation from the chains of economic determinations, of restituting him in his human wholeness, of enabling him to find unity and harmony with his fellow man and with nature" (p. 3). Marx was primarily concerned with discovering a way of socially organizing work that would make it possible for individuals to recover, and develop, their sense of humanity *through* their work.

Such concerns predominated in the work of the early Marx, who famously argued in *The German Ideology* (in Feuer, 1959) that the ideal social organization of work would "make it possible for [a person] to do one thing today and another tomorrow, to hunt in the morning, fish in the afternoon, rear cattle in the evening, criticize after dinner, just as [that person has] a mind, without ever having been a hunter, fisherman, shepherd, or critic" (p. 254). At first blush, Marx's vision might seem to embody a selfish posture toward work of a different variety than what Luther saw in the old monastic orders. However, for Marx the ideal worker engaged in these activities was "not Playboy but Prometheus...: a heroic individual engaged in a variety of challenging, self-directed activities of social value" (Campbell, in Applebaum, 1992, p. 447). For Marx, work would be highly varied and seamlessly integrated with life, and would contain an ethical injunction to provide some sort of social value. Of course, this Marx, with his liberating vision of work as spiritually restorative of human nature, was largely forgotten by both critics and adherents alike throughout the twentieth century (Fromm, 1961). The writings of the early Marx, then, represent one of the moments in the Euro-American tradition of thinking about work where the possibilities for a greater unity between work and life were recognized and celebrated.

What Do These "Key Moments" Mean Today?

The separation of work and life, and its consequent bracketing of ethical spheres, is not a natural arrangement, but rather one that is necessarily contingent. It is made through communication and changes over time and in different places. A quick look at considerations of work, in what the anthropologist of work Herbert Applebaum (1984) terms "non-market" and "mixed" societies, illustrates this contingency. Applebaum argues that three features distinguish work in non-market societies. First, work is an integral part of the "total cultural fabric" (p. 2), seamlessly woven with other aspects of the society, including kinship relations, religious obligations, and taboo. Second, the communal dimensions of work are foregrounded, even if such work is not wholly voluntary or devoid of self-interest. Rather, it is notions of reciprocity (Mauss, 1950/1990) that govern work's communality, and in this reciprocity work becomes a gift to the community. Finally, Applebaum (1984) observes, work in non-market societies is task-oriented rather than time-oriented. That is, workers are devoted to the completion of a task at hand, rather than to the completion of a specified duration, such as a shift. This distinction is particularly significant for our argument here, given the observation that societies with task orientations to work draw the least sharp lines between work and life (Thompson, 1967).

Of course, it would be tempting to argue that the emergence of the "salariat" in twentieth-century Euro-American economies—that body of workers paid a salary and not tied to shift or hourly work—represents a move to a different orientation toward time. Such an argument, however, would miss the way time itself often serves as a symbolic token of work done. That is, the productivity of salaried workers is often subtly evaluated through the amount of time spent working, regardless of tasks accomplished. This cultural expectation is captured nicely in an episode of the situation comedy, *Seinfeld*, where George discovers that if he leaves his car in the parking lot at Yankee Stadium, everyone will think that he is the first in to work and the last to leave, leaving him free to do very little work at all even as he is celebrated for his work ethic. While the way time is valued may have shifted for large portions of the workforce, the centrality of a time orientation has not.

These historical views remind us that we construct the notions of what counts as work and that our collective, contemporary views of work are neither as natural nor as inevitable as they may seem but are instead the result of socio-cultural processes that could have unfolded differently. Take the famous scene where Tom Sawyer (Twain, 1876/2008) lures his friends into whitewashing the fence for him "because it's fun." For a more serious example, health insurance companies employ medical professionals to screen requests for coverage. For the most part, these employees are charged with identifying how the fewest claims can be compensated, rather than seeking the best care for their insurance customers. How would this work be different if insurance organizations employed patient advocates rather than claim analysts? Both cases illustrate that the way we view work today could have been otherwise. And it is precisely in the "otherwise" that we can see the ethical choices that we argue are at the heart of how we speak about work. Reflecting on how we talk about work (to ourselves and to others), then, becomes an important exercise in developing our own ethics of work.

Why Disconnect Work from Life?

We began this chapter with a discussion of how colloquialisms such as "just doing my job" and "not personal, just business," and the colloquial separation of "work" from "life," serve to bracket consideration of the ethical implications of both the content and the form of our work. It is important to note, however, that each of these colloquialisms contains a more positive ethical potential as well. For example, another common usage of the phrase "just doing my job," rather than deflecting responsibility for the consequences of our work, instead seeks to deflect attention from the worker. For example, James Knight's book *Just Doing My Job* (2006) tells the stories of Australian police, firefighters, and paramedics who dismiss their acts of heroism as part of their normal course of business. Similarly, "it's not personal, it's just business" can be pragmatic too. An advertisement on Monster.com for a sales position at a recruiting firm counseled potential employees about the nature of the job, stating: "You sell yourself to companies to get their business, then you sell your opportunity to candidates. Some will listen to you and work with you, but many will not. You need to be OK with that. You must be OK with rejection. It's not personal, it's just business" ("Insurance Recruiter," n.d., para. 9). Here, the phrase deflects people's attention away from the fact that business is, in fact, incredibly personal and that if one were to take too close to heart the inevitable rejection that "goes with the territory" of sales, one would jeopardize one's ability to do the job, and one's self-esteem would suffer.

Finally, the separation of work and life does have a certain ethical usefulness. In a blog post alluding to an action taken in the war in Iraq, Army Specialist Brandon Stewart wrote, "I did something today I wish I didn't have to but it was necessary. I'm so confused in my life if you can call my existence a life. What this place is all about is work. Not life" (2007, para. 5). Here, Stewart, who finds himself fighting in a war and called to do things he opposes, draws the distinction between work and life as a matter of moral self-defense or rationalization.

The work–life separation and balance can also have a practical utility. For example, many women entrepreneurs strategically draw barriers between work and life in order that they might preserve their home as a sanctuary from work (Gill, 2006). In short, the danger is not so much in the use of the expression, which may often be useful. Rather, the danger lies in taking such expressions too seriously: "Entrepreneurship [as a form of work] may offer flexibility in work-life, but can concomitantly have consequences for the entrepreneur who neglects a non-work identity" (Gill, 2006, para. 56).

Chances are, when you think of work, you think of whatever it is you do that earns you your paycheck—your job. But, what happens if you begin to play with the term "work" in its broader sense, to explore other meanings of the term in your life? When does your work feel more like play or activism? Alternatively, are there moments when your leisure feels more like "work"? Do you have character flaws or bad habits that you are "working" on? Relationship problems that you are trying to "work" out? The point is, as much as we immediately associate work in our lives with our paid employment, we talk about work in our everyday language in a far more expansive sense. What all of these different uses of the term "work" share in common, to return to Muirhead's (2004) definition, is a sense of *compulsion*. Much like the word "work" itself, "compel" has both positive and negative connotations. One might say, "I am *compelled* to work at this job because I have no other choice, given my need to survive in the market." On the other hand, we often find work *compelling* when we experience *flow* (Csikszentmihalyi, 1991) or feel connected to some greater purpose.

Reconnecting Work with Life

If work is at its core a compulsion, then the challenge we face is to bring the positive and negative meanings of the term more closely together by discovering how to make the work we are compelled to do compelling to us. But we are likely to remain frustrated if we keep work separate from the rest of our lives, leaving the work sphere to be defined primarily by instrumental calculations. We should not consider work a space where we justify behaviors that would not meet the ethical standards we hold ourselves to in the "rest" of our lives.

Relatively infrequently do we see and discuss the connection between ethics and work. Instead, when we think of ethics as something that individuals encounter in moments of crisis, work appears as a normal and unproblematic state of affairs, punctuated by moments of dilemma in which we are called upon to make ethical decisions. Such a view of ethics is grounded in the deep individualism that enables the "bad apples" to defend themselves during a corporate ethical crisis.

Robert Bellah and colleagues' influential *Habits of the Heart* (1985) identifies two distinct forms of individualism in the United States: a *utilitarian* individualism, in which the individual immerses herself or himself in work, finding satisfaction in the trappings of (primarily financial) success; and an *expressionistic* individualism, in which the individual retreats from the public world of work, finding success in the private realm of personal relationships, hobbies, and the like. For Bellah et al. the problem is that both of these forms of individualism adopt a self-oriented view toward work, one that ignores the public dimension of work in the service of others. Here is a form of essentialism, of the reduction of ethics as exclusively the domain of the individual. What Bellah and colleagues argue for instead is a "reappropriation of the idea of vocation or calling, a return in a new way to the idea of work as a contribution to the good of all and not merely as a means to one's own advancement" (pp. 287–88). These researchers call on us to think about our work in terms that transcend individualism and to see the connection between our individual work and other institutions.

Three Questions for Consideration: Putting Excellence and Ethics to Work

One particularly useful way of taking to heart the call of Bellah and his colleagues is to think of *vocation* as "where your deep gladness meets the world's deep need," as the theologian Frederick Buechner wrote (in Palmer, 1999, p. 16). What is particularly provocative about Buechner's definition is its flexibility. Here, a vocation requires a sense of both individual and social satisfaction. If you work only to fulfill personal goals, whether to get rich or to indulge in whim, it's not your calling. If, on the other hand, you altruistically sacrifice your own interests to take care of those in dire need but get no sense of personal satisfaction from doing so, that's not your calling either. The key, then, is to find the intersection of the two perspectives.

Reflecting critically on how your work influences the possibility of human happiness is an important part of your response to this question (in the tradition of virtue ethics): "How shall I live in a way that facilitates the experience of eudaimonia?" In order to practice virtuousness with excellence in our work, we must make work something that we not only *do* but also think *and talk* about carefully and deliberately. So, here are a few questions that might help you reflect on work and its role in how you live and find meaning in life.

1. What counts as *work* in your life? What are the terms and images you most commonly associate with working? Do you or people you know talk as though being ethical "is hard work" or "adds to your workload"? What are the consequences?

2. How does your work connect to the wider society, including the ways you've experienced this connection as socially reinforced and rewarded? Identify the experiences or relationships that revealed (to you) that you and your effort mattered to others. Why were those memorable, and what did they teach you about virtue?

3. Finally, you might simply ask yourself what your greatest joy is, and how might it serve the world's greatest needs.

4

Being a Professional:
Problems and Promises

Now we seem to have replaced the ideas of responsible community membership, of cultural survival, and even of usefulness, with the idea of professionalism. Professional education
proceeds according to ideas of professional competence and
according to professional standards, and this explains the
decline in education from ideals of service and good work,
citizenship and membership, to mere "job training" or "career
preparation." (Berry, 2000, p. 130)

What Do We Mean When We Say, "Act Like a Professional"?

Consider the story of Erin Brockovich. In the film of the same name
(Grant, 2000), she has a confrontational meeting with representatives of a utility company where tables turn over the rejection by
Brockovich's firm of an offer to buy out the victims of a toxic leak-
age into a neighborhood that the firm is representing. The scene is
tense, emotional, and in some ways, surprising, not only because
of the response of Brockovich and her boss but also because of the
very different ways in which they enact what it means to be professional. Brockovich does not at all fit our idea of the "appropriate"
legal firm employee, nor does she have her boss's confidence at first.
She dresses in a hip, funky, sexual, and therefore "unprofessional,"
manner. She says what's on her mind, without much forethought,
with no artifice, with no pretensions, and without resort to legal jargon. She doesn't compartmentalize roles and behaviors the way we

expect most people in U.S. society to do as they cross the invisible but acknowledged threshold from the personal to the professional. In this and other situations we keep asking ourselves (often unconsciously), Does this person embody the idea/ideal of the professional? After all, once a category like "the professional" gets established, we inevitably look for ways people either fit or don't fit it.

In this case, seeing the character outside of work and coming to understand her internal motivations allow us to identify with her and so put aside our concern that she act "like a professional." We therefore allow an apparent outsider into our circle of acceptance. So, by the time of the confrontational meeting, where Brockovich gives an impassioned but also very specific account of the harms to her clients (i.e., the members of a community clearly hurt by the company's policies), we are already strongly identified with her. She tells off the opposing attorneys, using some colorful language, and we cheer her on as the attorneys for the corporation leave in frustration and failure. We identify completely with Brockovich at that point, seeing the entire situation, and the other characters, from her point of view.

In fact, there are several lessons in this story. In the scene described above, we see clashes of values, principles, power, and images. This much is easy, in a way. But, let's consider how the film leads us to identify with the main character and then ask ourselves: Would we respond similarly in the work and public settings we inhabit? Would we accept the style of the heroine as within the range of acceptable behaviors for a "professional" at our place of work? Would we even recognize, let alone applaud, such an agent as a heroine or hero in real life? Without the benefit of a compelling narrative and the cinematic suspension of disbelief, would we let Brockovich in the door of our own law firm or other situation? Or would we leave her to sit in the waiting room until she withered and finally gave up? In fact, how do we typically respond to the Erin Brockovich–like people in our work, in politics, and in the media? This popular story reminds us of how much the person becomes the message when professionalism is assessed: professionalism is at once an embodiment of societal ideals and an in-your-face representation of who matters and who doesn't (Ashcraft, forthcoming; Cheney & Ashcraft, 2007).

Of course, there's a risk in pursuing this particular line of questioning: we might begin to see professionalism as too wrapped up in the character and agency of a person. In emphasizing individual "characters," we may lose sight of the wider character of ethics in the cultures to which we contribute and which shape us. So we need to consider more broadly how to define professionalism in our own places of work and employing organizations. The professional world is both a narrower and more exalted domain for us than it would be if it were "just a job." While there is certainly variability by job, some common themes can be seen. In the area of financial planning, for instance, frontline service providers are expected to be cool, distant, and objective, and to "not to really think about people." Yet when they are asked about their work struggles, the individuals occupying these positions report the emotional tensions and the ethical dilemmas of handling cases in which clients are in dire circumstances. As one thirty-year veteran of the profession explained to researchers, "Financial planning is blood pressures, emotions, and people" (Miller & Koesten, 2008, p. 8).

These examples reveal strong tendencies, biases, and sometimes root metaphors (like the machine or the race) that guide our behaviors in work and professional life. As we'll discuss in chapter 5, in fact, the machine metaphor, with its apparent amorality (a machine doesn't use consciousness to make decisions, have values, or register feelings—at least not yet), underlies a great deal of organizational thought and practice (see Burrell & Morgan, 1979). We sometimes talk about organizations being "well-oiled machines," and this has its advantages for performance; but what does this mean for the people within them and how they relate to one another? If a person is part of a machine at work or in his or her profession, does it make much sense to talk about autonomy and discrimination or choice? Cogs don't choose to turn; they get turned by other forces. But, if work is not really like a machine—even when it looks that way, as in a factory—then what's the best way to think about it?

In chapter 3, we looked at the world of work in general, focusing on individuals' relationships to it. In chapter 5 we will consider the role of the employing or governing organization in all this. In this chapter, we will consider that domain we call "the profession," examining both the benefits and limitations of professionalism as we typically understand, frame, and enact it. As we will see, professionalism can compartmentalize rather than extend ethical practice, essentialize "quality" in certain persons and groups (even in images of what the professional ought to look like), and alienate some classes in society from others.

Where Did the Professional Come From?

The Rise of the Professional Classes

There is no general agreement among sociologists as to what counts as a profession, yet many people seem to learn from social cues what can be reasonably accorded the label (McDonald, 1995). We joke about "the world's oldest profession," and cartoons sometimes show attempts by "cave people" to distinguish themselves by distinctively modern credentials. It is, in a way, as futile to try to identify the actual starting point of professionalism as it is to look for the first organization in history (or the first conversation). The point is that professions in various forms have been around for hundreds of years. Professions, like corporations and labor unions, have pre-industrial antecedents in the forms of guilds, which represented associations of people, often craftspeople, with similar expertise and interests (Larson, 1977).

As the sociologist Andrew Abbott (1988) explains, it makes sense to analyze not just individual professions but also professions as a system because of the way they evolved together on the principle of jurisdiction (e.g., in pharmacy). But, especially in the United States and other highly individualistic societies, we aren't accustomed to thinking this way: we tend to make attributions of competence, authority, and integrity to individual persons while failing to see the larger social context in which anyone's professional status can be understood. As one of our colleagues in the College of Engineering at the University of Utah points out, civil engineering is often derided as a "softer science" because it involves a closer connection between engineers and the public, while the "hard science" of bioengineering involves engineers in work affiliated more with doctors, medical researchers, and the practice of medicine. In this case, as in many others, the company we keep can either elevate or reduce professional status. Still, one's profession is a jurisdiction that expresses a profession's claim to moral competence, in addition to technical competence, and, in a certain sense, superiority over non-members. In fact, as a society we expect certain things from professionals that we don't normally ask of non-professionals, and one of those is substantial mutual regulation (Dzur, 2008).

Jurisdiction is a natural extension of specialization: it refers to an arena of authority but also responsibility. With it we attempt to formalize the domain of a profession and the rights of those who practice it. This is socially useful, even essential, for the division of labor to function with some degree of order. To formalize a profession we turn to those in a particular professional group, who have earned the right to make determinations about what counts as "good work" or "a job well done." We allow them to set standards, which we, in turn, respect and apply. This often involves an explicit social contract; even when it does not, there is an implied consensus that governs our choices as we act as members of the profession. The next time you visit your family's doctor, consider this: the modern Hippocratic Oath, taken by most medical professionals upon conferral of their professional status, includes the promise to refrain from making diagnoses or performing procedures that can be better administered by other medical specialists. It is an interesting thought experiment to apply this principle to all professions and to consider what the world would be like if everyone were as conscious of observing the limits of their expertise as they are about protecting and celebrating their expertise.

For a group of professionals with a common purpose and self-governance, the consequences of assiduously respecting the boundaries of a jurisdiction can sometimes be devastating, as in the case of eugenics in the late nineteenth and early twentieth centuries. Eugenics developed out of the work of Sir Francis Galton, becoming a perverse sort of profession. Galton, building on but also departing from the work of his cousin, Charles Darwin, in the mid-nineteenth century, offered what he saw as a socially and biologically scientific approach to the advancement of human civilization. Eugenics advocates argued that practices such as forced sterilization and the prevention of inter-racial sexual relations would improve society. The communication scholar Marouf Hasian (1996) points out that framing eugenicists as scientific professionals was key to making the oppressive, racist, and sexist outcomes of eugenic knowledge seem acceptable. For large groups of people in U.S. society, eugenics provided a dispassionate and responsible way to create a progressive society, and other professions played roles in establishing that legitimacy. Juridical rhetoric that seemed neutral contributed to the Supreme Court's endorsement in 1927 of a Virginia law permitting forced sterilization (Hasian & Croasmun, 1992). While the lawyers and judges aimed to act professionally, that Supreme Court decision resulted in the compulsory sterilization of the mentally ill defendant Carrie Buck. Were the so-called scientists who were practicing eugenics suited to establish guidelines for others' procreation? A more basic question is, Should *anyone* have that power? How did legal professionals deny the fundamental biological rights of individuals by affirming the rights of the state and professionals to make such decisions? These are serious questions that should remind us of how easy it is for professions to slough off or drift away from their larger social responsibilities (Dzur, 2008). It's also a reminder of the necessary interdependence of professions and why mutual oversight among the professions, in addition to regulation within professions, is so crucial: the strict compartmentalization of ethics needs to be resisted, even when the experts in an area seem to "know best."

Specialization, Diversification, and Division of Labor

Specialization is a horizontal dimension of work, and it represents one of the three main dimensions of structure in organizations and society. The other two are hierarchy, referring to vertical order, and formalization, pertaining to the degree by which certain organizational relationships are institutionalized and preserved, moving from the informal and spontaneous to the formal and predictable (Cheney et al., 2004). Specialization is a kind of compartmentalization; it defines and labels areas of work activity seen as sufficiently different from one another as to merit their own "place." A profession, then, gets associated with its own body of knowledge, sets of practices, and status. An expectation of specialization accompanies professional status—we don't really *want* our lawyer to be a plumber as well. This is precisely why the late 1970s *Saturday Night Live* routine called "Theodoric of York, Medieval Barber," was amusing: Theodoric used his knife both to conduct surgery and to cut hair. In effect, his was the profession of the sharp knife.

Today we're above combining and thereby blurring distinctions between professions. On the other hand, we appreciate the risks of excessive specialization and bureaucratization that Max Weber (1978) warned us about nearly a century ago. Although specialization allows us to determine a professional's bona fide qualifications so that we can decided who is "in" and who is "out," specialization often creates unnecessary barriers to collaboration between those practicing different skills while working on the same problems.

Of course, subdividing the domain of knowledge within professions, professional associations, and employing organizations has notable consequences. The cultural anthropologist Mary Douglas (1986) observes that economists, as professional academics, have developed a "self-definition [among] various professions. Economists are the strong theoreticians in the social sciences. The institutions around them are based on many...[sets] of analogies" (pp. 64–65). These analogies became the basis for what counts as professional knowledge in economics. Doing professional economic work means distinguishing between luxury and necessity, between philosophy and applied science, between intangible and measurable things, and so on. Economists, as Douglas explains, carve out their knowledge domain by focusing on the latter terms in those pairs.

Professional economists also distinguish themselves and their areas of expertise even further; there are professional circles centered on macroeconomics, econometrics, international economics, organizational/

industrial economics, and such—just like there are different types of doctors or engineers. However, Douglas argues, using the example of domestic food system management, "The result is that policy makers and administrators *pay attention to* recurring deficits in food availability instead of to the balance of exchange entitlements through the whole society" (p. 65, emphasis added). Thus it seems that attention to food *security* is a more ethically inspired way to examine the problem of scarcity. Yet—and this is Douglas's central point—economists' professionalized knowledge is ethically loaded up front, but loaded differently for different areas of application. From this we see that we can make meaningful distinctions both within a "family" of professions and within any particular profession.

Douglas (1986) is basically saying that institutions, such as the professions and professionalism, help social groups figure out what terms, concepts, and bits of information "hang together." Because professionalism is often rooted in the mastery of specific domains of knowledge, it can be difficult, even debilitating, to figure out from whom to seek information and how to weigh data and recommendations. In complex situations, as when considering treatments involving nuclear medicine, the specialization of labor fosters quite a communication problem, socially speaking.

We say that specialization is "horizontal" because although professions exist side by side, as specialties, it is quite important to look at them in terms of their status and relative positions on the "ladder" as well. We find hierarchies within professions even as professions themselves are ranked within society. Recall our example from the field of engineering. While most people probably think of all engineers as having a particular social status, engineers themselves often differentiate among themselves according to the presumed level of difficulty or the acknowledged expertise involved in each type of engineering (civil, mechanical, chemical, biological, etc.). But what about the broad social esteem of engineers as a whole? Engineers aren't represented in the popular media the way doctors or lawyers are. There is no television show like *Grey's Anatomy* or *Boston Legal* that features engineers.

The 1965 film *The Spy Who Came In from the Cold* (based on the John le Carré novel), subtly displays the system of internal ranking in the East German Intelligence Service. The character Alex Leamas, a defector from a British spy agency, is vetted by the East German Intelligence Service, moving up the hierarchy at each step of the process. Two East Germans evaluate him; in each session, the superior in rank treats his occupational inferior with condescension and even disdain. The display of rank takes a humorous twist when Leamas is transferred further up the ranks for additional vetting, and the former superior becomes the new interrogator's ill-treated inferior. In this display of ranked relationships we also see how the culture of rank is preserved by communication of and experience within an organization's culture.

We all know that some professions are ranked and compensated more highly than others, and these rankings are affected by the politics of race, gender, and class (Ashcraft, 2007; Ashcraft & Mumby, 2004). As the sociologists Charles and Grusky (2004) explain, the degree of segregation along lines of gender is astonishing when one looks not only at industrialized societies but at the world as whole. There is an implicit and sometimes explicit "different but equal" standard applied to those entering and advancing within professions that persists even as egalitarian ideals spread in the wider society.

In the case of the clergy, there are different ecclesiastical barriers (and rewards) for women than there are for men; (aspiring) clergy with non-heterosexual orientations face yet other barriers. These barriers are not easy to overcome, as we see in the growing schism that occurred in the global Anglican Communion over the ordination of openly homosexual bishops (Kirby, 2005). In this instance, African members of the church are at odds with those in the U.K. and the United States, bringing class, racial, and regional differences to light even as the focus was presumably first on gender and sexuality. Who counts as a legitimate leader in this profession may lead to the breakup of the Communion and the creation of truly separate hierarchies and sets of allegiances in addition to different professional requirements.

From the analytical standpoint of Emile Durkheim (1964, 1996), modern society works largely because of the interdependence of people in various professions and jobs. The carpenter needs the teacher, and the social worker needs the computer programmer. But this account of interdependence still begs several questions: Which professions are truly necessary? Which professions actually contribute to social betterment? Important for us: Which professions, as typically structured and practiced, encourage ethical reflection? And, finally, which professions actually deal with ethics directly rather than keeping it on the margins of awareness and vision, in a vault that is only occasionally opened? After all, professionalism can sometimes mask ethical transgressions, even when we are reflecting on our own behavior (Chugh, Bazerman, & Banaji, 2005).

For example, George found that when he was teaching Chinese midlevel managers about leadership theories in 2000 *the main thing they wanted to discuss was moral–practical conflicts at work.* A few of the managers politely interrupted George's presentation to say that because there was normally so little time for such discussions with their colleagues they were anxious to talk about it in the classroom. Moreover, these experienced managers understood well why there is so little time for ethical reflection in the course of most professional work: the sheer pace and the premium placed on certainty don't often allow for it.

The Solidification of Associations, Standards, and Certifications

This need for an ethical space also takes us back to studies of early industrialized society, à la Durkheim (1964, 1996), and then to the present to consider how professionalism is as much a social as an individual matter. Durkheim saw professionalism as an important means of linking individual identity and performance to the needs and goals of the larger society, arguing that "there is no form of social activity that can do without the appropriate moral discipline[, and] each part [of a social group or profession] must behave in a way that enables the whole to survive" (1996, p. 14). Thus, for Durkheim, there was no role for the isolated professional, nor was there any sense of removing professional behavior from key ethical concerns. Still, he remained aware of the special demands that each profession carries with it.

Consider also the cases of osteopaths, massage therapists, and life coaches, to take three varied instances of professionalization. Each of these occupations moves farther from our ideal of the profession, thereby challenging us to articulate the essence of professionalism. Ask yourself: is there something inherent in a profession, or is it a label that (groups of) people use to make claims about the work they do? When we examine the language of professionalism, it seems that a profession isn't as much a social fact, as Durkheim would put it, as it is a persuasive way of speaking about work and the relationships that mediate among professionals, customers, and society (Lair, Cheney, & Sullivan, 2005). With doctors of osteopathy, we find a group striving for legitimacy alongside an established and powerful group of professionals: medical doctors (MDs) (Miller, 1998). With massage therapists, we find a group trying to distance itself from less respected forms of their work (K. R. Sullivan, 2007), simultaneously trying to separate themselves from the sexualized versions and images of their work while struggling to retain the sensual, healing, connecting dimensions of it. At stake are their individual reputations and the very legitimacy of their profession. With executive and life coaches, we find a new form of consulting defining itself in a space between existing professions, using a catchy label to gain attention. In such cases, roles and identities became closely linked to real and perceived ethical practices. Integrity thus refers to the integration of professional practice and personal identity as much as it indicates a general trustworthiness. And we determine the trustworthiness of a person or institution over time, considering many messages and actions. Professions do not gain respect overnight, and some struggle with it continuously, partly because of the politics among professions themselves (that is, the pecking order) and partly because of their own internal problems (like inconsistent application of standards or public scandals).

As professions are formalized, they gain legitimacy in the eye of the state while they acquire the authority to accord status to members. Members, then, must appeal to both the professional association and the state for their own legitimacy, their ability to, as it were, hang out a shingle. But this process is double-edged, for like all organizations, professional ones take on a life of their own over time and can become singularly devoted to their self-aggrandizement. This is especially true when they see their status threatened (as with Garrison Keillor's fictional Professional Organization of English Majors, from the long-running radio show *A Prairie Home Companion*), or when they want to be acknowledged as genuine contributors to social welfare and the smooth functioning of society (take the Public Relations Society of America, for instance [see Boyton, 2002; Liu & Horsley, 2007]). In either of these cases, however, professionalization can be used to create a sense of distance and mystery, classic strategies in the accumulation of power (Sennett, 1980).

Consider again the profession of engineering. Professional organizations representing the various disciplines of engineering help legitimize that work as professional. Many engineers are certified by societies as professionals—unlike, say, doctors or lawyers—after four or five years of undergraduate study. Also, as with clinical psychology practices today, nominal social status may remain even as things like pay, insurance, and the chief professional association's collective political clout diminish (Owens, 2007).

The Rise of New Groups, Categories, and Classes

The formation of groups is an important aspect of professionalism, and this applies both across professions and within organizations representing various parts of a profession. Some professions are highly formalized through (often institutionalized) rites of passage. Once we have established certification standards for a profession, as was done in the United States for physician assistants in 1975, that field is seen to have "made it" as a profession. Other professions are much more loosely assembled and have comparatively little authority to set standards and police their members. "Personal organizers," who sort through the clutter of home and/or office, are good examples of this (Belk, 2007). This type of profession was virtually unheard of until the 1990s; now some people see it as crucial. Like all organizations, professions begin as informal collections of people, although this may be difficult to remember when we encounter a long-established professional organization like the American Medical Association (AMA). Eventually, many professional organizations accrue power and resources far beyond what was initially imagined. The AMA and the American Bar Association, for example, have huge lobbying arms.

Architecture provides a good illustration of how a profession evolves and grows in size and influence. Architecture is the practice of designing built environments for specific human needs and goals within the limits of available resources. As a number of contributors to the volume *The Architect: Chapters in the History of the Profession* (Kostof, 1986) point out, architecture was a craft before it was a profession. Craftspeople would share and invent patterns of design representative of certain cultural traditions; although certain patterns and informal associations emerged, architecture was by no means a specialized profession. Tschumi (1996) describes the functions that architecture served as it became recognizable as a profession: "Historical analysis has generally supported the view that the role of the architect is to project on the ground the images of social institutions, translating the economic or political structure of society into buildings or groups of buildings. Hence architecture was, first and foremost, the adaptation of space to the existing socioeconomic structure. It would serve the powers in place, and, even in the case of more socially oriented policies, its programs would reflect the prevalent views of the existing political framework" (p. 5). Today there are numerous professional organizations for architects, among them the American Institute of Architects, the American Institute of Building Design, and the National Organization of Minority Architects.

If all goes well for the "professionalizing" group, the legitimization of those groups by the state and other institutions follows. This process is vital to the recognition and often the sustainability of a group. If we focus on changes in the image—and autonomy—of the pilot from the 1930s to the 1960s, we can see that this process took some surprising twists and turns in the United States and Europe. For example, what happened to the swashbuckling image of 1930s-era pilots? What happened to the heroines? In just a few decades, the most common image of the airline pilot transformed from a heroic, adventurous, swashbuckling man or woman, to a buttoned-down, quasi-military, bureaucratic white man.

The transformation and the narrowing of professional options and representations were breathtaking, as the communication scholar Karen Lee Ashcraft (2007) found in her wide-ranging analysis of professionalism for commercial pilots. Above all, the case of commercial pilots shows how multiple social, economic, and political influences work in the development of a profession. Job segregation in this and other fields routinely revolves around class, race, gender, and often nationality, but the groupings and the status markers are not necessarily static (Ashcraft, 2007, forthcoming). A great deal of the shaping of the profession happens through "the constitutive force of communication/discourse in the context of historical [and] material possibilities and constraints" (Ashcraft, 2007, p. 30). Thus, we must look carefully at the interplay of categories and the physical circumstances that both give rise to them and are shaped by them.

Clearly we are considering professional ethics as a much bigger tent than it is usually assumed to be. In most of our treatments of ethics at work, we have shut ourselves and our society off from broader and deeper understandings of the meaning of work, our way of being, and the implications of our choices—even mundane ones like how to respond or react to someone else's contribution to a meeting. As the anthropologist Helen Schwartzman (1989) shows vividly in her accounts of meetings at a mental health center, how we respond to impassioned pleas in meetings can be constrained both by images of professionalism and by organizational rules. For example, when is it okay to express euphoria or sadness or anger? Rationality becomes as much a norm for behavior and image as it is a logic of how premises and plans fit together. We don't usually think of these communication-style issues as relevant to ethics because we are so accustomed to pinpointing ethical moments or decisions rather than seeing ethics as an ongoing dimension of who we are and what we do. Thus, ethics remains in the little box of occasional adornments, or as a sidebar to life's conversation, just as it did for many of George's undergraduate students. While concern about morality animates them, analytical discussions of ethics do not. How often do we consider the implications of our ways of being at work and how we talk about who we are at work? Not often enough, we would argue. And we lose a great deal as a result.

Reconsidering Professionalism

Professionalism: Both Divisive and Helpful

Durkheim's *Division of Labor in Society* (1964) isn't usually considered to be a very critical book. However, in its commentary on labor and social relations in the nineteenth century, this book offers the seeds of understanding for how modern industrialized society separates us even as it helps us get things done and function as part of an entire system. Durkheim offers a detailed account of the differences between pre-industrial and modern societies, arguing that how work is organized is an important element of the social glue that makes society what it is. Moreover, Durkheim offers a kind of "moral particularism," accepting that the standards of one profession may not necessarily or completely apply to another; thus, the ethical guidelines for a lawyer may well be of a different nature than those for a physician. Still, Durkheim sees certain responsibilities as transcending professional communities, and these include deference to state authority (that is, abiding by the law) and altruistic motivation (avoiding dominating self-interest, or making appeals to an internal ethical motive). *The Division of Labor in Society* also highlights deeper fissures and forms of segregation. Three manifestations of this are notable in our society today: the use of professional jargon, the trend toward less rather than more access to higher education, and what has become known as "the digital divide." Let's consider the various angles on several new or still-emerging professions in terms of these aspects.

At the time we wrote this book, the Wikipedia entry for "life coaching" made reference to several professional organizations. It was suggested that the article be merged with entries for "coaching," "business coaching," and "personal coaching," and the neutrality of the article was disputed. As yet, this field has no governing bodies or supervisory mechanisms, and all major professional associations (e.g., International Association of Coaching, International Coach Federation, European Coaching Institute) are privately owned. Or take "hacktivism," where we see a wholly new form of unpaid activity that is trying to overcome its outlaw status and assert itself as a positive social force, even a social movement. There are different kinds of hacktivists, of course. Some of them try to set standards for their activities to put distance between themselves and the more "renegade" members of their networks. It's not always well known that many hacktivists see their work as part of a higher calling, especially when they are committed to open-source software, free access to information, and the removal of the shroud of secrecy concealing the activities of many governmental and private institutions (Van Buren, 2001). Writers of computer viruses even distinguish between "real virus writers" and "script kiddies," who simply "cut and paste" other's creations. And as one journalist's (C. Thompson, 2004) interviewee points out, the distinction can gloss over serious ethical considerations: "If you're going to say [virus and worm writing] is an artistic statement, there are more responsible ways to be artistic than to create code that costs people millions" (p. 72).

Professionalizing a "Non-professional" Activity

When we look at professionalization as a process, we realize that certain aspects in the "life" of work can be lost along the way to recognition, bureaucratization, and legitimacy. A good example of this is the set of activities and jobs associated with peacemaking around the world. In his keynote address to the International Peace Research Association biennial conference in Calgary, Johan Galtung (2006) bemoaned the growing "professionalism" of peace studies and peace work because it can emphasize the wrong set of motivations and inadvertently limit the dynamism and creativity of these activities. Galtung's remarks suggest how professionalism can quickly slide from a responsibility to the world outside the boundaries of the profession to an insularity from that world, to an arena in which professionals speak with other professionals about the outside world without ever fully engaging it. Further, when others see peacemaking as a profession, they may be discouraged from participating because of the assumed expertise required. At the same time, they may keep their own profession, such as law or medicine, segregated from the peacemaking profession in order to maintain its standing. This is another type of abstraction that occurs when presumably positive aspects of professionalism serve to remove the practitioners from the very set of practices to which they are committed in the first place.

The lessons here are several. Professionalism developed over the long term; it didn't just appear on the scene as we talk about it now. Professionalism both associates and dissociates people. As professions develop, those associations can become more formal and bureaucratic, but new senses of professionalism are always developing. In other words, our very notions of professionalism are always, to at least some extent, "up for grabs." At a time when commonly held assumptions are fragmenting, we can turn a critical eye toward representations of professionalism in the popular media to better grasp the implications of that fragmentation.

We might even ask about the unforeseen implications of professionalizing the "ethics industry" in business, with the rise of ethics officers and routine systems of compliance, along with now well-established codes of ethics for most organizations and groups of professionals. In what ways is this both a welcome development and a potential source of narrow thinking? When we think of the patterns and effects of professionalism more broadly, as dimensions of our struggle to formulate and control "the good," we can see how they operate at multiple levels and not just in predictable ways.

Professionalism in Popular Culture

Pop cultural representations of professional life are often plainly fictional, or at least heavily embellished. Even when they're "real," they tend to be exceptional and sensationalized, as we find repeatedly in the scandals that bring down stars. Think of how our expectations for sports heroes, politicians, and entertainment stars change over time. Recent articles on tarnished baseball and basketball stars in the United States have lamented "the loss of professionalism" (e.g., M. S. Schmidt, 2007), yet seldom is that idea defined other than with passing references to illegal drug use or angry outbursts, sometimes with racist undertones. But surely there's more going on here. This is part of the spectacle and the problem of professionalism: just getting our arms around it is difficult. Professionalism remains a powerful, emotionally and ideologically charged, yet little understood image (Cheney&Ashcraft, 2007).

Recall how the character of Erin Brockovich defied our expectations for professional behavior in a complex mix of style and behavior that is at once unacceptable and laudable. We believe that issues of style deserve to be taken seriously; they establish and reinforce expectations of professionals. Now let's add a few more examples. The eVoice voicemail service, for instance, promises that client organizations, including one-person companies, "get the professional sound in minutes" (http://home.evoice.com/s/r/evoice_evr). Their sales pitch relies heavily on equating the use of technology with a professional style and image. Take also the "professional" business lessons of *The Apprentice* television show and its overall message (Lair, 2007). As much as it presumes to portray behaviors that lead to success in the business world, the series offers its viewers a particular professional aesthetic, a subtle argument that being professional is as much about style as it is about substance: throughout the program, people whose dress and behavior deviates from professional norms either find their potential for success limited or are outright punished (the leisure suit–wearing, guitar-playing contestant Danny from the third season stands out here). Recall our earlier reference to the TV show *Survivor*, particularly for how it purports to teach us quite a lot about teamwork, competition, and truth (Thackaberry, 2003). We can also point to films such as *Michael Clayton* (Gilroy, 2008), where a character experiences a turning point in a rural pastoral scene that seems to touch him at a new, deeper level, prompting self-examination. Under the heavy cloak of professionalism, the "fix it" man for a corrupt corporate law firm had for years justified his work as reasonable, effective, and worthwhile. In one of the final scenes of the film, Clayton adopts the language of a lawyer who has realized the self-denying and socially destructive nature of work in the firm, cynically referring to himself as "a janitor" and, even more strikingly, as "Shiva, God of Death."

The theme of wholeness crops up in Denis Johnson's recent novel *Tree of Smoke* (2007), showing what stress can do to social-ethical systems as well as to individuals' sense of purpose. Johnson's novel follows Skip Sands, who begins his work with the U.S. Central Intelligence Agency as an idealistic, patriotic, hardworking young professional just before the United States entered the Vietnam War. Sands is quickly bewildered by the apparent lack of ethical standards or coherent purpose guiding the people, American and Vietnamese alike, waging war in Vietnam. Other characters struggle, and largely fail, to return to peace in the United States after serving as soldiers overseas. William Carlos Williams's (2000) short story "The Use of Force" evocatively describes a physician's intimate feelings as he performs his professional duty when examining a young girl during a house call. The execution of those duties, seemingly in the girl's interest, reveals a sort of betrayal of her as well. All of these examples portray protagonists who wrestle with the relationships between ethics and the nature of their profession and specific work tasks. The featured characters are troubled not just about what to do in a specific situation; they are also struggling over how ethics should apply to their lives.

Biographies can be especially revealing in this regard: an award-winning book on J. Robert Oppenheimer (Bird & Sherwin, 2005) chronicles his professional "fall" as he reevaluated his own career as a nuclear physicist and head of the Manhattan Project, which developed and tested the first atomic bomb in New Mexico in 1945. In Heinar Kipphardt's 1968 play *In the Matter of J. Robert Oppenheimer*, the protagonist recalls, "The dropping of the bomb on Hiroshima was a political decision—it wasn't mine....I was just doing my job" (p. 13). In the end, Oppenheimer felt part of neither the military–scientific establishment nor the peace movement, and he lost his credibility with both. He was in a professional and personal place struggling largely in silence. In this example we can plainly see how work, ethics, and identity are intimately intertwined. Oppenheimer's biography reveals how he shifted from framing his work in a largely personal–technical way to framing it in a moral–personal one. As with so many issues, the framing is crucial. "Professional" talk, ironically, often leads us away from ethical–moral considerations as we get wrapped up in questions of "doing the best job." As we have stressed in the previous chapters, "good work" isn't always what it may first appear to be (see Fischman et al., 2004).

In fact, expectations for professional behavior and style infuse our society, sometimes reinforcing and sometimes actually creating differences that wouldn't otherwise exist or be so pronounced (Ashcraft, 2007; Cheney & Ashcraft, 2007). We know we attempt to essentialize professionalism in things as superficial as dress, as in the case of Erin Brockovich, but we may still ask where all these sets of expectations come from and how they shape identities and interactions. For example, in a study that connects personal interviews with popular discourse, Holmer-Nadesan and Trethewey (2000) culled themes from self-help literature and talked to women entrepreneurs to examine how they both draw upon and resist certain cultural messages. The authors concluded that "[entrepreneurial] success is contingent upon realizing an entrepreneurial ideal that is ultimately held to be unattainable because of unsightly (feminine) leakages that always/already reveal their performances as charades" (p. 224). Certainly, in the United States an expectation of a mildly positive but cool emotional expression, a style that has been analyzed historically (Stearns, 1994), and also in terms of gender, race, and class, is the most often expected behavior associated with professionalism (see, e.g., Tracy, 2000). A study of firefighters (Tracy & Scott, 2006) points out that they felt like "rock stars" when traveling about town in their trucks or when entering situations fraught with physical danger. However, the firefighters also explained that this image was threatened by their having to perform much of the "feminized labor" (as the authors put it) of caring for others, which is part of day-to-day work for firefighters. The preference for the more "masculine" image of firefighting came, in part, from the general public's perceptions of firefighters and their work reflected in remembrances of September 11, 2001, calendars featuring muscle-bound firemen, Hollywood movies, and so forth. These are among the many stories we tell about professionals and how we think about professionalism in our society.

Rethinking "Common Sense" about Professionalism

We think of professionalism as an unalloyed positive force, yet when we look more closely we see where an overemphasis on professionalism can lead people astray. This is apparent in the United States and elsewhere in terms of press coverage of the foibles and falls of sports stars. In the steroids scandal that has plagued major league baseball in the first decade of the twenty-first century, the emphasis has been on high-profile players such as José Canseco, Roger Clemens, and Barry Bonds, with less examination of the professional *culture* of baseball as an institution. But the abuse of performance-enhancing drugs in baseball cannot be understood without considering the issue in the context of the immense pressure on players to meet and maintain the exacting standards required by their lucrative contracts. Or consider the case of Showtime's critically acclaimed series *Dexter*, whose protagonist, Dexter Morgan, is portrayed as a sympathetic serial killer. As a serial killer, Dexter is a consummate professional who not only kills his victims with exacting technical precision but selects those victims—all murderers themselves—by his own "code," which requires a stricter standard of proof than the criminal justice system. He has a more discriminating sense for *their* accountability than for his own. But no matter how much Dexter wraps himself in the cloak of professionalism, he remains a serial killer. The point is that professionalism as an ideal is considerably more ambivalent than we usually consider it to be.

Professionalism Is a Common Aspiration

If indeed the category of professional applies to everyone, it becomes meaningless; it's like calling everything "urgent" (as with most express mail labels today). On the other hand, if we use the professional distinction simply as a way of creating classes, we divide society unnecessarily and indicate that certain groups are simply not as worthwhile as others. This is quite evident in the traditional hierarchical arrangement between physicians and nurses, and it has surfaced in new ways as the corporatization of medicine in the United States has threatened the traditional autonomy of doctors and blurred the lines of authority between them, nurses, and administrators (Bartlett & Steele, 2006).

On a broader level, it is relevant to consider the global "digital divide," especially in the ways that networks of professionals span geographic boundaries but become more removed from other segments of the citizenry (Castells, 1996). This "exclusionary segmentation" occurs in both the domain of work and the domain of leisure. Emmison (2003) says of the relationship between "cultural mobility" and professional status that "[it] can be identified initially in a clear differentiation between an inclusive mode of cultural practice, in which people participate actively in a wide range of activities and possess broad competencies across both high and low culture, and a restricted mode, in which participation is more passive or conservative and confined to relatively narrow areas" (p. 217). He notes that "[the inclusive mode's] structural location lies with the professional and managerial class. The restricted mode...is most clearly exemplified in the manual working class" (p. 217). Emmison explains that the sheer mobility of professionals serves as a sort of status distinction, separating them as a networked class from nonprofessionals. Many professionals are, literally, free to move about in the society.

Control and Expediency Versus Expertise and Quality

"Quality," for example, is often determined in rather narrow ways. This can be seen in many programs called "quality control," "Total Quality Management" (TQM), and "excellence." The names of managerial programs and regimes are, like any such labels, subject to transformation, narrow application, and self-caricature. Any organization worth its salt stands on the assertion of excellence, and many will demonstrate that commitment by pointing to procedures and processes they have adopted. A classic example of this is the TQM movement, whose heyday was in the 1970s to the 1990s.

The original formulations of this approach emphasized several facets of organizing. Those first approaches to TQM actively engaged employees by combining careful self-reflection (at the individual and organizational levels) with an ethic of proactive participation.

However, fairly narrow technical procedures were often instituted to facilitate, manage, and track progress. Some later applications of TQM emphasized the program's use of technical measurement and largely ignored participatory practices. Other applications gave only lip service to the detailed technical requirements of TQM, in effect using a popular new label to describe business-as-usual. Despite these variations in how "quality" is ensured and communicated, one element is common to the later interpretations of TQM: they aimed to engage employees in an all-encompassing, management-oriented program. In the end, the application of these kinds of systems can be as much about routine, predictability, and control as about quality and quality improvement (Zbaracki, 1998). The result, in this case, is "a TQM that serves as a sort of least common denominator, uniting many elements underneath the overall term total quality management" (p. 630).

In this trend, as in so many others, the demands of the organization itself can dwarf broader standards of professionalism. In some cases, as studies of legal firms show, the dedication to particular organizational procedures can take attention from broader professional principles, as two business professors found in firms that were globalizing (Faulconbridge & Muzio, 2008). These researchers found that the distinction between adherence to a broad base of professional norms and adherence to an organization's norms become blurred in cases where a firm is striving to maintain consistency among far-flung offices. The problem can be seen especially in how committee work is structured and valued. The authors conclude by advancing the term "organizational professionalism," which we will revisit in chapter 5.

Professionalism's Moral and Technical Dimensions

Professionalism involves not just accomplishing segmented or atomized tasks, or even completing a degree or major project, but also reflecting on the role of a person and the larger group of professionals in society (Boyte, 2004). How does one immerse oneself in one's work for the sake of excellence, typically understood by one's employer and one's peers, yet keep an eye on the big picture of work, achievement, and contribution to society? For many people engaged in what we commonly call professional careers, this kind of reflection is not only possible, but also necessary.

For example, the Texas State Library Management Training Program lists these criteria: training, intellectualism, autonomy, judgment, independence, service, dedication, and pride (www.tsl.state

.tx.us/ld/tutorials/professionalism/criteria.html). Notice the combined expectations for training by other experts and the stress on the autonomy of the professional employee. The professional is supposed to internalize not just knowledge but also certain values so as to practice effectively and to "be" a professional. In fact, these are the types of characteristics (and by extension, benefits) we count on as we engage other "professionals" by contract or less formally. Signs of such legitimacy may be seen in academic degrees, training certificates, bonding, association membership, and so on. Even without formal contracts to govern them, the relationships between members of a profession or between them and their clients still lean upon a diffuse notion of social contract that is the architecture of trust in the society.

These attributes come to be applied not only to clearly defined bodies of work but also to whole categories of employees who do not share the same body of knowledge or type of job. In fact, this is exactly what has happened with many temporary, seasonal, and subcontracting or outsourcing relationships, as what has come to be called the "contingent economy" has taken a greater and greater share of the workforce (V. Smith, 2001, 2006). In areas as diverse as publishing and human resources consulting, the ranks of "itinerant professionals" have grown. According to the management scholars Barley and Kunda (2006), these contractors are more and more adept at packaging their own abilities and forms of expertise to gain the attention of potential employers. Still, even when these contractors are stably employed, the temporariness of the employee–employer relationship casts a negative shadow on their position, subordinating it from the start to those of permanent employees. Because of the instability of their employment, itinerant professionals rely heavily on their ability to network and try to maintain a reputation that extends beyond the net of potential employers. For Barley and Kunda, this represents a new kind of professional practice, one that does not have moorings in particular areas of employment, professional associations, or consensual standards.

Professionalism That Rules Out Ethics

In a particularly striking scene from the movie *Boiler Room* (Younger, 2001), Ben Affleck's character, Jim Young, tells a room full of young men who hope to be junior investment brokers, "Now, let me tell you what's required of you. You are required to work your fucking ass off at this firm. We are winners here, not pikers.... People come and work at this firm for one reason: to become filthy rich. That's it! We're not here to make friends. We're not saving the fucking manatees here, guys. You want vacation time? Go teach third grade public school." People might not be so direct or vulgar in real life, but it is not uncommon for the instruction to "be professional" to imply that one should not be too concerned with ethics, family interests, and the like.

The experiences of whistleblowers can attest to the dismissal of ethics in many workplaces. Steve Wilson and Jane Akre are investigative journalists profiled in the documentary *The Corporation* (Bakan, Achbar, & Abbott, 2004). The two worked for Fox News. An early episode of their show, *The Investigators*, dug into the science of engineered bovine growth hormone, specifically Posilac, a product promoted by Monsanto. Akre and Wilson recount how Fox News management vetted, curtailed, and attempted to quash the story after Monsanto issued threats to pull advertising funding and initiate legal action. Wilson recalls telling his boss, "This is news, this is important, this is stuff people need to know," to which his boss replied, "We just paid $3 billion for these television stations. We'll tell you what the news is. The news is what we say it is." After being fired for insubordination—ultimately, they refused to soften or censor the story—the two journalists went public. In this case, Wilson and Akre were instructed to violate some of the principles most basic to professional journalism in order to protect the interests of their employer. When they refused to contain or compartmentalize ethical standards, they were ordered to do so.

What's going on here? Asserting that one is a professional or insisting that one will adhere to standards of professionalism is a common strategy for whistleblowers who feel that ethical authority trumps supervisory authority or bureaucratic expediency (Perrucci et al., 1980). Akre and Wilson discussed their internal negotiation with Fox over the story to demonstrate that the company was not living up to the ethical aspirations that ought to guide the behavior of journalists and news organizations. The intended effect of Wilson and Akre's whistle-blowing was to generate social control over the actions of Fox and members of other news organizations, that is, to establish tenets of (un)ethical or untoward action by way of public example. As Meithe and Rothschild (1994) point out, an act of whistle-blowing does not have to be "successful" to be useful or effective, in that such activity may generate unwanted attention or public outrage or may stimulate action on the part of those empowered to do something about a situation.

But remember, to be a whistleblower, one must have a prior relationship with the person or organization that is exposed (Meithe & Rothschild, 1994). The moral–professional status of whistle-blowing can be ambiguous (Bouville, 2008). Whistle-blowing almost always involves violating an order or attempting to change routines. In some cases, whistleblowers contravene unequivocal policies or laws. So, while a whistleblower might claim an obligation to "professionalism" or "right behavior," he or she might also break labor contracts, fail to meet responsibilities to clients, or disregard other ties that bind, so to speak. Similarly, whistleblowers might take right action only after injustice or retribution is visited upon them, even though their accounts of blowing the whistle emphasize the agent against whom they're protesting. This was certainly the case with Akre and Wilson, who spoke up only after being fired and undertaking a lawsuit that, though ultimately unsuccessful, could have brought them a monetary reward. The real-life tobacco company executive portrayed by Russell Crowe in the movie *The Insider* also comes to mind; the character eventually explains the public threat that the industry's deceptions pose, but only after being berated and unjustly treated by his former employer.

In this way, whistle-blowing is often about divided or competing loyalties. But it also involves the question of where one places one's trust. For one's employer may trust you to be loyal to them even as that employer requires you to violate the trust invested in you as a member of a profession. In fact, many organizations' and institutions' compensation schemes may inadvertently (or even consciously) reward disloyalty and distrust. As the global financial crisis unfolded in late 2008 and early 2009, it became clear that, in many cases, lenders and traders were responding to rewards for excessive risks, often profiting on rebate fees for transactions that should never have been allowed in the first place. A few farsighted and concerned financial analysts sounded the alarm about these practices, but they were not taken seriously until banks and other financial services began falling like dominoes (see, e.g., Cotts, Burton, & Logutenkova, 2009).

Given complex and ambiguous motives and conditions, when are acts of whistle-blowing ethically required? When are they practically necessary? When are they strategically wise? Also, is obedience to an employer any more or less responsible than to a professional association's documented code of ethics? Let's rethink the assumptions of that question. The most problematic aspect of whistle-blowing as laudable professional behavior is what it communicates about justice in relationships and social organizations. The role of the individual is central. As Bouville (2008) points out, the question of one's obligation to go public, and the personal risk involved, adds to the practical pressure and moral complexity of these situations. But "just doing one's job" by pursuing duty to an employer or technical excellence or efficiency is just as suspect. At the U.S. Federal Aviation Administration in 2008, a surprising number of employees stepped forward with concerns about abuses of authority and failures to adequately protect the public. The National Public Radio journalist Wade Goodwyn (2008) reported that the George W. Bush administration claimed that the surge in internal complaints and whistle-blowing demonstrated that the organization was functioning properly. In one sense, that's an appropriate assessment. It was Arendt's argument in *Eichmann in Jerusalem* (1994) that the Holocaust of World War II was made possible by people's unwillingness to question authority.

Our argument is that transgressive behavior such as whistle-blowing is more than just right or wrong. Its most important function is opening up individual and organized action for discussion by posing questions where there might otherwise be unqualified certainty. Whistle-blowing offers specific organizations, members of a profession, and whole societies the possibility to engage the kinds of conversations about ethics that we're promoting in this book. Opening our work contexts to the possibility of dissent and counter-commonsense expression promotes such conversations. Research has demonstrated both that contexts amenable to dissent produce better and less extreme collective decisions (Sunstein, 2003) and that they make participants more willing to dissent in the first place (Kassing & Avtgis, 1999). The promise of whistle-blowing and other forms of dissent is to allow for the insistent reintroduction of ethics into our conversations about work and professional life.

Professionalism Redefined

A recent online survey of more than six hundred members of the online community iStockphoto (Brabham, 2008) shows that many people gravitate to the term "professional." Early analysis of the data has shown that the "crowd" gathered at iStockphoto is remarkably homogeneous and that the vast majority of participants label themselves as photography "professionals," not "amateurs." Brabham (2008, personal communication) has speculated about the meaning of such uniformity this way: "getting paid = going pro"; the logic here parallels notions of athletic professionalism. So it's hardly surprising that there is a continual trend to relabel jobs in many fields. But consider also who is behind each of those efforts. Both the individual and the group can be somewhat deluded by the move to call, for example, all Wal-Mart employees "associates." Re-labeling is not necessarily a reflection of or a step toward empowerment, as people in many mind-numbing or low-paid jobs well know. That is, simply calling someone a professional does not automatically confer on them the rewards, rights, and social status of other so-called professionals. Being employed as a residential or industrial cleaning professional is a good example. The company The Cleaning Authority refers to itself as "your cleaning professionals" (see cleaningauthority.com). Their service mark, "life's too short to clean your own home," suggests a certain hierarchy: some professionals are too busy to clean their own home, and other kinds of professionals clean those homes. Who cleans the homes of the "cleaning professionals"?

As we discussed above, specialization is one means by which people define the emergence of a profession. Specialization can narrow our vision of the world even as it encourages us to focus on a particular domain of work and society. With that narrowing of vision can come a loss of purpose and certainly an inability to communicate well across the boundaries between different jobs and different professions. What do you make of the following statement from Errol Morris's 1999 documentary *Mr. Death*, about an execution expert? Fred Leuchter—a man who consults with U.S. prisons on the technical points of execution-device construction, maintenance, and operation—describes the uniqueness of his occupation: "It's not anything different than any competent engineer could do. The difference is that it's not a major market. A lot of people are not interested and are morally opposed to working on execution equipment. They think that somehow it's gonna change them." But later Leuchter adds, "We must always remember, and we must never forget, the fact that the person being executed is a human being."

Thinking beyond the Usual Professional Suspects

How Do We Socialize Professionals?

Bear in mind the importance of "the company that a symbol keeps" and "what goes with what" (Burke, 1950/1969). We should attend to symbols that get attached to one another, becoming fast companions. On the subject of this chapter, do we regularly associate "professionalism" with "objectivity" and, if so, what are the practical implications of that? As the sociolinguist George Lakoff (2002) has explained, how an issue or a person or a case is framed up front is extremely influential. The findings of a recent study of the language of U.S. law schools in the United States by Elizabeth Mertz (2007) reveal much about how certain expectations for professionals are expressed and passed along, often only implicitly. In her study of law school socialization from a linguistic perspective, the researcher examined not only the texts of legal education but also the classroom dynamics, that is, the entire scene in which legal education occurs. A number of Mertz's findings are striking, but what was especially disturbing is that she found that law school texts and interactions in law school diverted students from considering the moral dimensions of their budding careers and the limits to legal thinking itself. Ironically, this diversion was accomplished through a particular adaptation of the Socratic method, where instructors *refocus* the discussions toward the responses they desire and frequently away from any questions seen to be outside the established questions of a case. Good evidence of how discussion is directed is the frequency of "uptake" measures in the classroom: students watch and wait to see whose comments will be "picked up" and therefore reinforced by the professor, the one who is shaping what it means to "think and talk like a lawyer." Similar situations can be found in the education of doctors, where, "technical skills emerge as fundamental, while interactive skills (if encouraged at all) are secondary ... [devaluing] relationship-centered approaches to the practice of medicine" (Coulehan & Williams, 2001, pp. 599–600).

Mertz (2007) found that the structural assessment of relevance and success tended to narrow discourse, rewarding students whose remarks fit neatly within the mold and winnowing out comments that might expand the boundaries of discussion. In addition, as students were steered away from the content and contexts of legal cases, they inevitably structured everything in terms of stock legal arguments and precedents. This meant that the capacity for a given social context or issue to redefine or reframe the discussion was largely lost. Ethicality became essentialized in a *method*. Because nearly all of the cases were about conflict, the lack of reflection beyond what was determined to be the appropriate legal method served to reinforce the supremacy of the method itself and to deflect considerations about legitimacy and morality. For Mertz, the power of the language and discourse of legal education and socialization lies in their ability to shape worldviews and, in fact, to legitimate one worldview. Similarly, Jack Coulehan and Peter Williams (2001) note that the predominant approach to medical education creates doctors who treat diseases and injuries rather than care for patients. This sort of education, the title of their article says, "vanquishes virtue." These are just two examples of the importance of language as used within professions and within the discourse of professionalism.

A "true professional"—regardless of the kind of work he or she does—is expected to assume practical and moral responsibilities beyond those prescribed by what is traditionally know as a social trusteeship notion of professional responsibility. The social trustee-ship model, which developed over the past two centuries, generally promotes an apolitical view of the professional. The implementation of this perspective can actually hinder critical reflection and neces-sary corrections in policies because the moral status of the profession itself is not examined (Dzur, 2008).

On the other hand, if a profession becomes too politicized, we can't really trust its practitioners to keep a balanced perspective on their own activities or to be open to a range of ideas and interests. Accordingly, we are suspicious of any field that purports to be objec-tive yet clearly allows cronyism instead of making appointments to positions based on expertise and bona fide occupational qualifica-tions. In recent years in the United States, for example, the legitimacy of many judges, and their rulings, have been called into question because the officeholders appear beholden to those who elevated them to their posts (Burr, 2008).

Okay, so professionalism is a mixed bag, when we look at how it plays out in our society. What this means for ethics is that we're not just talking about the ways professionals behave but also about the "behavior" of professionalism, itself. What do we mean by this? Well, this shift in thinking gets us beyond strictly individual acts deserving praise or condemnation and prompts us to treat professionalism in terms of how it operates in the larger society. At this level, relatively little has been said, but a few powerful critiques have been offered. Jeff Schmidt's *Disciplined Minds* (2000) looks at the training of physi-cists and argues that in the quest for discipline and objectivity, new professionals are stripped of the ability to ask big questions, to chal-lenge authority, to dissent. Especially through graduate and profes-sional training, the emphasis on objectivity can mean, in practice, that new members of the field are fearful of "sounding too political." The status quo is then privileged as an apolitical, natural position, and the opportunity for challenges to accustomed practices is lost. The sociol-ogist Diana Crane (1972) used the term "invisible college" to describe the community of colleagues, across sub-disciplines, that influences professional scientists more than do members of their home depart-ment or their university's administration. Groups of like-minded specialists develop their own distinctive standards, usually avoiding conflicts with those of other groups (see Crane, 1972, esp. ch. 5). But as Jeff Schmidt (2004, personal communication) argues, over time, "The ethical edge of many professions gets blunted by the force of conformity."

Professionalism and Its Broader Ethical Imperatives

We have already seen how professionalism can be equated with style, as in choices of dress, patterns of consumption, and so on. So, why is this a profoundly ethical problem? One poignant illustration comes from George's experience at the University of Colorado at Boulder. One day when he was having lunch at little Chinese restaurant across from campus, he overheard two undergraduate students discussing a business professor that one of them had as an instructor. The male student described the professor as "excellent": dynamic, knowledge-able, and "totally cool." Then he paused, as if he had misgivings, and the female student asked, "So?" His response: "Well, but he drives a Chevy." With this simple statement, the student not only bought into prevailing stereotypes about consumption and personal style but also indicated his willingness to dismiss the well-supported credibil-ity of the professor to judge him by one simple consumer choice. This was an instance of extreme essentialism: the reduction of an entire set of professional expectations to one's accessories. In this case, what passed for "common sense" was, at base, pretty nonsensical.

But there's more. This take on professional "packaging" can be a way of *coding* certain gender, racial, and class preferences, just as we saw in chapter 1 in the case of the African American human resources conference (see B. J. Allen, 1995, 1996, 2007; Ashcraft & Allen, 2003). To "talk like a professional" is to adopt certain linguistic and other sym-bolic conventions that serve to identify one as a professional person. These conventions may "attach" themselves to other conventions— masculinity, heterosexuality, and whiteness, for instance. By recon-ceptualizing professionalism this way, we may use it as a vehicle to preserve the oppression of certain groups just as we employ it to elevate our collective standards of performance at work.

Further, a stress on professionalism can conceal the actual diver-sity of jobs in our economy, as when the mainstream media and adver-tising for technology exaggerate the extent to which our work is all "knowledge based" (Cloud, 2001). This concealment sometimes goes so far that people no longer see the vast array of jobs performed, how many of them involve physical labor, and how abusive the working conditions many people endure are in this presumably postindustrial society. In the 2007 film *Ghosts*, illegal Chinese migrant laborers are completely concealed as they travel across Asia and Europe only to encounter horrible work conditions (in addition to secrecy) under the thumb of a boss who serves as an intermediary with employers. This is but one reminder of the many dark sides of the global economy and the invisibility of so much work in our world (see Bowe, 2007).

In a way, our language for work and workers tends to make whole segments of society invisible by emphasizing the jobs and people who count. We often push the invisibility in another way, too, by asking many laborers, such as maintenance workers, to keep out of sight. In researching environmental-activist groups, Brenden has noticed that people will speak of "keeping him/her on a leash," meaning preventing individuals perceived as likely to "erupt" emotionally from having visible roles in sensitive group meetings. These kinds of comments are occasionally paired with the remark that "this is a professional setting." These control moves reflect anxiety about what it means to be an activist and how one should act in that role in the public sphere. For some people, the illusion is preserved that the entire society is, in a sense, professional in both style and orientation toward work.

Professionalism, Historically and Culturally

The very term "professionalism"—like consumption, efficiency, or entrepreneurship—will undergo transformations in meaning as the term gets unattached from certain ideas and images and attached to others. We've already discussed how professionalism developed through the increasing stratification and segmentation of labor in society. This is one way of describing what happens with a term over time, but we can look at cultural variation in this way as well. Perhaps we can see this best in the "occupational segregation" of barbers and hairstylists (Rich, 2009). Until the mid-1700s or so, barbers were often surgeons as well. Even after barbers' work was separated from that of doctors, it remained a kind of public work. The dressing of hair, especially women's hair—the practice of cosmetology—remained largely private, however. It wasn't until the technological, stylistic, and economic advances of the 1920s that salons were widely available to the public. As well, cosmetologists began to displace barbers by the 1960s, when cultural shifts made the *styling* of men's hair and appearance more widely acceptable. "Bodywork" has not always taken its present professional form in popular discourse. The same goes for marketing and public relations, human resources, and a whole array of work categories. Professionalism, as we know it, evolved: it's not "just the way it is."

Police work presents another, perhaps even more powerful, example. In a recent ethnographic study of everyday police work and police culture, the communication scholar Robert Ballard (2008) found that police work contains a set of assumptions that are quasi-militaristic, specifically positing a "battle" between cops and criminality. This culture creates the mindset among officers that "the police are entitled to be authors, have a right to be in control, and view every situation as a threat to personal safety, where unethical forms of interaction are always justified no matter the situation" (p. 333). Usually the police encounter people in distress or reaching out for professional assistance and simply wanting a helping hand. The quasi-militaristic training and culture of the police does not equip officers for these kinds of encounters with the public, who they are, in fact, employed to serve. Ballard cites the "need to do policing better...a policing operation that exercises fitting ethical responses in situations where danger is a legitimate threat as opposed to the more social work–type situations that call for a different kind of communicative response" (p. 370).

Ensuring Professionalism for Good

Although we've tried to emphasize how professionalism can be a force for good in society, we feel that the good that professionalism promotes is largely taken for granted in our society; people overlook how professionalism bears on their personal happiness in addition to bettering society. This connection to personal happiness is, in fact, central to Aristotle's understanding of *eudaimonia*, according to the most recent interpretations of his *Nicomachean Ethics* (2002): the goal is to engage in a process where one's happiness is intertwined with ethical practice and society's needs. As the political theorist Albert Dzur (2008) argues, "Professionals' claims—to privilege or jurisdictional control—must be redeemed only after close scrutiny by those affected by them" (p. 77). For Dzur, professionals of all stripes have a responsibility to serve and be responsive to the public, and that's a stance that makes vaulted professionals a bit more vulnerable than they usually are in popular thought and culture.

Let's now consider how professionalism creates connection, not distance; fulfillment, not alienation; how it takes a stand rather than relying solely on a false sense of objective neutrality. The entrepreneur and environmental activist Paul Hawken (1999) recalls his realization that business itself is unsustainable, ecologically speaking. Coincidentally, he came to this realization at the exact moment he was called to accept an award for his business's environmental performance. He recalls, "I stood there in silence, suddenly realizing two things: first, that my company did not deserve the award, and second, that no one else did, either.... It was clear to me in that moment that... commerce and sustainability were antithetical by design, not by intention" (pp. xi–xii). Instead of distancing himself from the business world, Hawken rededicated himself to new visions of commerce, organizing, entrepreneurship, and professionalism.

In the end, *professionalism is a nexus of concerns about who we are and what we do at work—and beyond*. For that reason, we should examine it carefully, more thoroughly than we usually do. Professionals take on certain responsibilities to society just as they do to themselves. These identifications can challenge the easy partitioning of right and wrong, personal and professional, desirable and inevitable, and so forth. The professional is also accountable to the community of practice (that is, others in the same field) and his or her employer. And, as we have shown in this chapter, the language of professionalism, for better or for worse, both enables and constrains people at work. Sometimes, being morally responsible may mean resisting an order, going public with private information, or leaving a job or career altogether (Perrucci et al., 1980).

What about My Career as a Professional?

We use the word "career" so unthinkingly that we forget about its origins and its different senses. The *Oxford English Dictionary* online (1989) defined the term using several major categories, with early formulations referring to the running of a horse, a racecourse, and, later, rapid and continuous action. The final and most contemporary entry for "career" is of most direct relevance to our discussion:

> a. A person's course or progress through life (or a distinct
> portion of life), esp. when publicly conspicuous, or
> abounding in remarkable incidents: similarly with reference
> to a nation, a political party, etc.

This usage has its earliest roots in the 1800s connecting to foreign and diplomatic service, the dictionary notes. However, other permutations of the word in the *Oxford* entry are connected to one's personal life (e.g., "career girl").

Today, particularly in Anglo-American societies, we view career as belonging to the individual, and scarcely consider what it means for the larger society (Buzzanell & Goldzwig, 1991). This is true for many individuals as they contemplate their own career paths and shifts; it is also true for those who write about careers. This trend is among the most important limiting the ethical horizons of many professionals, we believe. How, then, do we take the best of Durkheim's classic emphasis on professional communities, those with legitimate expertise and ways of helping society, without endorsing elitism for elitism's sake? This we see as both a moral and a practical question lurking behind a broad-based discussion of professionalism today. (The other two important trends, as we discuss elsewhere, are consumerism and, for lack of a better word, "contingency.")

When one thinks of her career as embedded in a network or a web of social relationships, she is less likely to take her career simply on her own terms, as a possession or an achievement, and will instead ask questions about the effect of her actions on others. When a career is taken out of the larger social context, it is alienated, or separated, from others. Careerism, as the sheer advancement of individual interests, becomes rational and may even be perceived as necessary from this standpoint (Buzzanell, 2000).

What can we say about people who offer a service to others without hoping for compensation, perhaps even refusing it? One very unusual profession, or at least avocation, is that of pet psychic. George knows such a professional, and whenever anyone talks about her services to pet owners, people typically react with cynicism. However, as soon as they learn that she never takes money for her services, their attitude shifts toward genuine curiosity and respect (though they may hold on to disbelief).

Our differential expectations for salaries in the three major sectors are similarly tied up with notions of service, and that's why society as a whole is much more tolerant of extravagant CEO portfolios than of high pay for government officials or executive directors of nonprofits. Still, we sometimes maintain contradictory expectations about those in service professions, such as educators and the clergy, as when we say, "Well, they couldn't have made it in business." We want it both ways; we want people to be inspired to do less lucrative work because they are "called" to do social good, yet we want to insist that people really are motivated primarily by money.

As discussed in chapter 3, a *calling* was originally associated with religious or religiously inspired service, and still evokes that sense, as in the language of the Roman Catholic Church and some other religious organizations. However, the term gradually came to have a more general meaning, that of a connection between one's work and the needs of society. The idea is that by choosing a particular line of work, one is inextricably part of the fabric of society. Thus, the notion of complete independence from that society—as in treating one's work as merely a personal "possession"—becomes unthinkable.

Let's look at two examples, one from the published work of a CEO and another from George's fieldwork at a worker-owned cooperative in Spain. Yvon Chouinard, the founder of the clothing company Patagonia, writes at the start lines of his book *Let My People Go Surfing: The Education of a Reluctant Businessman* (2006), "I've been a businessman for almost fifty years. It's as difficult for me to say those words as it is for someone to admit being an alcoholic or lawyer. I've never respected the profession. It's business that has to take the majority of the blame for being the enemy of nature, for destroying native cultures, for taking from the poor and giving to the rich, and for poisoning the earth with the effluent from its factories" (p. 3). With Chouinard, we see a man struggling with his identity as one type of professional. He struggles with being a businessman because of the ethical misconduct he associates with doing business. He resolves that contradiction by insisting that business ought to be accountable to social contexts. Many businesses and businesspeople embrace social responsibility, as did Adam Smith, in his day. At the same time, it is increasingly common for professionals to talk about how they do business in terms of their *own career* as much as in terms of their shared profession.

When George was conducting his research on the worker cooperatives at Mondragón in the Basque Country, Spain, in the 1990s, he found that this more individualistic view of career was beginning to take hold in the workplace and in the community. Younger (then twenty-something) employees were more likely to talk about their careers as "mine"; accompanying (and perhaps fueling) this trend was a greater readiness to relocate. One midlevel manager in his early thirties told George, "Our outlook on the world is more open than that of the previous generations. We see ourselves moving around for professional advancement and then perhaps coming back here to retire." Importantly, this trend came under increased scrutiny with the economic crisis of 2008, as the cooperatives (now the seventh-largest private firm in Spain) are concerned with renewing their ethical–social core even as they deal with long-term financial stability and environmental sustainability (Cheney, 2008b).

The professional has additional responsibilities, grounded in his or her relationship with the profession, and in the profession's relationship to the larger society. For us, the definition of a "true professional" requires making a voluntary effort to expand the profession's stock of knowledge, skillfully sharing knowledge with those new to the profession, and "establish[ing] criteria of admission, legitimate practice, and proper conduct" (Solomon, 1999, p. 55). We could say that the true professional "pays forward" his or her indebtedness to those who came before them and practiced those same criteria.

In her book on the language and culture of the U.S. high-tech arena, Paulina Borsook (2000) spent a lot of time listening to conversations at professional conferences. She noticed not only a "portable" perspective on career but also a worldview that some would describe as libertarian. That is, high-tech professionals tended to celebrate innovation, individual accomplishment, and technological celebrities while simply ignoring or decrying the public investment that makes the high-tech world possible. Borsook points out that *Wired* magazine, in its early years (and often still) remained male-centric even though more women than men used computers, and commonly made reference to spontaneous and collaborative Internet constructions, even though the Internet's elements had been established by government entities. In the end, the language of these high-tech professionals cast the world as a place rife with cutthroat competition, more amenable to individual accomplishment than to collective advancement, and populated by people who make career decisions before ethical ones.

Our challenge to you, the reader, is to consider how the professional is embedded within a group or a community, and how that person or class of people demonstrates service and accountability to the group. How can you create space for discussions about ethical responsibility in the course of your own career?

The members of Utah Physicians for a Healthy Environment (UPHE) undertake just this sort of discussion. Along the Wasatch Front in Utah, pollution frequently makes air quality poor and unhealthful. This paragraph from the "About Us" page of the UPHE Web site references the community, local environmental conditions, *and* professionals' expertise and responsibility: "The Utah Physicians for a Healthy Environment is a small group of health professionals with concerns about health risks currently present in our environment. This is based on recent articles and convincing evidence in the medical literature showing that more people have coronary and cerebrovascular (heart attacks and strokes) events when air particulates (one form of air pollution) are high." The founding UPHE anesthesiologist Brian Moench is now an active participant in environmental efforts along the Wasatch Front. His personal and professional ethics move beyond the domain of his practice and into his community. At the same time, his professional credentials signal to others that he is knowledgeable and that he has their best interests at heart. So, Dr. Moench's professionalism works on several fronts simultaneously, connecting community issues to his medical practice and shaping his public persona. This case is a reminder of how codes of ethics are a starting point but not an end for our professional efforts.

What Does It Mean to *Have* a Professional Career?

Dr. Moench provides us a good example of an individual who has reflected and acted upon his professional code of ethics and the duties associated with it. Here we invite you to consider what being a professional means in the line of work you are in or hope to pursue. Below, we've reproduced three questions from the organizational communication scholar Patrice Buzzanell's *Career and Work-life Survey* (2007). Take a moment to reflect on the lessons from this chapter and on the meanings you (perhaps implicitly) ascribe to professionalism and careerism.

1. Using your own metaphor (my career is like a roller coaster, a winding path, a rocket, an expedition, etc.), complete the following: My career is like—.

2. If you were asked to give career advice to a new member of your profession and you knew that this frank counsel would go no further than this person, what would you tell him or her?

3. How can my *success* as a professional best be judged? To whom am I responsible, and who is best served by my work?

Keep in mind several issues as you conduct this thought experiment. To which individuals and groups or institutions do you feel responsibility as you respond to the questions above? Are those people's interests always consonant, or do they sometimes conflict with one another? What particular or specific *behaviors* do you highlight in your responses, and how would you *account* for them? And, importantly, how might your responses change over time, as in, say, later stages of your career?

If you find that the questions raise moral quandaries for you, or remind you of past dilemmas you have faced, consider the lessons of A. O. Hirschman's *Exit, Voice, and Loyalty* (1970). Hirschman proposed that people make one of three responses to their perception of decline or wrongdoing in organizations and the state. Facing obstacles, they may give up membership, leaving the firm or group. Alternatively, they may voice their concerns through proposition, petition, consultation, or protest. Or they may place their faith in the collective, going along with "the way things are." Hirschman's list was later expanded to include neglect, exhibited by those lacking commitment and giving up on the possibility of change (Rusbult, 1987). If your responses to the questions above seemed challenging because of aspects of the situation (like your boss or working conditions), what would you do? What would be the consequences of such action, and which opportunities might be lost in your taking that action? Are there options beyond those presented here? As we'll see in the next few chapters, the basic rules for ethical action—in organizations, in markets, and in other contexts—are negotiated through the language we use. Communication about professionalism, organization, and markets profoundly influences how we answer the questions above, and how we act on those answers.

5

Reconsidering Organizations as Cultures of Integrity

More often than not, discussions about ethics in organizations reflect only the "individualistic approach" to moral responsibility. According to this approach, every person in an organization is morally responsible for his or her own behavior, and any efforts to change that behavior should focus on the individual.

But there is another way of understanding responsibility, which is reflected in the "communal approach." Here individuals are viewed not in isolation, but as members of communities that are partially responsible for the behavior of their members. So, to understand and change an individual's behavior we need to understand and try to change the communities to which they belong (Brown, 1989, para. 3–4).

The Organizational Is Political and Rhetorical

The first photos of Iraqi prisoners that emerged in 2004 from Abu Ghraib prison in Iraq shocked the collective U.S. conscience, demanding explanation. Secretary of Defense Donald Rumsfeld and the rest of the George W. Bush administration quickly framed the photos as demonstrating mistreatment of prisoners at the hands of individual soldiers: the classic "bad apples" defense. As the defense goes, soldiers of questionable character under immense duress took out their frustrations on the prisoners in their care, overzealously exceeding the boundaries of morality, the law, and their authorization: as General Mark Kimmit remarked in the *60 Minutes II* broadcast that first broke the Abu Ghraib story, "Don't judge your army based on

the actions of a few" ("Abuse of Iraqi POWs," 2004). Of course, given
the widespread allegations of torture (extending to the detention
facility at Guantanamo Bay, thousands of miles away), the bad-apples
defense strained credulity from the start. Kimmit's remark attempted
to direct public attention to the overwhelming majority of soldiers
nobly serving their country and following orders with distinction;
what his remark also sought to do was to deflect attention from a different *few:* the leaders setting military policy.

We now know that torture was not limited to the isolated acts
of a few renegade soldiers but rather was encouraged by a broader
imperative to gather intelligence in "the war on terror," and authorization for this torture came from the highest levels of the White
House (see Warrick, 2008). For example, the now-infamous John Yoo
"torture memo" was used to grant widespread approval and a legal
defense of the interrogation techniques practiced at Abu Ghraib,
Guantanamo Bay, and elsewhere (Mazzetti, 2008). And yet we also
know that torture was not undertaken simply in response to orders
flowing down the chain of command from the Pentagon and above,
including from Defense Secretary Rumsfeld (Shane & Mazzetti,
2008). As Alex Gibney's award-winning 2008 documentary *Taxi to the
Dark Side* poignantly demonstrates, *cultural* issues were involved as
well. An entire web of messages, from superiors and peers, served
to tell interrogators at Bagram Prison in Afghanistan: "This is what
is expected." In short, the slide toward the practice of torture at Abu
Ghraib and elsewhere cannot be viewed solely as an individual ethical failure but rather should be understood as an ethical failure at the
organizational level as well. Thus, ethical responsibility is not exclusively an individual matter; nor can it be conveniently assigned to
formal rules and regulations.

The organizational path by which the U.S. military exercised
torture finds a disconcerting parallel in the more familiar organizational context of the corporate world. Two documentaries about the
wave of corporate scandals in the early twenty-first century trace a
disturbingly familiar path. An early scene from the documentary *The
Corporation* (Bakan, Achbar, & Abbott, 2004) nicely captures the predominant frame through which the popular business press portrayed
the wave of corporate scandals that involved some early twenty-first-
century bad apples. In this scene, an almost minute-long montage of
talking heads attributes the epidemic of scandals to the actions of a
few bad apples. Such attributions are perfectly understandable, yet
they fail to acknowledge, let alone account for, systemic problems,
including the question of how to consider an organization's agency

or its capacity for ethical or unethical action. In the case of Enron, it is difficult to imagine the actions of just a few bad apples completely toppling the U.S. energy giant. And, as the 2004 documentary film *Enron: The Smartest Guys in the Room* makes abundantly clear, it wasn't the actions of only Ken Lay, Jeff Skilling, and Andy Fastow alone that brought Enron down but also the complicity of energy traders who were gleefully working the system, and accountants who knew that what the company was doing was wrong yet failed to blow the proverbial whistle.

The point of the bad-apples segment of *The Corporation*, then, is to undermine the argument that individual actions alone—even when aggregated—can account for the ethical lapses of organizations. *The Corporation* directs the "How?" question to the general structure of the corporation as an ideal type, or perfect model, whereas *Enron: The Smartest Guys in the Room* points more directly at how the nature of a particular organization produces such ethical disasters. These films shift the level of analysis from the person to the organization, moving the question of ethics from the lone individual to that of the collective. While the preceding chapter explored ethics and profession as both an individual and collective concern, in this chapter, we more fully direct our attention toward the collective dimension of ethics in exploring the nature of organizations themselves.

Folk Claims about Where and How We Work

On the surface, organizations are relatively easy to grasp, especially when we associate them with a leader or figurehead. In a very real sense, Microsoft is Bill Gates, and Steve Jobs is Apple. Even years after Lee Iacocca's departure, it is hard to think about Chrysler without thinking of him. Often, we take physical manifestations of an organization—a sign, a building, a logo, a leader—and allow these parts to stand in for the whole. This is what is called a *synecdoche*, evidenced in this example: "There are some good heads in this room." Of course, such identifications quickly fall apart when we think about them: although the "golden arches" might be a powerful marketing tool for McDonald's, they do very little to help us understand McDonald's as an organization, including what it is like to work there. Where, for example, does McDonald's begin and where does it end? Consider the dimensions of McDonald's presence in our collective consciousness: We jokingly add "Mc" before a word or phrase to suggest that it is cheap, quick, and minimally satisfying. McDonald's is an "official

sponsor" of the Olympics. Ronald McDonald, the restaurant's epony-
mous clown mascot, has been a Saturday-morning cartoon character
and the leader of an exercise video. The embroidered polo shirts and
visors that are McDonald's employees' uniforms might come to mind
when you are asked to think about the restaurant. Other people will
think of such things as fast-food companies' use of genetically modified potatoes and hormone-treated beef, low-wage jobs, the health
effects of fast-food diets (see Morgan Spurlock's *Supersize Me*), and
the corporate pursuit of those who would tarnish a well-polished
image (see Franny Armstrong's controversial documentary *McLibel*).
In short, the vision of two "golden arches" evokes a lot of characteristics and actions but also diverts attention from others.

In this manner, synecdoche simultaneously directs and deflects
our attention. Another figure of speech, called *metonymy*, uses something *not* part of something else as a representation of it. One example
from the restaurant business would be, "The ham sandwich is waiting for his check." When it comes to understanding organizations, we
resort to both synecdoche and metonymy, simply because the object
of our understanding is so complex and so difficult to grasp. We can't
help but represent an organization as something less and in some
ways different from what it actually is.

At least since Gareth Morgan (1986) first published his popular
Images of Organization, a great deal of research has been devoted to the
various metaphors we use to conceptualize organizations (see also
D. Grant & Oswick, 1996). These metaphors help us concretize otherwise abstract notions of organization by explaining, in more readily understandable terms, the intangible forces holding organizations
together. We use metaphors to explain how organizations work, what
they are, and how they relate to the people who inhabit them. They
are unavoidable: even in this last sentence, we've implicitly invoked
a metaphoric cluster through our choice of the terms "people" and
"inhabit"; other choices are, of course, available to us (e.g., "members," "employees," "cogs"). In short, even when we aren't aware
of it, we are almost always, inevitably, describing organizations and
our relationships to them in metaphorical terms; the way we metaphorically figure these relationships always carries various degrees
of responsibility or even duty to the other.

Thus, metaphors never simply describe the world to us. They
also imply *action* (Ortony, 1993), and it is here that the metaphors we
use to understand organizations take on an ethical tone. The manner
in which metaphors push us toward particular actions is neatly captured in Ruth Smith and Eric Eisenberg's (1987) analysis of competing

root metaphors in the 1984 strike at Disneyland. While Disney and its striking employees were in conflict over a number of issues, each side anchored its arguments in different prevailing root metaphors for Disney as an organization. Both employees and management attempted to lay claim to two root metaphors with long organizational histories: Disney-as-drama and Disney-as-family. Using the family root metaphor, striking employees were able to effectively claim that the Disney Corporation was violating a founding principle of its business operations. What is particularly, and ironically, compelling about the choice of metaphors is how they prescribe particular actions. The metaphor of drama highlights artifice, directing attention toward the economic role of employees as hired actors, consequently legitimating disputes over employment contracts. The metaphor of family, on the other hand, highlights the reciprocal obligation of social bonds, relegating economic relations to the background. After all, one doesn't go "on strike" against one's family (except, perhaps, in fits of teenage rage). Metaphors, then, operate at levels much deeper than surface strategy; their rhetorical influence shapes how we act in the world in ways that simultaneously undercut how we *think* we act.

The way that we talk about organizations has a profound influence on how we see them, and how we act in and around them. Organizations have such a significant presence in our lives that it is easy to take them for granted, as facts of life. When opening up organizational metaphors to close examination, their "givenness" quickly recedes. Here, we take a quick tour through several of our most common organizational metaphors, with an eye to the ethical implications of each way of speaking, and how each sets the stage for certain types of ethical issues and questions.

The Organization as Machine

Organizations, at least in the informal sense, have existed throughout most of human history. Our contemporary understanding of organization is an invention of the Industrial Revolution. It wasn't until the eighteenth and nineteenth centuries that the English term "organization" clearly diverged from its etymological sibling "organism" (both sharing the Greek root *organon*; Cummings & Thanem, 2002). The clear division of the terms occurred during the ascendancy of the mechanical imagination driving the Industrial Revolution, with early thinkers conceiving of organizations through the restrictive lens of the hierarchical division of labor, and the top-down command-and-control approach to communication that is oriented toward maximizing efficiency in a process leading from input to output (G. Morgan, 1997). The ethical imperative of the machine metaphor tends to be one of *efficiency*. By the second decade of the twentieth century, talk about efficiency became not only a hallmark of organizational life but also a preeminent cultural value in North America and in Europe. Owners and laborers alike ridiculed Frederick Taylor's Scientific Management in the 1880s, but between the world wars it came to be the most common way of putting together people, work, and bureaucracy. Scientific management helped organizations see themselves as complicated machinery, composed of intricate parts joined in prescribed relationships. The machine metaphor thus calls into question whether organizations or their members have any motives at all. When this metaphor is taken seriously, it can lead to questionable amoral framing of practices and decisions.

While the machine metaphor may have figured prominently in both the development and academic conception of the modern organization, it has since fallen out of popular favor (Cummings & Thanem, 2002). When we frame organizations as machines, "we tend to expect them to operate as machines: in a routinized, efficient, reliable, and predictable way" (G. Morgan, 1997, p. 13). But missing from such a description are the humans that comprise—and whose lives depend upon—such organizations. As a result, it is tempting to dismiss the machine metaphor as a relic of the past, as the cold, lingering remnants of the most extreme forms of Taylorism. What do you think of when reading "workplace-as-machine"? Do you think of iron smelting, toiling Soviets, coalmines, or one of Henry Ford's assembly lines? What about a university computer lab, a stock-trading floor, a design studio at a computer firm, or a state-of-the-art research hospital? While our popular images of the work organization may have shifted, this does not mean that we have left the machine metaphor behind. To see the continued resonance of the machine metaphor, we need look no further than the 1990s popular management fad of "re-engineering" (Hammer & Champy, 1995; Hammer, 1997), the mechanistic euphemism for the waves of downsizing that have disrupted the lives of hundreds of thousands of workers over the last decade and a half, often coldly and abruptly in the name of increasing efficiency and boosting the bottom line.

Consequently, the machine metaphor is challenged for good reason. However, Paul du Gay (2005) and others (e.g., Sennett, 2006) have argued that we should not reject its bureaucratic companion out of hand. After all, there's a sense in which machines demand less of us, to some extent in terms of time, but at the least in terms of emotional energy, when compared to the kind of care required by a living organism or family (as we'll see below). As one of George's students declared to a class of two hundred peers, "I like the machine metaphor because it doesn't expect so much of me!" If we work as part of a machine, we are not necessarily consumed by it, either practically or morally. But, then again, the organizational "machine" that governs our actions may become immoral because of its own presumed amorality. "Confined," or the industry-preferred "concentrated," animal-feeding operations (CAFO) are machine-like systems for producing animals. The density produces economies of scale, but this is partially because many costs are externalized to others, such as the animals, who experience an unnatural life; nearby human populations, whose health is acutely and chronically harmed; and groundwater, which becomes contaminated. The economic analysts justifying it, and the people managing and running the CAFO, are just doing their jobs, running the machine. As to the externalized costs, "it's the price we pay for cheap food" (Lee, 2003, para. 30), noted one woman critical of the nearby CAFO's debilitating health effects on her husband. But is a machine really amoral when it deliberately extracts a damaging price from unwilling others?

The Organization as Organism

While organization and organism may share the same Greek root, their etymological divergence has been thorough enough that "organism" has come to replace the machine metaphor, at least in academic circles (Cummings & Thanem, 2002). A wide variety of perspectives embrace the view of organizations as organisms; what they share in common is the recognition of organizations as "living systems, existing in a wider environment on which they depend for the satisfaction of various needs" (G. Morgan, 1997, p. 36). Machines, like organisms, can be complex and intricate, but the key difference is that organisms are *alive*; they have metabolic processes.

The organism metaphor is rooted, at least partly, in the Human Relations School of management, which held sway from the 1930s to the 1970s, and its much-heralded "discovery" of the importance of human connection in the workplace. It flourished when biology's general systems theory (von Bertalanffy, 1968) was imported into the social sciences, in general (think of references to the "body politic"), and into the study of organizations, in particular (e.g., Katz & Kahn, 1978). Working from the framework of the organism, Christensen, Morsing, and Cheney (2008) took the body as a root metaphor for their critique of corporate communications, arguing that when organizations style themselves as unified bodies they actually overestimate their own unity and ability to speak with a single voice.

This overestimation of organizational unity can impose an ethical demand by, ironically, figuring the organization as a corporeal being with bodily needs to be cared for. Providing for these needs, affording sustenance, then, may be construed as an ethical obligation for organizational stakeholders. In difficult times, we struggle to keep a business "alive," "feed" its bottom line, root out inefficiency because it "harms" its profits (and corporations must have "healthy" profits), and, as a last resort, use credit to provide a "lifeline." Once the corporation is transformed into a collective body, *in*corporation can suggest the process by which the corporeal being is formed. Health or vitality hence can be represented with organismic metaphors because they highlight lifelike qualities. And while both individuals and collectives can be said to evoke character, we're drawing on the metaphor of the organism when we assert that an organization is happy (e.g., "We're happy to serve you"), passionate (as in the Microsoft brand campaign, "Your potential. Our passion"), or feels any other emotions. When speaking of ethics, people often turn to the organism root metaphor and the sorts of metaphoric issues or challenges listed here. That is, they use the body as an ethical metaphor in order to direct attention to both the episodic (e.g., "anemic revenues") and enduring (e.g., as a quality of the organism: "a robust organization").

Yet when we use the organism metaphor to talk about organizations, we often stick with abstractions, focusing on the corporation as an accomplished noun rather than a process-related verb. It's fair, then, to seek an understanding of exactly the kind of organism that might serve as a concrete model for the corporation. Microscopic bacteria with flagella? Plants? A catfish? What about *people*, human individuals? Organizations, like humans, have agency, make decisions, enter into agreements, are accountable for their actions, make rights claims upon others, and so on. And, harking back to Aristotle, they deliberately seek and pursue a "greatest good," and these efforts reflect character. It is these human qualities that are emphasized by the next metaphor we discuss.

The Organization as Person

While chronologically predating the organization as organism metaphor, the notion of an organization as person represents the next logical step, representing a particular type of organism: the human. Here, we refer to what Jon Andersen (2008) calls a kind of organizational anthropomorphism, the result of merging the organismic metaphor with a desire to understand organizational agency. The result is the organization as person. While there's a clear ethical move involved in this metaphorical shift—bodies are easy to objectify; persons aren't— there's also a curious irony at work. In creating a metaphorical individual that acts, we obscure the action of the actual individuals in the organization. That is, if an organization is seen as a person, then it is the organization, rather than the people comprising it, that is responsible for the consequences of its "actions" (as if those actions were somehow independent of the humans engaging in them).

It is precisely such a diversion of responsibilities that differentiates this metaphor from the others. In addition to being employed in both academic and popular discourses of organization, the organization-as-person metaphor enjoys formal, *legal* standing as well, at least in terms of one particular type of organization: the U.S. corporation. Corporate personhood is a rights claim that the legal personality or entity known as a "corporation" is an extension of the human incorporators; thus, denying rights claims to corporations is tantamount to denying them to the individual human incorporators. In the United States, these rights are codified in the federal and state constitutions. The superficial similarities of corporate and human agents include being able to enter into a contract, standing as a party in a legal case, exercising speech, making decisions, and so on. These are traits also associated with human beings. That corporations act as delegates for the moral agency of its human shareholders offers a more interesting justification for this legal status (Werhane, 1985). In either case, this metaphor rationalizes constitutional rights for corporations. The consequence of privileging corporations with constitutional rights is substantial because it strictly limits the authority of government to exercise control over its legal creations because such interference might abrogate corporate-claimed rights such as free speech, due process, equality before the law, and so on (Mayer, 1990). Corporations now possess civil rights (Telecommunications Act, 47 U.S.C.A. §332[c][West Supp. 1998]). With corporate personhood, the metaphor of the organization as a person becomes powerfully real.

We can also see this personification in contemporary public relations moves, as organizations speak of themselves in the first person. Corporate Web sites' "About Us" pages give ample evidence of this trend, as they are usually rife with talk about what "we" believe and what "our" values are. Often the executives or public "face" of an organization provides testimony on these pages. Personification is plainly evident in Apple's 2006 "Get a Mac" TV ad campaign, which shows two actors on a plain, white soundstage. "Hello, I'm a Mac," says Justin Long, the slender, youthful, easygoing, and, perhaps most importantly, "hip" actor portraying the Macintosh computer line. John Hodgman, a portly, cynical man dressed in tacky business attire, sporting the haircut and eyeglasses of a 1980s Bill Gates, responds, "And I'm a PC." The campaign has been wildly successful, spawning a host of parodies and spoofs. The popularity and mimicry of this campaign attests to the power of portraying a company or its products as a person with enduring personality traits and social relationships. Of course, people exist in relation to one another, and the next metaphor we discuss highlights the social power of a certain kind of relationship: the family.

The Organization as Family

If we follow the progression of metaphors above, we come almost naturally to the organization as family. As the discussion of Disney's use of the family metaphor in response to striking employees (Smith & Eisenberg, 1987) demonstrates, the family metaphor draws attention to *all* of the members of the organization as being deeply interconnected by a sense of interdependent fates and affective bonds. As cozy as the family metaphor may feel, it may become an excuse for acting in ways tolerated in some people's homes but not acceptable to coworkers or colleagues.

The organization-as-family metaphor is widely popular, no doubt because some organizations mimic superficial familial circumstances, that is, a collectivity spending much time together, depending on each other for success and survival. Organizations themselves may invoke and reinforce this metaphor. This invocation may be implicit, as with the familial-like relations deeply ingrained in Japanese understandings of the corporation and its relationship to its employees (Kashima & Callan, 1994). Or it may be explicit: as the Denver, Colorado, company A&H Roofing proclaims on its Web site, "All of our employees and customers are like family to us" (http://www.ahroofing.com/about.html). Countless organizations describe themselves in similar language to appeal to both employees and customers.

The family image is attractive because it suggests strong social bonds. The metaphor encourages a deep loyalty to each individual and to the organizational unit as a whole. Consider the organization behind organized crime: the mafia as "family." Commenting on *The Godfather Returns*, his 2004 sequel to Mario Puzo's *Godfather*, the novelist Mark Winegarder observed the potency of the family meta-phor for the mafia as an organization, based in part on his interviews with low-level mafia members: "If it comes down to family, every-body likes to think they could kill" (in Pool, 2006, para. 48). In short, the family metaphor compels us to put the organization before our-selves and at the same time above question—or at least beyond ques-tioning the basic relationships. The ethical imperative of the family metaphor, then, is an abiding care for and loyalty to "kin." The family metaphor supplies motives for ethical action grounded in predeter-mined relationships, or at least the suggestion of them.

The problem, as the Disney case illustrates, comes when the reciprocity dimension of "family" is not present (Smith & Eisenberg, 1987). Family obligations are reciprocal, and serious ethical concerns arise when the metaphor is invoked to induce the loyalty of organiza-tional members but is not reciprocated by the organization—as was often the case in the paternalistic corporations (note the familial meta-phor) that predominated in the mid-twentieth century. Several recent accounts of career employees who had dedicated themselves to their employers, only to be cut loose when the bottom line needed improv-ing, speak powerfully of the personal devastation that results when organizations fail to live up to the obligations implied by their invo-cation of the family metaphor (e.g., Sennett, 1998; V. Smith, 2001).

The Organization as Culture

The metaphor of culture represents, for us, the last step in the pro-gression of metaphorical ways of speaking of organization, extending beyond relationships in a close-knit family to relationships between people sharing common beliefs, assumptions, and practices. While the family metaphor may be widely used informally, the culture metaphor is more formally popular, dominating both academic and popular man-agement understandings of organization for now nearly two decades.

The culture metaphor was an evolved sociological and anthro-pological response to the systems perspective that had dominated academic research in the 1960s and 1970s (Ouichi & Wilkins, 1985). Adopting culture as a metaphor encouraged researchers to focus on the implicit dimensions of organizational life, facets of organiza-tional experience requiring interpretation that cannot be easily and objectively identified and measured. Because the holistic view of an organization afforded by the culture metaphor is so central to our arguments about the relationship between organizations and ethics, we offer a more through discussion of this metaphor below.

The Unavoidable but Overlooked Ethics of Organization

The partial description of the metaphorical ways of speaking about organization presented above represents a transformation of the organization into a progressively more human entity: from machine, to living being, to individual person, to family, to culture. These are the most popular metaphors for organization, although we have seen and heard others, such as zoo, garbage can, robot, mirror, and circus. Taken in sequence, each way of speaking about the organization—particularly organizational relationships—opens up a greater possibility for ethicality. Still, we should take care to avoid the misrepresentation latent in each metaphorical description, that is, viewing an organization as a given, as a thing. Such views privilege organizational entities over processes, presenting "organization" as a noun rather than a "verb" (Bakken & Hernes, 2006). Certainly, this way of speaking makes sense to us because it reflects how organizations present themselves to us every day. We see a letterhead, a sign, a building, and are presented with a seemingly stable entity that we might call a Dunder-Mifflin, a Starbucks, a Nokia. Viewing and speaking of organizations as if they were given "things" seems obvious and normal to most of us, but it presents us with several problems, two of which are central to our purpose here. First, this view presents organizations as existing in "a box," as closed and contained units that interact with, but are separate from, their environments. Such a view deflects our attention from an organization's two-way relationship with its context. Even more, this view encourages us to think of what happens *inside* of the boundaries of the organization as its own sphere of activity. Our tendency to think of organizations as captured by some metaphor simultaneously abstracts organization by reducing it to its symbol, essentializing organization to some kind of basic character unaffected by its environment or constituent parts, and compartmentalizes organization as a separate sphere of its own.

But what happens when we instead think of organization as something more of a process, as a way of "getting organized"? Think beyond the boundaries of the identifiable organization and consider how we coordinate our activities. Our emphasis shifts to *choice*: if organization is an ongoing accomplishment, then the way we organize is up for grabs. Consequently, the way we talk about organization is, too. As in our earlier claims about the other domains of professional activity, the choices we make in how we speak about organizations likewise influence the ethical possibilities we see in them.

The public administration scholar Robert Denhardt (1981) argues that organizations might develop a more robust ethics by shifting their attention to processes rather than tasks. That is, the ethical question lies less in what we do and more in how we do it. Virtue ethics also includes consideration of why we do what we do, that is, whether we are doing it for the right reason. Ethical practice is a ongoing process of reflection and activity. "Reflexivity" is a good word for what we advocate. Like reflexive approaches to ethical behavior, ethics itself—systems of ethical theories—developed alongside changed conceptions of the organizational form. To assess ethical practice within organizations, we should attend to the historical roots of the organizational forms we experience in everyday life.

How Did We Get Here?

We have suggested that how we speak of organizations (e.g., as a given or as an accomplishment) does, to a large extent, frame our ethical responsibilities in and to organizations. In this section, we highlight three key developments we view as central to the development of the ethical context of the contemporary organization: the advent of bureaucracy, the development of the corporate person, and the development of an increasingly short-term perspective for organizational decision-making. Taken together, these overarching trends show both how organizations seem to take on lives of their own and how these lives often get removed from ethical concerns.

The Development of Bureaucracy

Bureaucracy has a long history as an organizational form, dating back at least to the Qin dynasty in China. Anywhere humans have tried to govern large-scale collective action across relatively large spans of time and space, the social organizations designed to accomplish the task have included at least some elements of what we have come to recognize as bureaucracy. That said, our modern understanding of the bureaucratic organization began to take root as a result of the wholesale social transformation wrought by the Industrial Revolution, most famously documented in the work of the German social theorist Max Weber.

Weber (1978) treats bureaucracy as the ideal type, or utopian version, of an organizational form driven primarily by legal–rational authority. This organizational form is defined by a set of characteristics that includes a relatively rigid division of labor, an obvious hierarchical order, and a set of clear, "objective" technical standards determining who is qualified to hold each office or position, where each position is in the hierarchy, and which duties are associated with each office. Sennett (2006) observes that the overarching metaphor for twentieth-century understandings of bureaucracy was the military, in its clear, regimented, and top-down hierarchical structure.

Such conceptions of bureaucracy dominate the popular imagination, with the most prominent, popular uses of the concept conjuring negatives (e.g., the inefficiency and incompetence of "governmental bureaucracy" as opposed to "private enterprise"; Cheney, 2008a). It is easy to reduce bureaucracy to a formal structural arrangement, to take the organizational chart too literally. But as Sewell and Barker (2005) observe, Weber's interest in bureaucracy "lay in the vocabulary and grammar of organizations—systems of knowledge or discourses, if you will—and their relation to issues of how we are to conduct ourselves in those organizations" (p. 66). In other words, bureaucracy is more than just a conceptual structure allowing organizations to conduct their "business"; it is fundamentally a *mode* of conducting such business; therefore, distinctly ethical questions emerge about the nature of bureaucracy as organizational form.

At the broadest level, these questions are reflected in the intriguing duality of Weber's (1978) hopes for bureaucracy as a rational organizational form, and the fears stemming from his own realization of how bureaucracy was actually practiced. On the one hand, Weber saw bureaucracy's great potential to achieve social goods, using an abstracted, ideal system that could be applied in many different situations. Bureaucracy's promise, in Weber's view, lay with employees who, one hoped, would heed a calling to perform the duties of their position, accepting its limitation on their individual agency to further the collective pursuit of greater goods.

In practice, however, Weber (1978) saw that individuals acting in bureaucratic offices developed increasingly atomistic points of view that considered their actions only in terms of the purview of their bureaucratic position, a deliberate limitation on the scope of their relationships and consequently their scope of moral concern. Consider the approval processes practiced by most health insurance companies. Who makes the final decision as to whether you will be authorized or reimbursed for a procedure, test, or medication? It is unlikely that you have met or ever will meet this person. Yet they will pass judgment on your suitability for what might be a very significant operation or treatment. And how will they make this decision? They are, of course, more proximate to the insurance agency for which they work than they are to you. In other words, their primary concern is for their company's bottom line, as opposed to your health. Will they be encouraged to think of you in terms of an ethics of care or an ethics of utility based on "cost effectiveness"? Using Zygmunt Bauman's analysis of the Holocaust (1989), Jones, Parker, and Ten Bos argue that one of the factors complicating ethics in organizations is the creation of a moral distance between actions and consequences: "If the person who gave the order never sees the person who the order ultimately affects, then they will find it harder to care" (2005, p. 90). A bureaucracy can therefore limit the ethical scope of its members even as it aims at a broader good.

Another ethical dimension of bureaucracy is the manner in which it directs its members to narrow their ethical thinking, to consider only rules: "Bureaucratic organizations value conformity not innovation, [leading to] a situation where adherence to the letter of the rules becomes more important than their spirit" and "moral decision making becomes a technical matter: people only check whether they have abided by the rules" (Jones, Parker, & Ten Bos, 2005, p. 83, drawing on the work of Merton, 1940). Recall our chapter 3 discussion of the ethical implications of aphorisms like "It's just business" or "I'm just doing my job." Read the following story and consider the ethical consequences of either claiming or being instructed to "just do your job." One of our own family members briefly worked in a sales position for a company that offered various products and services to individuals wishing to establish online companies. After a while, this person began to realize that the service he sold to people (at no small cost) was likely little more effective than some diffuse information and advice already available in the public sphere. After this person approached his employers about improving the service, he was encouraged, and later told, to focus on "making the sale." Surprisingly, he found himself a less successful salesman, as measured in total revenue generated, when he approached contacts wanting to help them in their unique circumstances rather than "sell them" on the product. Ethics, in this frame, becomes not a broad, reflective matter, but rather the narrow, technical concern of whether or not one has properly complied with externally imposed standards. It is no more than what adults expect of well-behaved children.

Finally, bureaucracy is grounded in legal–rational forms of authority, so it is not surprising that the organizational form privileges a particular form of reasoning as well. That is, bureaucracy encourages its members to reason in accordance with Habermas's (1972) sense of "technical" rationality, which focuses on the empirically observable, the factual, and the predictable. Such reasoning is important and necessary but becomes problematic when it overwhelms other forms of human rationality, namely the "practical" reasoning that is grounded in common experience (as in project collaboration that becomes tacit and habitual) or "emancipatory" reasoning, the capacity to imagine how the world might be otherwise (as when a workplace finally refuses to excuse sexual harassment as inevitable, as "just the way it is"; see, e.g., Clair, 1993). In short, the privileging of instrumental reasoning in bureaucratic organization discourages much of the ethical reflection enabled by other forms of reason. Here we can see a problem with the colloquialism "It's not personal, it's just business": not only does it diminish the importance of the personal considerations in the immediate context in which it is uttered, but it also reinforces the more general practice by which bureaucratic reason writ large forecloses on space for the personal (Ferguson, 1984).

The consequences of such reasoning can be quite personal. Drawing on the function theory of the psychoanalyst Carl Jung, Denhardt (1981, p. 52) argues that because "the ethic of organization gives preference to decisions made (1) on the basis of specific 'factual' data, and (2) in line with strict logical functions," it privileges the psychological functions of sensing and thinking over intuition and feeling. The consequence, Denhardt argues, is that "the ethic of organization...provides a significant impediment to the individual's effort to achieve wholeness" (p. 52). Two examples highlight the level of the organization and the level of the individual operating within the organization: In the film *The Corporation* (Bakan, Achbar, & Abbott, 2004), the physicist and activist Vandana Shiva speaks about the development of the "terminator" or "suicide" genes for seeds; this gene causes sterility in the second-generation seeds produced by these first-generation seeds. The agribusiness giant Monsanto temporarily produced seeds modified with this "genetic use restriction technology," preventing the traditional seed-saving activities of farmers (i.e., Monsanto customers) and thus making them dependent upon the corporation from year to year. The creation of such a product, she noted, required a "brutal mind." That is, while the company followed a certain logic in creating and marketing the product, they likely never deeply considered the ramifications for farmers, communities, and "seed cultures" beyond their value to the company as a customer base.

But, you might say, I don't work at an "evil corporation." Who would answer that they did? The problem is that such reductive, instrumental logic increasingly extends to other organizational forms as well. Let's take schools of higher education as an example. Schools, both public and private, undergo accreditation. Accreditation requirements and processes are enforced by various public and professional organizations, depending upon location and the sort of curriculum taught by the school. Imagine that you work at a school applying for accreditation and are asked to testify that the school has implemented certain dispute-resolution procedures. The school has not done so but, you're told, is quickly developing plans to meet the requirement. With whom do your responsibilities and loyalties lie? Is "doing what's best for the organization" the right thing to do? Do you risk your job by resisting your workmates' requests for you to lie or risk it by jeopardizing the school's accreditation?

Recalling our discussion in chapter 4, we might ask what it means to behave "professionally" in this situation. Here again we are reminded of Whyte's *Organization Man* (1956), Sloan Wilson's *Man in the Gray Flannel Suit* (1955), and Marcuse's *One-Dimensional Man* (1964). Bureaucratic thinking, then, not only affects the ethicality of organizational actions and decisions but the ethical character of the bureaucrat trapped in his or her office. Bureaucracy assigns roles, and roles take precedence over individual preferences, including moral preferences. On the other hand, in Weber's view, bureaucracy as a whole may well be directed toward the public good, being imbued with a strong sense of values in addition to a commitment to high professional standards. This is why talking about organizations and our work as a part of them is so crucial: "Not only do we ask 'Who am I?' in moral analysis, we must also ask 'What am I doing?'" (Anderson & Englehardt, 2001, p. 238). Indeed, the latter is precisely the question Weber would have us ask regularly at work and with respect to our relationships with an employing organization. We all work within a broader cultural context, even if we are self-employed or solitary entrepreneurs. Regardless of what we're doing, we all need to consider the embryonic question in Aristotle's (2002) *Nicomachean Ethics*: "What is the object of my efforts?"

Our discussion of the ethical limitations of bureaucracy has, to this point, focused more on Weber's fears than his hopes, so we should be careful to end by detailing the organizational form's more "positive" face. Perhaps bureaucracy has gotten a bad rap in popular consciousness (du Gay, 2000, 2005). And so we tend to associate it with red tape and the mindless pursuit of "administrivia" rather than with establishing clear domains of expertise, setting performance standards, and making a commitment to the public good. Yet these are the aspects of bureaucracy that Weber explained and celebrated, even as he feared how people could get bogged down in their isolated roles and tasks.

Bureaucracy is designed to prevent fraud and corruption such as that demonstrated in the 1980s case of Crazy Eddie, Inc. Crazy Eddie was a U.S. electronics company with rather comical advertisements: "Crazy Eddie: His prices are *insane!*" From paying employees "off the books," to underreporting earnings, to overstating inventory, few of the company's operations were untouched by wrongdoing. How did "Crazy Eddie" Antar achieve such a thorough but profitable deception? Antar's nephew, Sam, earned an apprenticeship and, later, high-ranking positions at the company responsible for auditing Crazy Eddie, Inc. Sam Antar's interests, and his company's interests, were thus in conflict with the interests of public transparency, disinterested professional accountancy, and legal requirements. Ultimately, Sam testified against Eddie in court in exchange for leniency. The significance of this case for our purposes is that Eddie and Sam were able to undermine the beneficial features of bureaucratic organizations and thwarted the universal rules set forth by the Securities and Exchange Commission (SEC) meant to assure fair play in the market and honest dealings with shareholders. Sam's work for Eddie far exceeded that of any other accountant working as a bureaucratic functionary; Sam was not just active in auditing and documenting fraud but was complicit in designing and hiding it. (A detailed account of this case can be found in Wells, 2000a.) Further, assuming it had knowledge of the familial relationship, the accounting firm was culpable for permitting the professional relationship, given Sam's obvious conflict of interest. Bureaucracy is far from being a bad thing in all situations; when working properly, it can motivate good decision-making and help prevent unethical behavior.

Sewell and Barker (2005) observe that Weber's (1978) notion of the "ideal type" in general, and as it pertains to bureaucracy in particular, should not be taken literally as a perfect form materialized in a real world but rather as a heuristic that can be used to think about the world we encounter. Understanding the bureaucratic form, then, helps us develop "a critical appreciation of the practical and ethical implications of a life primarily lived in and through organizations" (p. 83). In other words, thinking about the features of bureaucracy helps us understand the ethical dilemmas posed in and by organizational life.

The Development of the Corporate Person

Earlier in this chapter we introduced the idea of the "corporate personality" as a metaphor for the organization and touched on some of the legal consequences of extending this metaphor into law. Here we briefly review its legal history under U.S. law and its effect on the ethics of organizations.

Corporations were originally royally recognized associations of persons; the point of incorporation was to ease capital aggregation. The thirteen colonies that comprised the pre-revolutionary United States were corporations chartered by the king of England. In this contract between the sovereign and the incorporators, the king maintained sovereignty over his creations. After U.S. independence, and with the experience of corporate tyranny in the collective consciousness, the incorporation process was delegated to individual states, with corporations created through legislative processes (Horwitz, 1977). The objective was to constrain incorporators to use the privilege of incorporation for the public good and to maintain democratic authority over them. The 1819 U.S. Supreme Court case *Dartmouth College v. Woodward* established a precedent that holds today; it states that incorporation is a contract rather than a piece of legislation. Given the constitutional constraints on government interference with contracts, this change substantially circumscribed government authority over corporate activities. Next was the recognition of the corporate personality as justifying the recognition of corporate claims to U.S. constitutional rights. This came about by way of another U.S. Supreme Court decision (*Santa Clara v. Southern Pacific Railroad Co.,* 1886). This resulted in further limiting government authority over its creations, enabling corporate managers to use federal courts to overturn laws that infringe on corporate rights claims (Ritz, 2007). Corporations now exercise many rights previously reserved for human beings, but not being human frees them from some limits that people have (e.g., unlike humans, corporations may have an infinite life, can avoid imprisonment, and can deduct criminal penalties from their taxes). The metaphor of the organization as a person may be recent, in terms of popular communication, but its history in law goes back more than 150 years.

The corporation is supposed to stand in singly for the collection of persons who are its owners and employees. With the acquisition of rights, this entity has tremendous defenses against the government; and with limited liability, corporations provide a firewall of responsibility to its shareholders and employees. This calls into question the entire idea of corporate social responsibility. Where does responsibility reside in this kind of organization? There's a clear irony here: the corporate person is designed as a metaphor to alleviate individual and group responsibility and limit liability for individual and group actors (such as the management team) within the corporation; yet when something goes wrong, the metaphor is suspended and individuals within the corporation are blamed: the "bad apples" defense.

The Development of a Short-Term Focus

Richard Sennett (2006) argues that the transition to a new form of capitalism over the last half-century has been marked by the turning of three "pages." First, the collapse of the gold currency exchange standards in the 1970s unleashed massive amounts of capital to be invested, resulting in a shift in the balance of power from managers to shareholders. This shift fueled the wave of hostile takeovers in the 1980s, sharply satirized in the Monty Python short film *The Crimson Permanent Assurance*, depicting corporate raiders as literal pirates, and skyscrapers as ships firing their file cabinets, which acted as cannons. Sennett's second "page"—the privileging of short- over long-term investments—follows from the first. As he observes, in 1965 pension funds held stock for an average of 46 months; by 2000, average turnover had been reduced to 3.8 months. Of course, this celebration of the short term is perhaps best embodied by the late-1990s emergence of the "day trader" as a cultural icon, trading online and driving up the stock prices of dot-com companies that had shown no actual profit. (The dangers of this short-term focus, and particularly of trading on perceived value instead of material value, are made abundantly clear by the 2000s dot-com bust, and again in 2008 with the bursting of the housing bubble, itself attributable to the transformation of real estate from a long- to a short-term investment.) Sennett's final "page" depicts a new capitalism, the rapid advance of information and communication technologies. Moore's law, which had held more or less true since 1965, held that microchip computing power would double every 18 months. Evidence now suggests that Moore's law is beginning to fail, but only because the average speed of the doubling of computing power is increasing (Markoff, 2002). These three trends have worked together to create a sort of perfect storm, pressuring managers to make quick and decisive decisions expected to immediately improve the bottom line.

The difficulties such conditions create for the possibility of ethics is captured by Slavoj Žižek's (2006) essay about the ethics of the popular prime-time drama 24, featuring the counterterrorist agent Jack Bauer doing whatever it takes to prevent an imminent terrorist crisis. Time, then, becomes a distinctive feature for framing the ethical scene or context. For Bauer, there is, literally, no time for "quaint" ethical qualms about things such as torture, a point reinforced by the onscreen countdown of the fictional day. As Žižek remarks of Jack Bauer and the other counterterrorist special agents, "They are something like the psychological equivalent of decaffeinated coffee, doing all the horrible things the situation necessitates, yet without paying the subjective price for it" (para. 6). Here again, we encounter the fiction that our lives can be separated into spheres in which ethics sometimes do and sometimes do not apply. As Žižek notes, part of the appeal of 24 is its argument that we can indeed suspend our ethics in the sphere of work without having to pay a price for doing so. Urgency becomes a principal, even dominant, shaper of the scene of ethical action, and in powerful ways limits the horizons of ethical conceptions and performance.

At some level, however, we know that there is a price to pay. As we've argued in chapter 3, the work we do profoundly shapes our sense of self (think of the Great Santini and the bathroom-attendant father.) And there's some evidence to support this. A study of the "Macbeth effect" at Northwestern University demonstrated that people are more likely to clean their hands after committing—or even contemplating—acts that contradict their own personal values (in Carey, 2006). We might be able to provide justifications for our willingness to act differently in different spheres of our lives, but such justifications do not shield us from the personal consequences of doing so. In a related vein, when we take the organization-as-person metaphor seriously, we can see what's compelling in Bakan's diagnosing the prototypical modern corporation as a "psychopath" (2004; Bakan, Achbar, & Abbott, 2004), following the guidelines of the DSM–IV.

If we return for a moment to the defense of bureaucracy (du Gay, 2000, 2005), we can see that one of bureaucracy's virtues is its stability and predictability. That is, bureaucracy moderates the speed and severity of change. After all, its rational basis is designed to secure such stability by situating power and knowledge in the office or position rather than in the person. Of course, in late twentieth-century economics, such stability has been turned from a virtue into a vice for its foreclosing possibilities for flexibility (a value that, in many respects, is replacing efficiency in the language of the "new" economy). This loss of stability presents an ethical challenge for the participants in these "new" organizational forms. This challenge stems from the very real threat to worker security that such flexibility poses: "Fear of losing our sinecure can sometimes make cowards and fools of us all; at the very least, it can lead to laxity, mediocrity, and the anesthetization of critical thinking" (Gini, 2001, p. 136). Ironically, the very forces that promise emancipation from Marcuse's one-dimensional society (1964) have instead simply substituted a different kind of one-dimensionality. We'll turn more directly to this theme below, but it is necessary first to explore how organizations concretely engage ethics as an issue.

How Organizations Typically *Deal* With Ethics

We have argued that organizations are important molders and representations of ethical dilemmas and moral decision-making and likewise mold our response to these dilemmas and decisions. Popular frames for ethics developed alongside organizational structures and imperatives, such as complex bureaucracy and short-term focus. Here we consider the implications and efficacy of three typical responses to ethics in the organizational world: ethical codes, ethics officers, and corporate social responsibility (CSR) communications. The first two responses are characteristically bureaucratic in that they provide "universally applicable" rules in formal language (that is, an explicit means of discrimination) and create specific work duties for enforcing code compliance, relying on clear roles and responsibilities, and a presumption that employees voluntarily take action. CSR and the growing public attention to and language about it can transform organizations, but there's also the chance that it's more a fashion than a genuine development of widespread cultural transformation (Zorn & Collins, 2007). In examining this, we might "read" the current trend toward CSR against the earlier popularization of corporate ethics codes.

Ethical Codes

Ethical codes were popularized in the 1980s as a response to the public's low opinion of business, and a rising demand for government to exert stronger oversight (Stevens, 2008). Ethical codes were often seen as public relations tools to present an ethical corporate image to the public and to stakeholders, in addition to serving as ethical guides for members' behavior. But ethical codes are ineffective when used as systems of legalistic control over the behavior of employees (Trevino

& Weaver, 2003). Instead, it is a focus on "culture and cooperation [that helps] create conditions where ethical codes are effective" (Stevens, 2008, p. 603). Many critiques of ethical codes focus on their often-vague language or their overwhelming attention to detail. Such critiques, however, approach codes from a position that both essentializes and abstracts them, treating ethics as if it were contained in the code itself. A more appropriate critique recognizes that such codes are "discursive instantiations of a system that does not encourage reflexivity on the part of organizational members in terms of ethical principles" (Canary & Jennings, 2008, p. 276). It is naive to expect that ethics codes can sufficiently document transparent organizational values or serve to clearly, effectively, and sufficiently communicate them to others. Instead, they must be understood as embedded within the organization as an entire system. In other words, no matter how explicitly stated, if the code doesn't match the culture, it's not likely to work.

The failure of organizational ethics can largely be attributed to a failure of managers' "moral imagination," argues the ethicist Patricia Werhane (1985). She is quick to point out that this failure is not attributable to individuals as much as it is to systems limiting the "horizon of the possible" for managers' thinking. Turning ethics into formal policy deflects attention from the necessity of ongoing personal and systemic reflection and adaptation. Hugh Willmott (1998, p. 82) points out that ethical codes purportedly fill in the "moral vacuum" created by the amoral nature of market capitalism, effectively directing attention from the ethical nature of capitalism as a certain kind of social–economic system. Werhane's and Willmott's criticisms concern a very widespread practice: 78 percent of the Fortune 1000 companies they surveyed had a formal code of ethics, and 98 percent reported using at least some form of formal document (Weaver, Trevino, & Cochran, 1999). The construction of these documents, these bits of organizational structure, is so common that we can conceive the act itself as a ceremony indicative of typically bureaucratic, culturally significant organizational operations. Indeed, organizational stakeholders make meaning out of the very existence or absence of certain structures, using them to infer certain motives on the part of organizations and their leadership (Meyer & Rowan, 1977).

We can think of ethics codes as ethical structures imposed by organizations. Here, Robert McPhee's (1985) observation that organizational structures serve as "shortcuts for communication" is particularly instructive. He points out that much of the communication in organizations is indirect, coming through structures "rather than [though] a direct social dialogue" (p. 161). So, for instance, naming someone supervisor or even superior is a shortcut, obviating discussion of who ought to give orders to whom; similarly, a printed meeting agenda often eliminates the need to discuss a meeting's precise purpose. Thus structure stands in for time- and emotion-intensive face-to-face communication. But, as McPhee recognizes, structure usually fails to predict behavior. In the case of ethics, the following may be one reason: a survey by the Ethics Resource Center found that government agencies were more likely to frame ethics in terms of "what must be avoided rather than what must be done" (in "Government in an 'Ethics Crisis,'" 2008, para. 12). This absence of communication can be as important as any presence is in a network of people and/or organizations (Knoke & Kuklinski, 1982).

For Willmott (1998), ethical codes attempt to colonize the ethical reason of organizational members and seek to instrumentalize values such as honesty and trust. But there are examples of organizations that do not simply try to essentialize and contain ethics in formal policy. Koernberger and Brown (2007) studied an innovative consulting firm that made researchers available to commercial enterprises in the interest of helping organizations in various sectors discover key opportunities for collaboration that they might not otherwise see. The firm, named Incubator, found that careful attention to ethics constituted the core of its business, which was grounded in researchers having free and full access to the top levels of client organizations, with executives knowing that the researchers would share that information with others. Incubator executives "chose not to develop a rule-based code of conduct but to create a 'living document' in which ethical dilemmas and solutions would be added as they occurred in practice. At the core of their ethical discourse was a belief in 'professional standards' as institutionalized in other professions, such as law and medicine, and the conviction that, in the long run, good ethical practice would be more or less automatically aligned with successful business practice" (pp. 504–5). At the same time, however, Koernberger and Brown reported that many Incubator employees used their twenty-page *Code of Ethics* as a marketing tool to convince clients of their ultimate trustworthiness. So, even a code seeking to operate inductively, presenting mini-cases and statements of general principle rather than stringent rules, nevertheless remains a code that can be presented as a static artifact, an ethical "calling card" of sorts.

There is communicative content in just how ethics are discussed in relation to policies and codes. While it shouldn't be "made into everything" (a colloquial way of describing essentialization), process does matter. In the winter of 2004, the Kenan Institute for Ethics at Duke University began work with nearby Capital Broadcasting (S. K. May, forthcoming). The four-month project applied the Institute's *ethics at work* methodology to produce a code of ethics for the company. Capital Broadcasting's experience is a superior example of dynamic treatments of ethical codes. Rather than diving into ideas for the code of ethics, the group initially focused on the process (as in Rawls's approach as he sought to identify the principles of an ethical system; see chapter 2). After agreeing on what constitutes a fair process, participants were more likely to abide by its results. The first step in that process featured a company-wide assessment. The assessment relied upon multiple dialogic tools such as peer-level focus groups, that is, situations of interaction and engagement. The second step was to bring together all employees (in eight groups that blurred division and unit boundaries, and professional levels, etc.) in a series of eight meetings lasting two to three hours each. In those meetings, the employees discussed the findings of the survey, identified common ethical dilemmas at work (via employee-created scenarios and cases) and discussed how to resolve them, identified the company's core values through a process of appreciative inquiry (i.e., identifying what works rather than what does not), identified the company's key stakeholders, created "do statements"—or specific responsibilities or duties—to each stakeholder, created a draft of the company's values and ethics code via a "writing group" designed to represent all levels and units of the company, brought in key stakeholders to provide feedback on the values statement and ethics code, and created an action plan for implementing the code and integrating it into company policies and procedures.

When we consider our personal agency, particularly our adherence to a code of ethics, it's apparent that participating in the creation of the code greatly enhances our sense of autonomy. Agency simply permits us a choice, but autonomy grants us the ability and satisfaction that arises from developing the range of choices. The company's success at institutionalizing their new code of ethics affirmed that ethics in general, and autonomy in particular, are highlighted in situations where we are free to define the set of available choices and also free to commit to them. Autonomy promotes responsibility.

The tension between policy and practice may be made visible in communication. In the cases presented here, Koernberger and Brown note (2007, p. 511) that the challenge was to conceive of ethics "not as a set of abstract values or as an 'object' that the organization could 'possess,' but as a discursive arena where people negotiated their identities and enacted their futures." Negotiating and enacting ethics in this manner is never accomplished *merely* through the publication of an ethics code or policy; it emerges from texts and behaviors that are part of complex interpersonal and systemic networks of interaction (see J. D. Johnson, 1992, for this view of structure). Above all, we should ask whether codes of ethics actually lead to the ethical improvement of organizations and professions (Johannesen, Valde, & Whedbee, 2008).

Ethics Officers

A second practice many organizations engage in as they consider ethics is the creation of a formal organizational position devoted to ethical issues. While creating such a position is not as widespread as creating formal ethical codes, Weaver, Trevino, and Cochran (1999) reported in their survey of the ethics practices of 247 Fortune 1000 companies that 30 percent had offices dedicated specifically to ethical issues, and 54 percent had one officer in charge of ethics. However, 54 percent of these corporations reported that that officer spent less than 10 percent of his or her time handling ethics issues, while 14 percent reported that their ethics officer dedicated more than 90 percent of his or her job to ethics.

This disconnect between title and duties is a significant problem for any organization hoping to encourage morally upright behavior among those involved in its day-to-day operations. Issues of ethics are inherently social, and so, too, should be ethics officers. Why? Ethics officers' positions' are manifestations of actions taken in the interest of ethics. (We're assuming that members of an organization aren't completely cynical about ethical action, of course.) Communication among organizational stakeholders is what *mediates* between organizational form and what can be designated as ethical action. Ethics officers are delegated the responsibility of making ethical action possible for organizational members by helping them to understand what constitutes ethical behavior. We can look at this from a "negative" perspective, also. Ethics officers can, at least, help forestall unethical behavior by reducing the sense of anonymity and isolation that many feel in bureaucratic settings, conditions that can promote bad behavior (see Zimbardo 2004, 2008).

Corporate Social Responsibility

Corporate social responsibility (or business for social responsibility) has been a popular way of framing business's relationship to society since at least the late 1970s (Carroll, 1979). The view runs counter to the neo-liberal economic take on the connection, perhaps best represented by the Nobel laureate Milton Friedman (1970), who held that the only responsibilities of a form are to make a profit for owners (such as shareholders) and to obey the law (and even to rewrite the law for business's benefit, if doing so is legal). From the neo-liberal economic standpoint, each sector, and therefore each type of institution, has its role to play in society. To ask a private enterprise, such as a corporation, to assume responsibilities for the society as a whole is to promote confusion about goals and, worse, to bog the firm down such that it cannot effectively meet its primary business objectives and stay true to its owners' interests.

Importantly, CSR has risen in popularity during the same three decades that have seen widespread corporate globalization, more mergers and acquisitions, frequent outsourcing of services, remarkable corporate mobility, and, of course, the dominance of regimes of free trade and privatization in many parts of the world (S. May, Cheney, & Roper, 2007). For many advocates of CSR, then, this set of policies is a necessary antidote to the excesses of unconstrained private interests and to the fact that corporations *do* influence the public sectors of nations and the world. Also, it represents a recognition that independent nation–states are losing power and that many countries' sovereignty is being eclipsed by multinationals' power. Still, some business leaders view the term "responsibility" as "too political"; consequently, since 2000 the environmentally oriented term "sustainability" has become more popular with some business groups that formerly identified with CSR (C. Allen, 2008).

For our purposes, "responsibility" is important on all levels of society, including organizational and institutional level. We might therefore ask, What does it mean for organizations *not* to be socially responsible? And what about strategic social responsibility, such as targeted philanthropic efforts, aimed at bolstering sagging corporate reputations (Porter, 2003)? Asserting the need for CSR begs the question of how best to *institutionalize* responsibility, as we discuss here and in chapter 7. The question of responsibility to what and to whom quickly arises, as in the much-heralded "triple bottom line" that includes owners, employees, and the larger community and environment. To be sure, responsibility needs to be accompanied by transparency and by accountability to more than just shareholders, or even the still-narrow category of stakeholders. We are again reminded of how our language for framing such issues can have powerful practical and policy implications.

As organizations seek to instutionalize such responsibility, many remain confronted by the question of how socially responsible can a corporation be without the visionary leadership of an entrepreneurial and longtime committed founder? Charismatic authority linked to social values can be a powerful motivator and the glue that holds such organizations together over time (S. Grant, 2005). But such "virtue" needs to be owned and enacted by all members of the company, lest they be lost without a new incarnation of the admired founder to guide their own ethics and to locate the company's distinctive role in the context of the field, industry, or market. An organization's ethical transformation may be initiated by one of its leaders, but ethical cultures are formed and sustained interactively.

Organizational Culture: Shaping and Sustaining Ethics

As we've suggested here, it is not so much that there is anything wrong with organizational efforts to establish ethical codes, ethics officers, or corporate social responsibility. Rather, it is that such efforts are often unsatisfying, creating the appearance of a commitment to ethics but demonstrating little underlying reality. After all, not long before its collapse, Enron circulated to all of its employees a detailed, sixty-four-page code of ethics, which turned out to be quite at odds with actual company practice ("Code of Ethics," 2000). For us, the key ingredient is *culture*. Culture, as a metaphor, helps us capture the tacit, implicit dimensions of life inside of organizations, dimensions that communicate more powerfully than explicit messages. In other words, more things are going on in the office than simply "getting the job done" (Pacanowsky & O'Donnell-Trujillo, 1982, p. 136). Focusing on the tasks done on the surface level—the level most directly targeted by the dos and don'ts that predominate in ethics codes—ignores the powerful messages being sent informally. For example, a risk-taking mentality was informally encouraged at Enron by the widespread stories venerating Jeff Skilling's and other top executives' dangerous adventures (Gibney, 2005). The formal aspects of the organization can tell us only so much about its ethical practices (Weaver, Trevino, & Cochran, 1999). To fully understand them, we need to understand informal communications; these are found in the realm of culture.

Culture: Something an Organization "Has" or "Is"?

Our earlier description of culture as a metaphor for organization overlooks crucial differences among those who adopt a cultural view of organization. Not long after the notion of "organizational culture" exploded in popularity in academic and managerial circles in the early 1980s—driven by Geert Hofstede's seminal academic study of the influence of national culture on local IBM branch offices (1980), and the popular success of Terrance Deal and Allan Kennedy's *Corporate Cultures* (1982) and Tom Peters and Robert Waterman's *In Search of Excellence* (1982)—the critical management scholar Linda Smircich (1983) identified a clear schism between two distinct ways of understanding what organizational culture means. On the one hand, culture was viewed as a *variable*, as something that (senior) managers can manipulate to achieve particular organizational goals. In other words, culture is a possession of the organization, something an organization "has"; it can therefore be reduced to a set of characteristics, such as rituals, beliefs, and symbols. On the other hand, some drew on the tradition of ethnography in sociology and anthropology to argue that culture was best seen as a *root metaphor*; in other words, as something that an organization "is." From this perspective, culture cannot be manipulated in order to directly achieve results, but, rather, must be understood before any effective action can be taken. Culture, in this second sense, becomes a broader scene for action: each new member can participate and perhaps shapes it in some way. Each of these views of culture has significant implications for an organization's effects on professional ethics.

The view of organizational culture as something that an organization "has" is often a top-down view of culture as an object that can be directly created or shaped by intentional managerial interventions. In a curious way, this parallels how we sometimes think of virtue, following the ancient Greeks, as coming *to* us, like gifts from the gods. Richard Barrett, the author of the book *Liberating the Corporate Soul* (1988), markets his services as a corporate consultant whose recommendations to his clients are based on a comprehensive survey of their organizational culture. Barrett's managerial approach to organizational culture is one in a long line of efforts to manipulate culture. These emerged in the late 1970s and early 1980s, particularly in the United States, as a response to the threat of Japan's economic success. Organizational culture, the argument went, was the key to Japanese success, so U.S. managers needed to devote their attention to issues of culture in order to maximize organizational performance.

At the same time that this managerial approach to organizational culture was developing, an alternative view was taking shape. The view of culture as something that an organization *is* argues that organizations do not directly control their culture. Rather, culture becomes a metaphor through which one can understand what "life" is like within a particular organization. This view of culture captures the intangible dimensions that make an organization what it is: the talk around the water cooler, the gossip from cube to cube, the rites and rituals unique to the organization, and more. From this perspective, one can't understand Google without understanding its free-wheeling dress codes and gourmet cafeterias, or the old IBM without its blue suits. This perspective does not suggest that managers don't influence an organization's culture, just that their influence is neither exclusive (members influence the culture as well) nor as strong or direct as they might think (or wish) it to be.

Organizational Culture's Formative Influence on Ethics

Each of these perspectives (i.e., "has" and "is") has value for organizational culture. While the view of culture as a root metaphor (*is*) may provide us with a deeper and more satisfying understanding of an organizational culture, it can often leave us without a clear understanding of how an organizational culture might ultimately be changed. And while the variable metaphor (*has*) may be overly simplistic in its understanding of the nature of organizational culture, it is nevertheless a useful tool for leaders seeking to change their organizational culture. The value of organizational culture as a construct for understanding ethics at the level of the organization, then, lies in our embracing the utility of both broad views of culture.

In this vein, the sociologist Tim Hallett (2003) offers an intriguing analysis of the role of symbolic power in shaping an organization's culture. For Hallett, who draws primarily from the work of the eminent French sociologist Pierre Bourdieu, the notion of symbolic power offers an alternative conception of organizational culture, one that recognizes the influence of structure while preserving space for agency. Hallett's arguments explore the relationship of organizational culture to ethical practice, grounded in an analysis of the demise of the accounting firm Arthur Andersen in the wake of the 2001–2 Enron scandal. As Hallett observes, Arthur Andersen's demise was quite ironic, given its long history as a respected standard of corporate social responsibility. Hallett documents a longstanding tension in the company between the Samurai (the ethical accountant) and the Merchant (the mercenary consultant), but the Samurai held sway, tied to key organizational narratives about the firm's founder. So, when Leonard Spacek succeeded Andersen, he established the Standards Group, "an in-house group of ethics watchdogs" (p. 142), and placed their office less than fifty feet from his own. This privileged the approach of the Samurai. When Larry Weinbach succeeded Spacek in 1989, he ran Arthur Andersen from New York, leaving the Standards Group in Chicago. This redirected power to the Merchants, and not long afterward, Arthur Andersen overturned a longstanding practice of counting stock options as an expense against profits (this change improved the monetary bottom line). For Hallett, these changes are certainly not directly causal but, rather, indicative of how "the Standards Group's symbolic power to define proper accounting practices had disappeared" (p. 143).

As Hallett's analysis of Arthur Andersen suggests, leaders have a profound role in shaping an organization's culture, but that culture is, at the same time, a force beyond the direct control of any manager. This tension reinforces the importance of thinking of ethics not only at the level of individual action but also at the collective level of the organization (Anderson & Englehardt, 2001). After all, individuals' actions inside an organization will be inevitably and profoundly shaped by that organization's culture: it's not simply a matter of "bad apples" acting unethically. Since managers inevitably influence organizational culture through their actions, they have a responsibility to consciously work toward shaping an ethical culture (Beyer & Nino, 1999).

Indeed, an emphasis on mindful habits—featuring deep awareness—is one way to infuse an organizational culture with conscience, explains the business ethicist Kenneth Goodpaster (2007). Analysts of organizations often put aside matters of conscience when they shift from the level of the individual to that of the organization. This is understandable because neither within the domain of ethics nor under law do we wish to suggest that a collectivity has a motive or set of motives in the same way that a natural person does. On the other hand, to leave the discussion there is to forsake the opportunity to consider how a value-based culture can cultivate virtue just as it can lead people away from it. As Seeger and Kuhn (forthcoming) argue, "Values are much more than corporate window dressing. Rather, they are woven into the fundamental structural fabric, taken-for-granted assumptions, patterns of language and interaction, and day-to-day routines of organizational life. They are enacted in the dynamic moment-to-moment processes of organizational operation at deep levels. In this way, organizations, their operations, activities and procedures, may be understood as the enacted product of a collective value system." Thus, an organization continuously engaged in reflecting on its own responsible practices sets both formal and informal examples for employees making all sorts of day-to-day decisions (e.g., see Chouinard, 2006). This is the real ethical potential of organizational culture.

Further Ethical Reflections Organizations as Our Creations

In this chapter, we've shifted our focus fully from the level of the individual to the level of the collective while maintaining attention on how the way we speak shapes the ethical dimensions of the domain we're exploring. Here we have repeatedly claimed that how we speak about organizations (as in the other domains covered in chapters 3, 4, and 6) has a profound influence on the ethical actions both of organizations as social actors and of the individuals within them. Here we'd like to end our arguments about organization with a brief exploration of the ethical possibilities of alternative ways of speaking about organization. We'll loosely follow the development of the chapter in reverse, discussing first an alternative conception of organizational culture before reconsidering the metaphors we use to describe organizations and then, finally, exploring an expanded role for choice once we no longer take organizations as a given.

First, an important caveat. Throughout this chapter, our discussion of organization has implicitly centered on understanding organizations as *corporate* organizations. There are, of course, other forms of organization and organizing—such as nonprofits and for-profit cooperatives—that we somewhat overlook in our corporate gloss on "organization." In many respects, our choice of focus is inevitable. After all, the corporation is the dominant social institution of contemporary capitalist society (Deetz, 1992), and its dominance is important for several reasons. First, the corporate form is where the overwhelming majority of professional work we address occurs. More importantly, these other forms of organization are increasingly pressured to adopt corporate-like forms, particularly as corporate discourse is increasingly pervasive across organizational spheres (e.g., Chiapello & Fairclough, 2002; Thrift, 1997). Our focus here is not meant to ignore alternative organizational forms. Nevertheless, in acknowledging our somewhat necessary bias here, we hope to highlight, once again, how our way of speaking subtly shapes our understanding. That is, our implicit reliance on corporate understandings of organization has inevitably deflected attention from other potential models of organizing. Such awareness is crucial to any rethinking of what "organization" might mean or look like.

Rethinking Culture: Culture as Something an Organization Is "In"

While the variable ("has") and root metaphor ("is") perspectives outlined above each represent a longstanding and well-supported approach to organizational culture, here we'd like to playfully suggest a viewpoint grounded in a different proposition: culture is something that an organization is "in." Here culture becomes *context*: it is outside of organization, seeping through its porous borders, subtly but inexorably influencing the culture on the inside. Consider, for example, the way that ironic popular representations of organizational life—as in the television sitcom *The Office*, the film *Office Space*, and the comic strip *Dilbert*—might engender in employees a sort of cynical resignation to "the way things are." Or we might think about how popular management books (*What Would Machiavelli Do?* [Bing, 2002]), television shows (*The Apprentice*), and films (*Wall Street*) are use an admittedly mixed metaphor to portray the business world as a dog-eat-dog, cutthroat, corporate jungle. Do such portrayals even slightly influence the ethical behavior of individuals and organizations in the "real world"?

Of course, it would be very difficult to determine the exact extent to which culture writ large influences the cultures of concrete organizations themselves. Our point here is not to measure that influence but rather to suggest that we consider the role that such representations play in our broader cultural conversations about organizational life. That broad cultural events would not have at least some influence on organizational life, though, is hard to imagine. Consider, for example, the bizarre case of organizational mimicry that occurred in Provo, Utah, when a manager allegedly performed waterboarding on one of his employees as a motivational exercise (Alberty, 2008). In that case, an employee is suing his supervisors and employers at Prosper, Inc., an executive coaching firm, for using a crude version of the torture to demonstrate to salespersons "that they should work as hard on sales as the employee had worked to breathe" (para. 1). Here we can see culture as a context, as something an organization is "in." Recall our discussion at the outset of this chapter. Administrators within the U.S. political and military regimes have spent great effort denying that certain treatments of prisoners amounted to torture. And they claimed that when torture occurred it was not a systemically produced phenomenon. But what does this have to do with corporate culture at a typical firm? Recall the times you've been instructed to work "as if your life depended on it." That metaphor is telling, inasmuch as it elevates and essentializes organizational behavior as survival. When we sort out the implicit and explicit dictums of the innumerable messages and examples concerning everything from work in the "corporate jungle" to the treatment of "detained enemy combatants," we can see that broad cultural patterns can exert an ethical influence on organizations themselves.

Conceiving culture as an organizational context is compatible with both the variable and root-metaphor perspectives on organizational culture. What the "in" perspective does is direct our attention toward the broad cultural resources shaping our understandings of the possibilities of organizational life. By invoking context in this manner, we seek to spur a broader cultural conversation to help us think of ethics in a different way, one that might reshape how we think about ethics in an organizational context.

Rethinking and Re-expressing Our Metaphors

Another way to rethink organization itself as an ethical domain is to reconsider, or even revise, our common metaphors of organization. There are two possibilities here: we can either explore overlooked dimensions of our current metaphors or find new ones that direct our attention to more ethically desirable possibilities for organization.

In terms of reconsidering our most prominent metaphors, let's take, for instance, the less-explored possibilities of the organization-as-person. If we recall our earlier discussion of the corporate person, we can see latent opportunities that direct our attention directly toward the ethical character of an organization. That is, we can ask what kind of person is the organization, and what kind of person ought it to be? An interesting segment in the documentary *The Corporation* explores the collective behavior of the corporate person and its psychological "diagnosis" according to the diagnostic standards of the DSM–IV, the authoritative source for mental health professionals. While such comparisons may perhaps be overdrawn, by thinking carefully about what type of person the organization is, we can ask perhaps less dramatic, but equally provocative, questions, such as, What does it mean for an organization to have integrity?

In addition to reconsidering our popular metaphors of organization, we can also rethink the way we talk about organization by exploring new, or at least less prominent, metaphors as well. The critical management scholars Peter Fleming and Andre Spicer undertook a 2007 study of acts of resistance in organizations and came up with an interesting set of alternative metaphors that reveal the possibility for choice and agency in refiguring and reconfiguring organizations.

Starting with the notion of organization as a *prison* (see also G. Morgan, 1997), Fleming and Spicer argue persuasively that when we take organization as a given, we often feel trapped by it: "When we enter an organization we intern ourselves and give away the freedoms enjoyed in the rest of our lives. We allow cretinoid managers to tell us what to say and when we can move our bowels. We adhere to a strict set of rules (both written and unwritten) that govern what we do and how we think. We accept the micromonitoring of everything from our keystrokes to our attitude. And, what is even more surprising, millions of us accept these mind-numbing and spirit-crushing regimes every day, and are often grateful for it" (2007, p. 4). Fleming and Spicer's argument here suggests that accepting organization as a given encourages us to throw up our hands and abdicate our own autonomy, and with it the possibility for Aristotelian virtue. It is much like the commonly expressed argument in political campaigns that "if you don't get tough, mean, and nasty, you'll never win." This is exactly the kind of rationale vividly illustrated in *Boogie Man: The Lee Atwater Story*, the 2008 *Frontline* documentary about the late political "operative" for U.S. presidents Ronald Reagan and George H. W. Bush. Atwater suggested that his commitments weren't to a particular set of policies or to a specific ideology but to the game itself.

With the tacit support of those around him, nothing but winning mattered. Only on his deathbed, in 1991, at the age of forty, did he express regret about the "damage" he had done to the political culture and organizations of the United States by making "dirty tricks" part of mainstream political strategies. Where such strategies prevail, it is easy to see how many individuals willingly relinquish their own capacity for ethical decision-making, particularly in a radically contingent, short-term economic environment (Sennett, 2006) in which they may be grateful simply to be employed.

As we've illustrated, metaphors imply action, however, and compared to the metaphors of machine, organism, family, and culture, *prison* makes organization distinctly unpalatable. Fleming and Spicer suggest two alternative metaphors with which to view organization. First, they suggest that an organization can be seen as a *playground*, where acts of resistance can "poke fun at the corporation" (pp. 4–5). An episode of the sitcom *The Office* illustrates this metaphor. While regional manager Michael Scott and his lackey assistant, Dwight Schrute, are away from the office for an afternoon closing on Michael's new condominium, the rest of the office escapes their mind-numbing duties with an impromptu "Office Olympics," complete with yogurt-lid medals for the winners. When Michael and Dwight return early, the rest of the staff recovers what's left of their act of resistance by performing what James C. Scott (1992) would term a "hidden transcript," holding a closing ceremony that Michael thinks is in his honor. The result of the Olympics is an act of small-scale resistance, of play, which at least opens up a greater space for action for Dunder-Mifflin's office drones. A second alternative metaphor suggested by Fleming and Spicer is that of the organization as *parliament*. Here, invoking the images of the rowdy House of Commons during the British prime minister's weekly question time, Fleming and Spicer are seeking entailments, or implied meanings, of a metaphor that suggest people competing to "have their voices heard" (p. 5) and to be acknowledged as a self-governing people rather than loyal (or at least compliant) subjects.

Each of these metaphors seeks to move our understanding of organization and, as a result, our understanding of the actions we can and should take, from the prison (where passivity is the key to survival), to the playground (where we are free to poke fun), to the parliament (where we are required to speak up and be heard). Fleming and Spicer draw our attention to organizations not as given accomplishments but as spaces where processes play out as a result of the choices we make, reminding us that "we are always implicated in an ongoing struggle to establish a particular kind of organization" (2007, p. 6).

Challenging the Given and Highlighting Choice

We began this chapter by exploring the ways in which we tend to talk about organizations as a "given," as static nouns rather than active verbs. The ethical importance of such descriptions is that we are encouraged to accept organizations as they are, as a reality to be navigated but not changed. It therefore only makes sense to critique organizations (or organizational contexts such as the market) for their ethical shortcomings to the degree that choice is involved in their constitution (Jones, Parker, & Ten Bos, 2005). So, what choices do organizations make? The management scholar Jeffrey Pfeffer (2006) has argued that, for the last several decades, organizations have made explicit choices to disavow their nature as communities (another metaphor to consider) but have attempted to frame such choices as not choices as all but rather economic necessities (i.e., "the market made me do it!"). We need to begin to speak of organizations in ways that do not *reify* them, that do not make them and their environments more solid than they need be. A broader view of ethics requires that we speak in a manner that engenders not only a greater range of choices but also a sharper awareness of choice itself.

To help recognize the agency available to you in your work with and use of language in organizations, consider the following questions.

1. What metaphors shape your understanding of the organizations you work with today? What would such an organization look like with a different metaphor—perhaps one you have not considered before? What difference could that shift in perspective mean for ethics for the organization and its members?

2. What memories or cultural experiences can you point to as particularly significant turning points in the development of your ethical character? Was an organization, or its representatives, part of anything you remember? Now shift your focus a bit: have you been a part of or heard a story about a *whole organization* changing so significantly that its members were explicitly concerned with the relationship among ethics, work, and life?

3. Think of an exemplar unethical organization or an example of unethical organizational conduct. You can use one of the cases we discussed in this chapter. If you were a member or leader of that organization, what would you do to intervene, if you were to take any action? How would communication be part of your efforts to steer the organization back toward virtuousness?

The choices that organizations and the people working in them make to shape cultures of ethics are critically important, but these choices operate within broader social, political, and economic contexts. For most contemporary organizations, a major context is corporate and consumer capitalism. Corporations are explicitly charged with making a profit and, increasingly, nonprofit and governmental organizations have to define themselves similarly. The ethical organization, then, is always confronted by seemingly amoral market demands. But what are the various ethical possibilities for the market itself, and for its effects on organizations, the professions, and work? This question is the focus of the next chapter.

6

Seeking Something More in the Market

For all their power and vitality, markets are only tools. They make a good servant but a bad master and a worse religion. They can be used to accomplish many important tasks, but they can't do everything, and it's a dangerous delusion to begin to believe that they can—especially when they threaten to replace ethics or politics. (Hawken, Lovins, & Lovins, 1999, p. 261)

Introduction: Setting the Record Straight on Market Magic

Let's start with an overused and little understood metaphor. Adam Smith's *The Wealth of Nations* (1976b) is often crystallized in the image of the Invisible Hand, interpreted as a guiding force that both animates and guides the market—and by extension, all human affairs. The image simultaneously makes the market concrete and mystifies it as an external authority beyond our reach. In this way, the metaphor is used to cover both a powerful empirical presence and an undefined metaphysical force. Smith used this image *just once* in his monumental work. Despite this fact, the Invisible Hand has become a powerful and commonly invoked representation of economic forces—providing a clear example of how people can grant the market and its symbols a life and power all their own.

Smith's market was not as cold, calculating, or impersonal as many commentators would have it seem. To the contrary, according to the business ethicist Patricia Werhane (1991), the idea of the Invisible Hand was also used just once in Smith's other and far less famous book, *The Theory of Moral Sentiments* (1976a). In this book, the image of a distant, omnipotent force is countered by a caring force; here is not an impersonal market unaffected by social values and human feelings (and failings) but rather one where empathy and compassion played huge roles in complementing and restraining self-interest. Indeed, Smith opens it—a book that he regarded as a companion to *The Wealth of Nations*, according to Farrell (2002)—with a passage that sounds very much at odds with the typical summary of his thinking: "Howsoever selfish man may be supposed, there are evidently some principles in nature, which interest him in the fortune of others, and render their happiness necessary to him, though he derives nothing from it except the pleasure of seeing it" (Smith, 1976a, para. 4). Rather than assuming that humans are driven solely by selfish needs and that the Invisible Hand channels such selfishness for the benefit of society, Smith recognized that humans are predisposed both to altruism and to self-interest, and saw the market as something that required countervailing forces to prevent its being destroyed by its own excesses.

As it turns out, Smith's market(place) wasn't so impersonal after all. Smith's conception of markets was one in which person-to-person bonds were essential, and fully absentee landlords or financiers uncommon. In his time, most economic transactions were conducted between people who knew each other and were concerned for one another's well-being, if only because they would see each other on the street. Thus, the market was far more than an abstraction for Smith. The Invisible Hand, "about which so much has been written," Werhane notes, "is not [in fact] the force that drives Smith's ideal political economy" (1991, p. viii). This revelation casts a whole new light on old ideas, as was captured by a *New Yorker* cartoon (Fradon, 1992) in which captains of industry, perched on a hill outside Darien, Connecticut, look off into the distance for an actual Invisible Hand of the Marketplace.

Our experiences of markets and economic life are influenced "all the way down" by how we communicate. In our talk about the market, we assume quite a lot about its ethics and our own. These assumptions facilitate the invisibility of communication about the market. For example, on the "Numbers" episode of the public radio show *This American Life* (Updike & Glass, 1998), the host, Ira Glass, interviewed Will Powers, an employee at a marketing firm. Mr. Powers's boss asked him and his colleagues to practice the principles of brand marketing in their relationship with a friend, family member, or close acquaintance. "Will chose his wife," Glass tells us. It's fascinating to hear Mr. Powers speak of his wife as "the customer/client," himself and his affection as "the product," and their relationship as "the organization." To "improve his brand" Will "focus-grouped" his wife and conducted an informal "brand ladder analysis" about what she valued most in him and their relationship. Throughout the interview, Will speaks enthusiastically about this use of marketing language to make sense of his personal life. But, later in the interview, Will offers a somewhat different reflection, noting, "I think the reason this was so powerful is [that] we actually sat down across from each other and it was just us, totally focused on each other, you know? There was no other distractions, you know... And she actually wrote it down, you know, 'This is what's important to me.' It's almost very elementary, spelling it out." Was this the magic of the market, so to speak? Or was it just a novel technique to get Will to have a deep and direct conversation with his wife about their relationship and her needs? It's certainly not the *only* way to have such a conversation.

Whether Will Powers's experiment was successful or not and whether one ought to use the frame of marketing to participate in a marriage is up to you to decide. It is fairly clear, though, that Will took for granted that his employer had the *right* to ask him to do this, and that thinking about his wife as a "product" and himself as a "service" was ethically unproblematic. We use this example to demonstrate two things. First, the language of the market can seem natural to us in contexts where it might otherwise be fairly alien. Sometimes, we don't even recognize that we're using it. And second, the assumptions and consequences of using market rhetoric are often difficult to identify but very significant, especially for ethics.

Four Folk Claims about the Market

Endless Expansion

Deirdre McCloskey (1985) describes what she calls "the rhetoric of economics" as an insistence that markets and other economic institutions are amoral and completely natural: The market "is what it is, does what it does," and so on. One of the things the market supposedly does, almost by definition, is try to expand. This is something Marx (1976) understood keenly, even though the capitalism of his day was governed more by the imperatives of production than by the engine of consumerism. An extreme present-day example helps illustrate this point: twice in recent years the Pizza Hut corporation sought to project its logo onto the face of the moon (Gibson, 1999). Space represents the last frontier for advertising and marketing—for the signs of privatized consumption—we might say, given that a corporate logo on the moon could be seen from the oceans and the two poles. We are accustomed to thinking of the market (and parts of it) as having no real limits, with ever-expanding possibilities for both investors and consumers.

The impulse to colonize everything with commerce extends market boundaries far beyond anything ever imagined by Adam Smith (1976b) or even by the advertisers of the mid-nineteenth century (or, for that matter, those of the first half of the twentieth century). The economist Robert Heilbroner (1972), who is well known for his ability to translate economic ideas for popular audiences, notes significant differences between the market of Smith's time and that of ours: "Today's market mechanism is characterized by the huge size of its participants: giant corporations and equally giant labor unions obviously do not behave as if they were individual proprietors and workers. Their very bulk enables them to stand out against the pressures of competition, to disregard price signals, and to consider what their self-interest shall be in the long run rather than in the immediate press of each day's buying and selling" (p. 57). Size matters when it comes to the market and its players. This is precisely why George likes to ask managers in major corporations, "So, who or what is the market?" They first look at him quizzically, but they are soon challenged to consider the roles of their own big businesses in comprising what we refer to collectively, and often quite casually, as "The Market." This is one step toward prodding others to consider their own professional responsibilities and those of their employing organizations for that thing we typically locate outside our moral and practical reach.

As economic recession deepened into a potential depression in 2008–9, a growing number of mainstream voices began to question the market's constitution. The Nobel laureate and economist Joseph Stiglitz (2008) remarked that most commentators debate what sort of recovery the U.S. economy will make. Will the downturn be short and precipitous but quickly reverse? Or will it be significantly longer but less "sharp"? Most people think about these sorts of recovery scenarios with images of the letters "V" and "U." Stiglitz believes, however, that the letter "L" is a better image to keep in mind, considering all economic indicators. He points out that the recovery and continuation of market expansion is made possible only with an ideology that presumes that markets inevitably must grow. Such a presumption, says Stiglitz, is another deeply ingrained cultural myth about how capitalist markets distribute resources and ensure well-being. In fact, that story about the market is part of what led up to and deepened the present economic crisis, since people presumed, despite evidence to the contrary, that all was well and times were good after the radical deregulation of U.S. and global financial markets. Regulation of investment, or intervention, is what Stiglitz proposes will expand growth and confidence. Economic policy that promotes a hands-off approach statistically and overwhelmingly benefits a very small minority, suggests Stiglitz, and is folly stemming from questionable beliefs about how markets (ought to) work.

Goods Without Goodness

Part of the mystique of the market is that it is cloaked in an aura of morality, implying that it offers "the best way." Yet, when we operate inside the market, we frequently shift to an amoral, realist position that is probably best captured by the saying, "It's just business," which implies that "if you question this arrangement, you're living in a dream world." It seems the market has it both ways; or rather, those who promote the market as the model for almost everything we do have it both ways: advocating market solutions is seen as right and true, while the internal workings of the market are considered beyond the reach of moral assessment.

It is remarkable how seldom the tension between these two market frames is noticed in economic reports, political discussions, or popular culture. But sometimes it is noticed. Soon after the invasion of Iraq by the George W. Bush administration, the Defense Advanced Research Projects Agency's (DARPA) plan for a "terrorism market" was leaked to the press. The secretive Department of Defense think tank planned to use the Futures Markets Applied to Prediction project to foresee possible terrorist threats around the world. The project's rationale was that people seeking short-term financial profit based on predicting terrorist attacks would help represent trends and possible threats. Then-U.S. Senate Minority Leader Tom Daschle recalled, "I couldn't believe that we would actually commit $8 million to create a Web site that would encourage investors to bet on futures involving terrorist attacks and public assassinations.... I can't believe that anybody would seriously propose that we trade in death.... How long would it be before you saw traders investing in a way that would bring about the desired result?" ("Amid Furor," 2003, para. 15). Should the market, in the interest of benefiting U.S. military intelligence, have been allowed to "work its magic" to determine the likelihood of terrorism? Or is such a proposition, as Oregon's Senator Ron Wyden put it, "ridiculous and...grotesque" (para. 16)? For the DARPA employees who devised the futures program, the "nature" of markets was very likely taken for granted, such that the use of the term no longer required any definition. This example demonstrates why we ought to question amoral treatments of market dynamics and language in our own lives and workplaces.

This is exactly what Robert Jackall (1988) did in his famous book *Moral Mazes*, one of the most important pieces of research on the everyday moral reasoning of people at work. As Jackall interviewed a variety of professionals, including public relations (PR) and marketing managers, he found that they typically let their ethics ride with the market. They let the market "dictate" what was acceptable. Discussing how PR strategies are formulated, Jackall observes:

> The decisive moment...comes when a managerial circle...
> decide[s] that a certain rationale "is the way to go," [is] one
> with which they "feel comfortable." Here morality becomes
> one's personal level of comfort vis-à-vis the anticipated views
> of others. The measure of that comfort becomes a confidence
> in the casuistry necessary to persuade others that one's
> stories are plausible and one's choices reasonable. (p. 189)

Combining bureaucratic expediency and careerist opportunism, many of the managers justified their behaviors as being within the perceived range of acceptability for their reference group. In surprisingly few cases were professional standards seen as elevating or aspirational. The most successful people in the organizations Jackall studied deployed an "ethos that...turns principles into guidelines, ethics into etiquette, values into tastes, personal responsibility into an adroitness at public relations, and notions of truth into credibility" (p. 204).

"Making It"

Now, how does the market get to be such an overriding frame of interpretation for action, including the determination of what is or is not ethical? The spectacular fraud committed by financier Bernard Madoff in December 2008 provides an example of how faith in monetary and market success precludes public scrutiny of ethically dubious work. Madoff nearly was a billionaire Wall Street trader well respected by his colleagues. His career reflected the classic myth we tell about work in the market—the Horatio Alger, pull-yourself-up-by-your-own-bootstraps sort. As a trader, Madoff had a reputation for providing steadily positive returns. His success, and his founding of an exclusive private investment firm, earned him clientele among the very wealthy and very famous. Comparatively unregulated hedge funds, large banks, and other private firms invested with his company. The only problem was that many of his investments and portfolios were bogus. Of course, there were plenty of warning signs, such as a Securities and Exchange Commission investigation in the early 1990s, private due-diligence research that found his results statistically impossible to reproduce, and the remarkable lack of transparency as to how his steady performance defied all reasonable expectations—even during Wall Street's recent heady years (2005–2007). And yet these same news reports acknowledge that his ability to conceal unprecedented fraud and duplicity was tolerated, encouraged even, by the consistent rewarding of reckless investment and greed (see Berenson & Henriques, 2008). The discussion of Madoff raised big questions not only about regulation but also about the integrity and responsibility of the investment community as a set of professionals.

The Harvard educational psychologist Howard Gardner (2008) and his colleagues spent ten years developing the Good Work Project, a systematic investigation into the application of ethics in the professions and how to stimulate deeper reflection and problem solving. After interviewing more than twelve hundred professionals between 1998 and 2008, Gardner and his colleagues concluded not that a significantly higher proportion of people are acting unethically at work and in the market than in the past (say, 30–50 years ago) but that there are many more "avenues of greed" to lure people away from good work that is excellent, ethical, and engaged. Gardner explains that the infusion of market models—and, we would add, market discourses—into every corner of contemporary life, including religion and the environment, has not necessarily served us well. Under the banner of collective governance by self-interest, we have pushed examples of other kinds of motivation and inspiration out of view. With few celebrated instances of pursuit of the common good for its own sake, it's little wonder that most ethical discussions at work concern merely compliance.

"Good work" entails excellence in terms of standards of quality, engagement in terms of deep commitment, and ethicality in terms of adherence to lofty principles that transcend the immediate situation. When the work, organizational, professional, and market environments support this tri-dimensional pursuit, it is a happy situation. Unfortunately, this match is increasingly rare across the professions (Gardner, 2008). This is partly due to the marketization of professions, explain Gardner, Csikszentmihalyi, and Damon (2001). However, it is also the case that "the market is as much a consequence as a cause of many phenomena" (p. 14).

Gardner and his collaborators' studies of specific professions are revealing. In the case of genetics in the 1980s, there was a beneficial confluence of factors affecting the field, particularly in that most geneticists felt little market pressure and retained the pursuit of knowledge as their primary commitment (Gardner, Csikszentmihalyi, & Damon, 2001). Research pursuits were often framed as the exciting discovery of basic scientific knowledge. Fischman and colleagues (2004) note that "when [today's veteran] scientists began their careers thirty or forty years ago, research for product development was not common. But nearly 80 percent of those [young scientists] with whom we spoke in the late 1990s cited goals concerned with identifying diseases and cures and developing pharmaceuticals" (p. 66).

Another example of a profession's marketization is journalism in the 1990s. Increasing concentration of corporate media ownership and deadline pressure caused journalists to narrow the range of their news coverage and sacrifice the depth of their reporting. Young professional journalists, examining their domain of work, "noted the increased competition that was forcing the domain to compromise its mission, and pointed to the sensationalism that was pervading contemporary journalism" (Fischman et al., 2004, p. 55). Moreover, Fischman and colleagues noted, "Only 35 percent of the young professional journalists expressed a commitment to the domain. On the other hand, [they readily used]...unethical tactics,...[and] seemed to lack a feeling of responsibility to the values of the domain" (p. 55). The authors of that study suggest that this cynicism is the result of professional value pronouncements that, in the market context, routinely do not match up with observed practices. Communication and conduct are supremely important in gauging others' (and engaging one's own) ethics and responsibilities as a professional.

Inevitability and Permanence

A major response to analyses like these rests on the idea that market advancement is inevitable and that any fundamental attempt to challenge it is misguided at best and subversive at worst. James Arnt Aune's compelling book *Selling the Free Market* (2001) helps us see how ever-improving market performance is cast as inevitable. As a basis for justification or excuse, the idea that "The economy is simply and always will be like this" goes considerably further than the argument that "Everyone's doing it." It actually says, "This is the way it must be, for all of us. Resistance is futile." In that way, this kind of rhetoric can become a self-fulfilling prophecy, ethically speaking, when we enter the workforce, an organization, or public life believing "It's a dog-eat-dog world."

Consider scenes from P. T. Anderson's 2008 film *There Will Be Blood*, where everything is collapsed into the universe of business competition, and even the sphere of the spiritual is recast in capitalist terms. The main character, Daniel Plainview, personifies market greed and expansion, consuming everything in his path to satisfy his voracious ambition, symbolized by an oil derrick that explodes and injures his adopted son. The larger market is seen as corrosive, but the film primarily focuses on individual ambition, almost as if the excesses sprang forth solely from Plainview's personality. In fact, the film is loosely based on Upton Sinclair's muckraking novel *Oil!* (1927). Sinclair, however, is far more explicit in describing the market's machinations and inherent weaknesses, preferring to see them as *systemic* rather than as residing in personal ambition and greed. But usually the system that paves ever more "avenues of greed" remains unchallenged because, typically, when popular culture verges on a critique of the market, it still slips back into the individualistic "bad apples" perspective.

A 1989 essay by Francis Fukuyama, a midlevel official in President George H. W. Bush's administration, introduced into public language a slogan that, like the image of The Invisible Hand, places supreme confidence in "free" capitalist markets. Proclaiming "the end of history," the author said that the model of advanced democratic capitalism in the United States would become the global standard. This declaration represented not only hubris but the assumed perfect equation of democracy and capitalism. In light of the past decade's challenges to the idea of a single "script" for globalization, Fukuyama (2006b) has since retracted, or at least significantly amended, his earlier position. Just as Trotsky's followers realized that "'real existing socialism' had become a monstrosity of unintended consequences that completely undermined the idealistic goals it espoused" (Fukuyama, 2006a, para. 9), so, too, has modern-day economic neo-conservatism, in its push for largely unregulated liberal market democracies now, everywhere, and at whatever cost, demonstrated the striking difference between the realized and the ideal.

Žižek (in Mead, 2003, para. 11; Žižek, 1994) vividly illustrates the assumed inevitability of forces such as the market when he describes changes in popular conceptions of "end of the world" scenarios. For fifty years after the end of World War II, the fear was that the world might end if the Cold War turned hot. Beneath this fear was the idea that two competing economic (and political) systems were clashing. In the two decades since the fall of the Berlin Wall, popular eschatology has shifted to embrace cataclysmic scenarios such as an asteroid strike or (the more likely) disasterous effects of climate change. As Žižek argues, what we seem to have lost is the belief that humanity, as a collective agent, can actively intervene to steer social development. In the past thirty years, we have again begun to accept that history is fate. Thirty or forty years ago, there were still debates about what the future would hold in terms of major political–economic systems: communism, socialism, fascism, neo-liberal capitalism, undemocratic capitalism, and so on. The idea was that if life were to go on, there were various social possibilities for *how* it would go on. Now we talk about the end of the world *as if it is much easier for us to imagine than a change in the political system or the economic structure*. The sense is that life on earth may well end (per various threats) but that, somehow, capitalism will persist.

Examining What We *Say* about the Market

When we see the market as controlling us, or at least defining the space in which we can operate, we lose sight of the fact that the market is a human construction. But that's not how the market is popularly imagined now. We use the term "the market" in many ways: it is elastic, powerful, and readily invoked in a variety of contexts. It is usually taken for granted, and in most instances used imprecisely. The term does a lot of jobs for us, socio-linguistically. A few years ago, George (Cheney, 2004a) decided to jot down the many ways people appeal to and talk about the market, in order to create a kind of folk taxonomy of meanings for it. He noticed not only the many ways people appealed to the notion but also noted that the term's users seldom defined it. The market operated as a "god term" in a great deal of popular discourse: a presumed foundational good that didn't require explanation, let alone defense. The multiple meanings of "the market" may be found in everyday interactions as well as all sorts of media, including contemporary career Web sites, TV shows, ads, and films. This list shows both the ambiguity and the appeal of the term. In fact, "the market," like other broad-based value terms such as "freedom," derives much of its power from its imprecision (Orwell, 1970). As a sort of super-ordinate being or proper noun, The Market commands credibility, incites passions, and invites loyalty, even if we fail to examine its practical implications—for democracy, for instance.

Here are ten ways that the market functions in popular discourse and the popular imagination, especially in the contemporary United States.

The Market as Exigency or Pressure

As an exigency—a condition or requirement for action—the market becomes both an excuse for untoward or questionable actions *and* a justification for presumably laudable ones. The market thus becomes a handy "because of" or "in order to" motive (see Schutz, 1967). We talk about the market both as something that propels our decisions and actions and as something we set out in front of us as a goal or something to reach. We say that "The market won't bear this," or that "The market doesn't reward that." One result is that we fail to think about what the market is and what it does when it becomes an umbrella for so many of our actions and transactions.

The Market as the Best Way

Markets are very often talked about not only as means by which to order the economy but also as the single best mechanism of discrimination and choice for the ordering of society as a whole. This attitude was exemplified well in the unbounded faith in the dot-com expansion of the 1990s, which demonstrated unrestrained confidence in certain economic sectors in the 1990s. This ultimately unfounded optimism is well captured in the 2001 documentary film *Startup.com*, which told the story of two friends who went into business together only to see it crash in less than a year when the dot-com bubble burst. As a Salon.com review put it, the film captured well the heady period of dot-com capitalism, a time "when a business plan and a confident handshake could secure millions of dollars in venture capital; when vision was more important than experience; when it seemed anyone could get filthy rich on an idea" (Stark, 2001, para. 1).

The Market as God

Religious scholars have observed how the market stands in for answers to all sorts of ultimate questions, especially in discourse supporting big business. Again, it's as if there is no need for further explanation, given faith in the market to handle everything (see, e.g., Bigelow, 2005; H. Cox, 1999; Welch, 1998). Appeals to the market represent a leap of faith not unlike the metaphysical claims of theological and doctrinal discourses. As Barbara Vincent (cited in Welch, 1998) found in her analysis of pro-market discourse in New Zealand in the 1990s: "At the heat of any religious movement there is a Power that transcends and humbles humanity, and that needs to be respected and followed for its adherents to find fulfillment....The Market and Market Forces play this role in the documents of the New Zealand Business Roundtable. The Market is powerful. It provides. It allocates fairly with an 'Invisible Hand.' It solves problems. It cannot fail. It is without error" (p. 25).

The Market as Amoral Frame for Action

As we've already discussed, invocations of the market create a frame within which moral evaluations may be avoided and moral justifications need not be provided. In class discussions, students frequently talk as if the market is a neutral space in which people act out their "human nature." Are doctors not disclosing to patients the full extent of an expensive procedure's risk or contractors fudging the numbers on an estimate to win a bid merely acting out "the way people are"? This evasion of morality has enormous implications for professional ethics in terms of how we carve up our professional and personal lives into pieces that receive varying degrees of ethical attention. Still, we often overlook the ethical implication of market behavior until we are forced to consider it, as in the stock market crash of 2008. Following the critique offered by the economist Herman Daly (1977, 1996), should we, and *can* we, merely "let the market grow and do what it does?" From a practical perspective, the market has very real, moral consequences.

The Market as Everyday Social Practice

What we do best as a society is shop, one might conclude from recent trends. After all, just after the terrorist attacks of September 11, 2001, President George W. Bush, in an address to a joint session of Congress, told the American public that one of the best ways that they could personally fight the terrorists was with their "continued participation and confidence in the American economy" (Bush, 2001, para. 71). This statement has been almost universally interpreted as a call for U.S. citizens to "go shopping" (an interpretation the Bush administration did not deny, despite criticism of the statement's seemingly crass materialism). Such an interpretation, however, would have been unimaginable during World War II, when Americans were encouraged to spend disposable income on war bonds, and even basic food items were rationed (see M. Jacobs, 1997). After all, the poster character Rosie the Riveter pinched her pennies and went to work. These days, the term "retail therapy" is used to describe how people use shopping to express themselves, alter their emotional and mental states, and feel better aligned with social expectations.

The Market as a Domain of Social Relationships and Bonds

The market is also a network, a web of relationships. Consider the image of the ancient Athenian agora or the hope of the Swedish architect Victor Gruen, who conceived of today's shopping malls, expecting them to offer a forum for all types of interaction and a revival of the public sphere (see Hardwick, 2003). But the shopping mall has turned out not to be a commons; it is private property, and its owners may decide who is permitted to enter, the kinds of assemblies that people may organize within the mall, and the content of visitors' speech. The variety of relationships within a public commons far exceeds the narrow relationships found in the mall. The types of social bonds we foster in these spaces are critical, because our present myopic focus on "the principle of immediate interest maximization...cripples our economy [and] weakens every other aspect of our lives together" (Bellah et al., 1991, p. 95).

The Market as the Purveyor of Consumer Choices and "Freedom"

We often talk about "consumer power" as if buying things is a kind of naturally endowed liberty that everyone may freely exercise. Think of comparisons people make between nations. Do people use language that suggests that peoples with "stronger" economies are somehow freer and more powerful? It is no exaggeration to say that "the market" is used as a stand-in for "society itself." This association represents a big part of the success of marketing itself, with its promises to discover what people want and offer it to them (see Laufer & Paradeise, 1990). Of course, while some markets can deliver hundreds of options for dog food, automobiles, and cell phones, they can't produce integrative communities, strong family ties, and clear consciences. Writes the pop musician Donavon Frankenreiter (2004) in his song "Heading Home": "You try to sell something that just can't be bought/You say it's the latest and the greatest, but I know that it's not/Be somebody you don't want to be/Didn't even exist last year, but now it's what we need."

The Market as Global Network

The market can also be understood as the web of interconnections among organizations (White, 1981). Here it's important to consider the world as populated by organizations, notably corporations. The global-network perspective implied is built on transactions among people, between people and organizations, and among organizations to create a total system that, in turn, guides transactions. Of course, this means that people with powerful relationships can preclude others from participating influentially in the network (Castells, 1996), just as the biggest corporations strive to crowd out competitors even while praising competition.

The Market as an Arena of Symbolic Play

Do you know people who are involved in investment clubs or who trade gold and goods in the "World of Warcraft"? In such contexts, the market is almost surreal, something removed from everyday experience and yet closely linked to it. With the hugely popular Internet-based game Second Life, players sometimes extend their moves to have actual, material consequences (Boss, 2007), buying and selling virtual real estate with hard currency (as opposed to virtual currency), and setting up digital sweatshops producing Second Life "value," subsequently sold for hard currency.

The Market as Myth or Meta-narrative

In the ways we talk about it, the market becomes not only what we do but also who we as a people are. Hodgson (1999) remarks on utopian treatments of economics: "The word 'utopia' fosters a likelihood of change and points to an unfulfilled future that differs from the present. In general, a utopia is a description of a desired world to come: whether or not such prognostications are feasible and whether or not such a desire is shared by others" (p. 5). His point is that economic thinking is often characterized by narratives about where we've come from and where we ought to go. Yet, these compelling narratives may tell just part of the story, one that is compelling but not necessarily accurate.

Summary

At first glance, ethics do not seem to be an explicit concern for these perspectives on the market's meanings. But let's take a closer look.

Ethics are implicated whenever we use language to frame the ways humans relate to one another. Talk about the market is one important type of such discourse, which seeks to answer questions about how we should live our lives, directions for conducting commerce, goals toward which we ought to work, and more. But one of the most important questions typically left unanswered by these formulations is, What is our role in the market? That is, who are we as we act within the market, as consumers, as capitalists, as professionals?

Deciding Who We Can Be in the Market

Throughout this book, we have raised questions about agency, or the capacity of a person or group to accomplish something in the world. In terms of professional ethics, we are especially interested in the moral dimensions of that question. How do we engage the ethical side of human affairs, how do we frame our ethical responsibilities writ large, our ethical aspirations, and what do we do about them? Ultimately, we are interested in the pursuit of *a* good life rather than simply *the* good life (Solomon, 1999). We have looked at the domains of work (and jobs) or professionalism (understood in terms of both advantages and disadvantages), organizations and industries (with their many forms), and the now the market. These represent both domains of activity and various ways of positioning our own activities and responsibility. We speak of "just doing our job," "acting like a professional," "toeing the line," and "bending to the will of the market." All of these are important points of reference in the world of work and in the ways we define our roles in and around the workplace.

An overarching question about roles and responsibility explores where we draw the lines. After all, they have to be drawn somewhere: we can't be held morally responsible for absolutely everything that goes on in our company or within our labor association or with a product we manufacture. In other words, when is it fair to say that some situational or external forces really did *make* us do it? When does the market have agency, or how does it appear to? These are not questions we are prepared to resolve, either in general or in the case of a particular ethical decision. What we can do, consistent with the entire line of analysis in this book, is explore how the question of ethical agency is framed in various work-related activities.

Karl Marx (1976) brought our attention to alienation and abstraction in capitalist economies. Appropriating the concept of alienation from the idea of separation of the Roman Catholic Church from its land after the European Middle Ages, Marx applied it to the ways we separate people from the whole products of their labors (as in the move from a craft to a factory system of production), how we remove control from workers' hands (including literal and figurative senses of ownership), and how we treat the economy as something outside of individuals' pursuits. In today's various conceptions of the global market, labor is often considered a domain of life separate from those activities in which we create connections with others, such as civic participation and consumption. Karl Polanyi (2001) observed that one effect of the Industrial Revolution was "to separate labor from other activities of life and to subject it to the laws of the market"; as a result, industrialization "annihilate[d] all organic forms of existence and...replace[d] them by a different type of organization, an atomistic and individualistic one" (p. 171).

These forms of severance or division are paralleled in our abstractions of the economy and the market. "Severance" is a term we hear in the context of severance pay, but the underlying meaning is largely forgotten. As Derek Sayer (1991) explains vividly, severance is one of the key aspects of the modern world: not only do we abstract things (like the economy from people) but we often pull things out of context, from their roots, and from each other. On this, the three founders of the study of modern organizations all agreed. Karl Marx (1976) called the separation of people from the results and benefits of their labor alienation. Emile Durkheim (1996) feared that specialization would remove us from one another and keep us from understanding the larger society. Additionally, Max Weber (1978) worried about the progressive rationalization involved in creating organizations where everyone would be, in his words, like "cogs in a machine."

Severance is the cutting of ties: of people to culture, resources to nature, people to people. To some degree, role-related boundaries are necessary in that we must circumscribe roles and activities. For a journalist, being usefully and responsibly objective means suppressing one's personal opinion or suspending judgment in order to understand events from multiple perspectives. When professional journalists act in their capacity as professionals, they need to distance themselves from events to perform an objective analysis. But here we can distinguish severance from role-related boundaries. Revisiting an example from chapter 1, we posit a photojournalist lucky enough to be the first person arriving at a burning house. A parent, with an infant, trapped on the second floor shouts, "Catch my baby!" A crude idea of severance dictates that the journalist refuses. Would this hypothetical journalist, in refusing to intervene, be acting ethically, professionally, or responsibly?

Of course, it is also likely that people make excuses for ethically questionable behavior by claiming that their personal needs or attributes are completely separate from the demands or characteristics of their workplace or the market in which they work. In the *New York Times*, the commentator David Carr (2007) reflected on the surprising lack of media coverage of a Circuit City plan to fire thirty-four hundred experienced sales clerks across the United States, writing that "media outlets could not be blamed for having a little fatigue when it comes to layoffs, which have become an organic part of American life" (p. C1). Notice how swift, sweeping firings at large companies are simultaneously invoked as normal, as part of everyday life, but also as distant enough to not merit attention. Market forces are composed of many interactions and individuals' perceptions, to be sure. And, yet, it is troublesome to say markets are just an aggregation of the purely economic activity of individuals. Severance is a denial of relationship.

When it comes to market magic, in a little-noticed sideshow we see how the market becomes a big box into which we put all sorts of responsibilities and accounts, especially when we question others or ourselves about actions that might be seen as harsh, problematic, and even immoral. George observed this in his decade-long study of the Mondragón worker cooperatives in the Basque Country, Spain, where managers who cited the market as a basis for corporate policy often could not point to the actual market pressures underlying their actions. Rather, the market became an essentialized category into which fell lots of decisions, made for a variety of reasons, including personal preference and expectations about "what a global corporation needs to do." Like these managers, we often readily surrender our agency to the market, perhaps even more than we surrender it to our jobs, professions, and organizations. Returning there in 2008, George found debate at all levels of the cooperatives about how to listen to and lead the market in the future. As a result of the global financial meltdown, managers and others were asking searching questions about which market signals were worth serious attention, not only in a strategic sense but in a moral one. Part of this discussion centered on the Mondragón Cooperative Corporation's capacity to recognize its own agency in making the social economy of the future (Cheney, 2008b). Not only must they be in the market, but also their power and values compel them to try to refashion it.

Three Big Assumptions, and Professional Ethics

Markets = Democracy

As we've already explained, two common presumptions are that the market is inherently democratic and that market economies equal democratic societies. Let's examine that assumption more carefully, considering how it is typically expressed (or taken for granted) and what its ethical implications are. The entire institution of marketing is built on the assumption that the best thing for that profession, and society, is to find out what people want (ideally, even before they know) and then to (magically) provide it. Marketing has thus a compelling democratic ethos; the institutions of economic interaction and democratic participation are uneasily fused in marketing discourse. What could be more democratic than this? What could be better than a system that lets everybody win (if they can afford to)? How could we run society better than this? Marketing itself becomes not only a profession but a model for everything from politics to health care to religion. Should it be surprising, then, that the market is the first solution people think of when they consider how to encourage corporations to act more responsibly, how to combat global warming, or how to bring former worshippers back to religion?

In the mainstream news media, in political discourse, and in many of our history books, the equation of capitalism and democracy is simply assumed. Almond (1991) points out that there are four possible relationships between democratic social systems and capitalist markets in any given society: both present, neither present, and only one or the other present. Yet, politicians and corporate managers often talk as though market democracies are the only actual or legitimate arrangement. Even those who recognize the distinction between a system of representative democracy and that of public choice in the marketplace consider the mechanisms of the market "a tolerable approximation" (Kuttner, 1997, p. 334). Along with this tolerance can come an attitude of acceptance for whatever is done in the name of either system; each one watches the other's back.

Markets = Consumers "Doing What They Do"

A third assumption is that our primary role in the market is that of consumers. Citizens have both rights and responsibilities, but consumers aren't accustomed to thinking of themselves as beholden to others. That is, when we shift our terminology to the consumer, as happened over the course of the twentieth century, responsibilities take the back seat. Amazingly, in less than a hundred years, the most common meanings of "consumption" shifted from two negatives—waste, and tuberculosis—to an overwhelmingly endorsed positive—shopping (Cheney, 2005). Perhaps this is why the *New Yorker* writer Adam Gopnik (1997) called consumerism "the century's winning 'ism'" (p. 80). The 1960s and 1970s offered two versions of consumerism: first, advocacy for consumer information, product safety, and product quality, as typified in the organizations launched and developed by Ralph Nader; and second, rising expectations, including confidence that the good life meant ever more affluence. In retrospect, it's quite fair to say that the latter form has won out, at least for now, bolstered by the folk logic of marketing: find out what people want and give it to them. Or, better yet, stimulate needs that the marketplace can satisfy (Ewen, 1976).

A deleted scene from the film *Borat* (2007), Sacha Baron Cohen's send-up of contemporary U.S. culture, offers a dramatic illustration of this point. In this scene, the Kazakhstani character Borat, amazed at the variety of products available in a U.S. supermarket, stands in front of the enormous cheese section, pointing to each individual item and asking the clerk, "What is this? And this?" The answer every time is "cheese." The scene continues uncomfortably for several minutes. The problem, of course, is not that we have too many choices in commodities. What Borat's persistent inquisitiveness reveals is that more does not always mean better. As Marcuse (1964) points out, choice among various brands or types of consumer goods is a paltry substitute for freedom.

We surround ourselves with commodities and even commoditize our own lives. These trends are founded in the notion of lifestyles, born in the 1920s (Ewen, 1984), when automobiles were becoming readily available to the middle class for the first time. It is important to note, too, that car advertising was designed to appeal to the audience's sense of identity, freedom, and status. Autos were not simply for transportation; they enabled one to free oneself from tradition: men could now take women on dates away from her family's home. The car was a conspicuous luxury and, like other expensive commodities, conferred social status, as Thorstein Veblen (1935) observed in 1899. Our cultural context influences and is shaped by our market activity and the language we use to talk about it. Take the following as an illustrative contemporary example. An active belief in the prosperity gospel, a theology purporting a causal link between religious faith and material wealth, makes "Christvertising" plausible. Want to connect your religious practice to your business work? There's a product for that! Christvertising is an alleged communications consultancy whose Web site boasts: "Whether yours is a small, big or internationally renowned brand, God's is infinitely larger" (see www.christvertising.com/who.html).

Some of us even treat ourselves as commodities. It is not uncommon for young people looking for their first professional job to say that they are marketing themselves. People are sold on an idea when they are persuaded. A team member provides a unique "value-added" to group processes. John Desmond (1995) explains that this sort of linguistic drift is indicative of a broader trend—namely, the increasing use of instrumental rationality and exchange value to make sense of everyday life. When everything and everyone becomes a commodity to be bought and sold, we can say that people engage in commodity fetishism. As E. F. Schumacher (1973) so poignantly wrote, we can't ultimately treat social relationships as being like revenue or we will spend them away.

Our concern is about how happiness relates to ethics and what that means in terms of how we do business: how we perform our work, relate to others in professions and other organizations, and participate as citizen–consumers in the market. Here again, our recent classroom experience is relevant. During more than a decade teaching a course on quality of work life, George found that students wanted to spend more and more time discussing the spheres of family, community, and consumption, in addition to their roles in for-pay jobs. As they considered their various roles and their relationships to what we call the market, many students started to question the notion that material goods are the key to happiness. Their realization is especially important because many of today's ads promise not only a cleaner body or more efficient transportation but even emotional and spiritual satisfaction for their buyers (Klein, 1999).

Of course, in colleges and universities it has become commonplace to describe students as consumers. In one way, this is entirely reasonable: it helps emphasize the accountability of the institution to its clients (McMillan & Cheney, 1996). However, the shift to the idea of consumer or customer has hidden negative implications as well. When we look for advocacy in the marketplace—say, in arguing that community health takes precedence over profit—what collective identity is usually invoked? People's speech often implies that being a consumer means that one cannot also be an activist (Kendall, Gill, & Cheney, 2007). Syracuse University, an early adopter of the student-as-consumer notion, was puzzled with the results of their policy change in the early 1990s, when they began to push the concept in all their publications and official communications. By the middle of that decade, the development office had noticed a sharp decline in graduates' contributions. When fundraisers asked some graduates to explain their relationship to the institution, they stated: "If I buy a car from General Motors, do they expect me to make voluntary contributions to GM for the rest of my life?" (Readings, 1996). For these graduates, a relationship redefined in purely transactional, commercial terms no longer had a hold on their loyalties or desire to do something extra for the organization. This powerful example demonstrates how marketized relationships can change the nature of connections between people. Market-based relationships can, nonetheless, deepen connections and be the basis for ethical activity, since "Among the most important dimensions of such 'civil regulation' [to promote business virtues] are consumer demand for responsibly made products, actual or threatened consumer boycotts, challenges to a firm's reputation by nongovernmental organizations (NGOs), pressure from socially responsible investors, and the values held by managers and other employees" (Vogel, 2006, p. 3). Still, the language of consumerism suggests something other than, or at least less than, this kind of regulation and responsibility. This is exemplified by the fact that our accounts of "being a consumer" involve the ideas of duty, accountability, and restriction far less than our accounts of being a citizen, employee, volunteer, or family member.

In a way, today's "marketing society" (a term coined by Laufer & Paradeise, 1990) is a logical extension of the notion of lifestyle: today's advertisements sell ways of life as much as they do products. Ads promise that products can do just about anything for people, even as some of them (such as MasterCard) claim that "money can't buy everything." But, of course, there ought to be limits to the marketing language we apply to so many relationships. While it might make sense to speak of marketing oneself to prospective employers during job interviews, does it make sense to talk about "diversifying your family's offspring portfolio" when planning to have another child, or to say that we're "invested in the long-term futures" of our church or spiritual community? Consuming isn't all that we do, and it isn't the sole measure of value in our lives, though Saturday at the local shopping mall may make it seem otherwise.

Market Performance = Happiness

A third assumption that we make is that the market and our role in it as a consumer is the most direct path to happiness. We receive hundreds, if not thousands, of messages every day to reinforce this notion. If the market, according to the utilitarian ideal, is designed to maximize happiness and minimize pain (or want), then aren't increased happiness and decreased pain and want fair measures to use when assessing market performance as a whole? A great unwritten but vital assumption of the economy and of economics is that markets are a central (even *the* central) venue in which and means by which people satisfy their needs and pursue happiness.

The contemporary research on happiness causes us to rethink work and consumption and, even more importantly, to rethink using the market as a model for practically everything today. The powerful idea of "miswanting" (Gilbert & Wilson, 2000), as described in chapter 2, challenges a foundational marketing assumption, which is that one should find out exactly what people want (or help them find out) and then give it to them. Shockingly, marketers now seek, as a normal part of their work, to mold people's identities to make them think of themselves as consumers first, and from a very early age (Schor, 2004).

Economists have long noted that the U.S. workweek began lengthening again, in the mid- to late 1970s, after three quarters of a century of reduced workweeks (Schor, 1992). At the same time, interestingly, the gap between the rich and the poor in the United States began to widen, after four decades of narrowing (Boushey & Weller, 2005). These trends are very likely intertwinded, and they bear on questions about equity, fairness, and happiness (Pollin, 2005). During this same period, the availability of goods and services and people's expectation of consuming these goods have increased dramatically. Consequently, only through overwork are many people able to afford their increased consumption (Schor, 1997).

Our argument is something of a back-door critique of the market. It begins with the "where people are already at" and then asks, "So, does the way you conceive of and engage in the market make you happy?" The political scientist Robert Lane's book *The Loss of Happiness in Market Democracies* (2000) makes precisely this point. Lane reviews all the available research to conclude that, generally speaking, there has been a decline in happiness in the biggest economies of the world and that the triumph of consumerism hasn't been altogether positive. In fact, Lane's research across areas from psychology to economics shows that there may well be diminishing returns in accrued happiness once people have met their basic needs. After reviewing empirical psychologically research, Myers (1992) concluded that monetary wealth in excess of the money needed to meet basic needs and secure a modicum of leisure time does not, on the whole, increase people's happiness. In fact, there can be a net loss, in terms of time and energy invested in working harder for that bigger house, a new car, and the latest technology and fashions (Schor, 1997).

Recent research on happiness provides the basis for questioning something that regularly goes unexamined in talk about the market: the selection of indicators of economic health. Since the late 1960s a growing number of observers has criticized the hidden assumptions and inadequacies of the gross national product (or GDP) as a holistic measure of a society. As the U.S. senator Robert F. Kennedy put it bluntly in 1968: the GDP "measures everything, in short, except that which makes life worthwhile" (Kennedy, 1968; for a historical discussion, see T. Clarke, 2008, p. 49). Coming from this perspective, researchers, consultants, and some political leaders have been working to revise our measures of economic health, starting with considering factors that are not ordinarily included in economic assessments, such as the strength of community ties.

But if there being stuff to buy and one's having the money to buy it fail to generate one's long-term sense of subjective well-being, what about achieving success, at least as measured by popular opinion? The developmental psychologist William Damon (2008) found that even otherwise bright, healthy, and respected adolescents felt intense dissatisfaction with their accomplishments. Many young people with admirable achievement records, says Damon, report never developing a clear sense of purpose, a deep sense of meaning, a "calling." In this book, we invoke the concept *eudaimonia*, or flourishing. How is it that "success," despite its implication of "good living," has left many young people feeling as though they have not flourished? Happiness ought to be part of the discussion about the discourse and ethics of the market because, as Myers (1992) points out, "happiness is both an end—better to live fulfilled, with joy—and a means to a more caring and healthy society" (p. 21).

The King of Bhutan's 1972 conference, which yielded the alternative indicator called "gross domestic happiness," inspires hope for reframing what counts as meaningful in evaluating a country's (or other entity's) quality of life. Since then, cities, regions, and even the United Kingdom have explored alternatives—sometimes citing the results of happiness research—including measures called genuine progress indicators (GPIs) (for details on such developments, see Anielski & Rowe, 1999; Costanza et al., 2004; Daly & Cobb, 1989; Talberth, Cobb, & Slattery, 2006). At the same time, culture jammers have sharply challenged use of the GDP; Adbusters created

a series of ads showing that subtractions from rather than addi-
tions to the GDP ought to be made for toxic waste sites and cancer
diagnoses—because those are things that we as a society want to see
minimized.

As problems with the GDP demonstrate, it seems that the market
is not good at providing happiness—that is, beyond a certain point.
The relationship of economics to happiness is complex and in some
ways riddled with paradox. The Easterlin paradox is the relationship
between material wealth and the sense of satisfaction and joy in life
that we described above: the connections between income and happiness have become less correlative even as national incomes for many
countries have risen dramatically. Why is this so? For one thing, people do reframe their needs and wants as their situations change mate-
rially and socially. There is no single or one-dimensional solution to
the question of how to measure happiness for purposes of linking it
to economic productivity and societal wealth, any more than there
is a single definition of happiness in all places and times. However,
the recent revival of interest in the happiness–economics connection
calls for a return to basic questions about what the economy is *for*
and what it is *doing*. As Luigi Pasinetti wrote about the role of communication in creating and strengthening economic ties, "We should
not fear to go straight...to discussing ends and social goals," including not only an equitable distribution of income but also social justice and the common good (2005, pp. 341–42). We have a dynamic
labor market that promises the possibility of great wealth accumulation. We have also developed a success-obsessed culture whose
messages suggest that happiness can be found largely at work, providing goods and services for the market. As the popular philosopher
Alain de Botton (2009, p. 106) remarks, "all societies have had work
at their centre; ours is the first to suggest that it could be something
much more than a punishment or a penance...[and to assume] that
the route to a meaningful existence must invariably pass through the
gate of remunerative employment." This assumption, however, does
little to ensure our happiness.

In the Market We Trust

This is a good place to consider a detailed example that captures the
role of ethics in market activity. It's both tempting and easy to claim
that the contemporary global economy is so new that it bears no
resemblance to earlier incarnations of globalism. Consider, however,

the case of "tulipmania" in seventeenth-century Holland, when the Dutch empire was a powerful economic force in the world. As you read this account of the historical crisis, consider how one social force—trust—played an enormous role, and then consider how trust was called into question in the global financial crisis of 2008–10.

Tulipmania

Tulipmania has long been held up as a moral tale of greed, speculation, inflated prices, and the inevitable plummet of the tulip market during the Dutch Golden Age. In the book *Tulipmania*, Anne Goldgar (2007) cuts through the sensationalism to provide a richer economic, social, and moral account. She argues that the effect was not primarily economic because most of the tulip traders could withstand price decreases, and many continued to trade in tulips after the crash. The real consequence was the destruction of trust.

Any trade in futures depends on trust, but none more than the Dutch tulip trade in the early 1600s. First, tulips did not necessarily bloom true from one year to the next, much less from one bulb to its offsets (growths that generate new plants). So a bulb could produce a rare and valued flower one year but a mediocre one the next, so there was no clear way to determine whether the bulb bought was the bulb received. Second, bulbs were pulled out of the ground in the summer so they would not rot; they were then replanted in the fall to bloom in the spring. Ideally, a buyer would see the flower in the spring and take possession of the bulb when it was pulled from the ground. But the tulip trade went on year-round, so it was common for buyers to trust sellers to provide the promised bulb when the time came.

When tulip prices crashed, buyers were naturally reluctant to make good on deals negotiated when prices were high. In addition, bulbs might be sold from the first buyer to the second, to the third, and so on, before the actual bulbs were delivered. So, if one buyer reneged, subsequent buyers had no choice but to do likewise. The tulip grower's honor was at stake, and sometimes his or her honesty could not even be proven, as when one buyer continually delayed coming to the seller's garden to witness the digging up of the bulb until the seller had to dig it up anyway for fear of rot. Goldgar argues that it was the destruction of credit relations and honor that was most consequential. This, in turn, caused people to fear that society was becoming disordered more than to fear economic loss, per se, especially in an economy that relied on honor.

Today's "Tulipmania"

When we wrote this section of the book, you could tune in to almost any news program—from CNN to NPR to BBC—and hear stories about the "crisis in confidence." This effectively means that people don't trust the existing order of social relations and agreements. It's really no wonder: we realize that perfectly normal market activity involves savvy investors engaged in risky behavior that would be considered suspicious in any other arena; lenders provide deceptive home loans to people they know will be unable to manage the accrued debt; and state leaders are inconsistent in rationalizing their decision to subsidize Bear Stearns, seize control of Fannie Mae and Freddie Mac, and allow Lehman Brothers to collapse.

Three Lessons

There are at least three lessons common to both the present and the historical events we have presented here. First, market activity is contingent upon the way we make sense of what is happening. As Deirdre McCloskey (1985) explains in depth, groups of people use language to convince themselves of what is going on among them. If contemporary capitalist markets operate as we've described, then ethics is abstracted and defined out of, or perhaps tightly constrained within, market activity. Yet, if our ethics inspire commitment to others, ruling ethics out of market practice undermines trust. There's good reason to think that markets don't always act in our individual or collective best interests. Most of the economic growth in recent history has been achieved by amassing wealth for very few people (Krugman, 2006) and exacerbating inequality between the rich and the poor (Boushey & Weller, 2005). This is a global trend, but not an inevitable one.

Second, we can see how essentializing the market as a mechanism for economic growth is, in fact, somewhat pathological. If a behavior is economically rewarded, but is destructive to the social fabric, should it be encouraged? The ethically informed response ought to be a resounding "No!" As noted in chapter 2, *our individual virtue significantly depends upon our participation in a virtuous collective.* So we again return to the problem of talking about markets as amoral. The crisis in the Dutch tulip market was deeply tied to people's identities as honorable actors. But, if market valuation reinforces immoral behavior, then the promotion of upright activity requires *extra*-market conduct in addition to market restructuring. This is one point that Appiah (2008) makes in explaining the inadequacy of thinking about ethics as mere *responses* to quandaries; a larger scope for ethics instead minimizes the likelihood that we enter quandaries at all. So our larger ethical conversation about markets should question growth. Do we fetishize economic growth, pursuing it even when that pursuit damages other values we hold dear (Hamilton, 2004)? The title of a book by Eric Davidson (2000) is a pithy reminder of the pitfalls of market fundamentalism and myopia: *You Can't Eat GNP: Economics as if Ecology Mattered.*

Third, a healthy pairing of market activity and democracy requires both cooperation and dissent. Dissent and dissenters, observes the law professor Cass Sunstein (2003), often ensure open access to crucial information and prevent groups from engaging in extreme behavior behind the scenes. (Sunstein, it should be noted, was appointed by Barack Obama to head the Office of Information and Regulatory Affairs, where he will oversee policy related to governmental regulation and the economy.) Journalism is often called the Fourth Estate, a label emphasizing an independent role but now commonly referring to the press's professional duty to balance objectivity and advocacy. Today's journalism is a profession increasingly subject to marketization (see Gardner, Csikszentmihalyi, & Damon, 2001). What happens when commitments to increasing cost effectiveness or the profit margin overrun the commitment to providing valuable information and ensuring fairness? At worst, the result is the denigration of a social function entrusted to a class of professionals (see Dzur, 2008, and our discussion in chapter 4). Short of that, curious practices take hold, as with a Pasadena, California, newspaper's outsourcing of *local* news coverage to a company in India (Pham, 2007).

Features of market systems can promote or inhibit behavior. Dissent is sometimes required because it highlights when and how patterns of social behavior do not provide for broad-based well-being. If we want to value different things, or want altogether different values, radical market restructuring is sometimes necessary. The journalist Ben Collins (2008) makes this point when he explains how the modern food industry continues to expand and be more profitable for investors but also persists in its failure to feed and nourish large segments of the global population. As our focus on communication suggests, a change in the public conversation about something can, in fact, result in a transformation of the thing itself.

Reflecting Further on the Market We Make

What kind of market, then, do we wish to make? And, how do we reframe them in more ethical terms? What makes market-oriented relationships meaningful, personally fulfilling, and socially valuable? The social critic Wendell Berry (1993) argues that maintaining a degree of economic freedom and healthy social relationships depends not upon some abstract conception of the public but instead upon the more concrete idea of *community*. Berry defines community as "a people locally placed, and a people, moreover, not too numerous to have a common knowledge of themselves and of their place" (p. 168). A nation—and in our case, a national economic market—ought to be thought of as "an assemblage of many communities," according to Berry (p. 168).

Considering the Market's Place in Community

Why center on communality and reciprocity in the marketplace? Take the relationship between community and food production. Bill McKibben (2007) found that eating locally for one year helped him reconceptualize food markets. In that year, McKibben was able to develop personal connections with the producers of his food and to ask questions about production processes. In the industrial food system in which most of us eat, we rarely have much sense of where our food comes from and what it consists of before we buy it. This, McKibben points out, is the result of system that makes for cheap food but also for unemployed farmers, environmental degradation, animal cruelty, and difficulty in implementing food-safety regulations. McKibben describes rewarding personal connections, joyful eating experiences, and, yes, a few new challenges from his yearlong experiment. He points out, though, that his change in economic behavior was inherently more environmentally sustainable and contributed directly to the durability of his community. What motivated McKibben was a desire to realize social good, to feel and produce social solidarity through communication, to consume conscientiously (Cheney, 2005).

In the end, communities built on mutually caring social relations are what produce happiness of the sort we're describing in this book. Lane (2000) argues that contemporary market economies crowd out those sources of happiness and well-being in favor of individual opportunity and material abundance. Individual satisfaction and amusement are a poor substitute for the rich public life that is possible when the idea of happiness is paired with trust, responsibility, and mutual support. The community institutions (and their functions) that create supportive social bonds are increasingly being replaced by expressly private organizations (Putnam, 2000). Frankena (1973) points out that the dilemma of the ethical egoist, one who holds that the pursuit of enlightened self-interest is the supreme and sole responsibility of moral agents, is, first, that we require others' help to live a good life, and, second, that we often experience well-being when supporting others.

Alternative Economics, Alternative Ethics

This chapter has explored the curious relationship between communication, markets, people, and ethics. The language of the market, we've argued, too often puts the workings of social, political, and economic institutions beyond the reach of individuals and collectives working to ensure ethical relationships and activity. There are very real examples of people working together to change social conceptions about what markets can be and about which values are foundational to them. The well-known historian and political economist Gar Alperovitz (2005) argues that U.S. and global economic systems show signs of *evolutionary reconstruction*, in which change is achieved through a combination of reformist and revolutionary activity (p. 235). Alperovitz lists several requirements of a political economy (which is a label for the dynamics of power in market relationships) to guarantee "a more egalitarian and free democratic culture": equality in decentralized democracy, economic security, sufficient leisure time, and "a culture of common responsibility" (p. 234).

There are many forms of alternative market exchange. What they have in common is their challenge to consumerism as usual. The ways we talk about production and consumption—and about work and play—in today's world emphasizes desire, and thus incompleteness and perpetual impoverishment (Stearns, 2006). Before consumer society, lifestyles, and such, explains Stearns, "luxury existed...but not the constant parade of changing fashions that would characterize modern consumerism" (p. 8). That perpetual revolution in technology and fashion, is ironically based upon an important constancy: "The principle that set the market in motion and kept it going was the inclination to satisfy self-interest through exchange" (Muller, 2002, p. 61). Research has shown that these processes have deepened inequality and threatened the ability of the market itself to distribute essential resources (see Lardner & Smith, 2005), leaving many people seeking substitutes.

But if we are looking for such substitutes, how can we talk about labor and exchange without the language of private enterprise for profit? Here we will briefly discuss a few notable examples. Despite globalization—now a cliché term—a number of communities have created and sustained their own currencies. These complementary currencies supplement the national monetary standard for exchange. Sometimes these currencies generate or are issued by local exchange trading systems (or LETS), which are more formalized local economic programs. Most complementary money systems are *only* local, inasmuch as the money may be issued and used in just one community or region. Susan Meeker-Lowry (1996) explains, "Community currencies are very helpful as a means of creating and sustaining self-reliance" (p. 458). They encourage participation rather than reward scarcity. They value local labor and trade by stemming the flow of money out of a community. And, while establishing new values through an alternative or local economic system can be difficult at first, the laborer being remunerated with such money is a member of one's community. Plus, that money asserts its value only in trade, so wealth must be shared and not accumulated. There are numerous organized bartering systems. Some track and barter time, such as LocalBucks (see timebucks.com) and Time Banks (see timebanks. org). Others create and manage a local currency; in the United States we find the Liberty Dollar, the Maui Dollar, and the Moab (Utah) Barter Coin.

Of course, we do not use only money to engage in economic exchange. Consider the gifts you give, whether birthday presents for family members, donations to local public media outfits, or volunteer time and effort for the benefit of a nonprofit organization. Have you ever received in-kind payment for services rendered? We'll discuss examples of these sorts of "gift economies" in more detail in chapter 7. As the social theorist Pierre Bourdieu (1990) has explained, choosing alternatives to money and (capitalist) market interaction are consequential, and demonstrate a very particular logic about value in exchange and relationships. In short, they communicate different values, and make possible different ways of organizing and interacting with others. Whether in the exchange of gifts, the establishment of a worker cooperative, or the creation of the World Social Forum in response the World Economic Forum, people find ways of engaging in alternative economies and markets.

Other kinds of economy are certainly possible. But what does alternative economics have to do with communication? Consider the fact that some of us engage in alternative exchange but still tend to associate talk about markets mostly with Wall Street bankers, transnational corporations, and the streaming stock quotes on the TV news. As the rhetorical theorist Richard Vatz (1973) put it, "Utterance strongly invites exigence" (p. 159). He means that what we talk about and how we talk about it actually helps make things more imaginable, and then doable. In the case of the market and ethics, we have too long spoken of one model. There are other ways of arranging human commercial transactions. For the study of professional ethics, this means we have a certain collective responsibility to see beyond "the way things are." When The Market becomes a substitute for more thoughtful and heartfelt examinations of our roles in society, or when ethics are disregarded altogether, we need to craft a new kind of *communication*. Innovations in the communication of ethics and economics can help us to envision new sorts of markets and ethics. We have to begin by breaking habits of talk about "how we (ought to) do things around here" that are without moral content.

Maintaining any habit, even a habit of thought, requires routine. Becoming too comfortable with the "normal" or "natural" story of anything is dangerous. This is especially the case with ethics in professional life and in the marketplace. David Kotz (2008), a commentator on the Web site truthout.org, points out the absurdity of Alan Greenspan's claim to have "found [himself] 'in a state of shocked disbelief' at the failure of self-interest to protect [the U.S.] banking system" (para. 1). Greenspan, of course, was the chairman of the U.S. Federal Reserve from 1987 to 2006. We have referenced the interdependent and global housing, credit, and bank crises that came to a head in 2008. These crises were made possible in the United States in part because of two regulatory changes made during Greenspan's tenure. Like many others, Greenspan trusted that (enlightened) self-interest alone could produce ethical and stable market relations. As we've pointed out, such faith is based upon a simplified reading of Adam Smith's economic theories and an essentialized description of markets. Today's economic crisis provides us a chance to rethink the assumptions about our relations to the market and to those within it.

We invented a language that helped promote the free hand of the market and create its results. We are now at an important moment, where we need to explore and share new ways of talking about the market based on values such as trust, solidarity, well-being, sufficiency, sustainability, and happiness. Such a market would be oriented toward *eudaimonia*, as complex as that concept is, and not toward the much narrower goals of growth and the accumulation of capital or, more broadly, "stuff."

Revisiting "What Works" in the Market

In the book *A Postcapitalist Politics*, the authors write about how our language supports and constrains the economic realities we face (Gibson-Graham, 2006). Citing Butler (1993, p. 2) they "[recognize] the inevitable *performativity* of language—its power to create the effects that it names" (Gibson-Graham, 2006, p. 2). The questions below invite you to reflect how the market language you use shapes your other views and options. Both ethically and practically speaking, your account of the market and your work in it *matter*.

1. How are our options for work—and work practices—shaped by market forces and appeals to the market? What does this mean for freedom? For the pursuit of happiness? For doing good in the world?

2. Do you *owe* it to the market to be a successful professional? If so, what does "success" mean? Where do your ideas of productivity, success, and a brilliant career come from? What are the most memorable messages you've received about how markets work and the role of ethics within them?

3. How can an organization such as a business stand outside the market? What do virtuous alternatives to an amoral market logic look like? How can we work within the system to change it for the better, perhaps to soften its harsher aspects or to make it responsive to more fundamental human and environmental needs?

7

Finding New Ways to Talk about Everyday Ethics

"Moral language, *as* language, is essentially public. The avowal and endorsement and revision of norms are conversational activities. It can't be unimportant that human beings spend so much of their days talking to other human beings (and yes, on occasion, being talked at)." (Appiah, 2008, p. 197)

The Power of *Talk* about Ethics

In a class discussion in 2008, Dan asked his students to engage the premise that ethics is almost always framed negatively, as a cost to business. While the class readily accepted this idea, a debate ensued over whether or not such a framing was a *necessary* outgrowth of capitalism. Dan's students generally shared a desire for a heightened sense of ethics in the business world, but most agreed that the needed changes were not realistic, echoing arguments like "ethical businesses just can't compete with unethical businesses." In short, the students framed ethics as a desirable goal but one that could be achieved only under certain (rare) conditions, and generally at great risk.

When Dan suggested that notions of necessity and realism were *themselves* shaped by a particular view of capitalism (recall our discussion of Adam Smith and the misunderstood metaphor of the Invisible Hand in chapter 6), many argued that the frequent sidelining of ethics within capitalism was a natural part of "the system" rather than grounded in a set of strategic choices. "The market *is* amoral," many argued, echoing a common essentialist claim. In other words, "the market does according to what the market is." Others in the class contended, more specifically, that "the only way the market can deal with ethics is by calculating costs to the bottom line." Translation: the market will be ethical only when the cost of unethical behavior becomes too great for the market to bear. Even those students most troubled by this perspective had a hard time seeing this amorality as anything other than inevitable; after all, the market *is* according to what the market *does*. Of course, from our perspective, the relationship between capitalism and ethics is neither predetermined nor one-dimensional. Rather, the role of ethics in the market cannot be separated from the ways we talk about and frame that relationship. Inevitability represents just one way of talking about the market, and this has implications for how we do our work, participate in professions, and serve organizations. "That's the way it is" is one common way to express inevitability and the impossibility of change—in perspective or in reality.

As we've suggested at several other points, the rhetoric of inevitability is often intensified by a kind of temporal immediacy, what the sociologist Ben Agger refers to as the "instantaneity" of "fast capitalism" (2003, p. 5). The rhetorical weight of this instantaneity was felt during the financial-market meltdown in October of 2008 as a means of promoting the U.S. Treasury Department's $700 billion "bailout" package. When the bailout was first announced, both President Bush and Treasury Secretary Paulson warned Congress against delay, advocating that the three-page legislation be passed *as is* because of the extreme urgency of the situation. The Republican presidential nominee John McCain proclaimed that he needed to "rush" back to Washington to secure passage of the package. Advocates on all sides of the issue accepted the pervasive sense of urgency and, to the astonishment of observers from across the political spectrum, acted without deliberation.

Our point here is not to take issue with either the bailout package itself or the truthfulness of the claims surrounding it but rather to point to the immense rhetorical force of urgency. Here, notions of fear and inevitability were used to create a need to act, and act now; there was no time for the luxury of debate and deliberation. There was no time for talk and, in a way, no time even for the illusion of democracy. The irony of this situation was not lost on many citizens who angrily charged that, if the government could suddenly assist Wall Street, why couldn't it offer more to "Main Street"? But as Žižek suggested

in his provocative commentary on the crisis, perhaps the appropriate response would have been to talk: turning the colloquialism on
its head, Žižek admonished leaders, "Don't just do something, talk"
(2008a). Žižek here draws our attention to the importance of deliberation, the danger of unreflective action, and the need for refiners rather
than deciders. But there's a subtler dimension to Žižek's admonition
as well. Drawing on the observations of the Nobel Prize–winning
economist Joseph Stiglitz, Žižek points out that even the expert
advocates of the bailout had no idea if the proposal would "work"
in a narrow, technical sense. Instead, they hoped that by forcefully
doing something, anything, they could help restore enough trust in
the market that frozen credit would thaw and resume circulation,
avoiding economic disaster. As Žižek puts it, "The bailout may work
even if it is *economically wrong*" (para. 2, emphasis added).

In other words, despite our popular separation of "talk" and
"action," talk *is* action, and action *is* talk (an idea well established by
philosophers of ordinary language). How is this so? Action necessarily carries with it a symbolic, in addition to an immediately practical,
dimension. In short, the market is not some place ruled by hard numbers and figures, untouched by the influence of words and symbols.
To the contrary, the way that we talk about the market has a very real
and powerful effect on its actual performance.

Of course, as we've argued throughout this book, the underap-
preciated power of talk extends to the domains of work, profession,
and organization as well. Just as there are certain myths about the
market, so there are myths about communication, and about ethics.
Here again we do not mean that myths are necessarily false. Rather,
we are using myth in the sense of a big story that carries with it certain ideological assumptions (Frye, 1957). As detailed in chapter 2,
myths serve as the grand narratives we tell about the world, helping
us organize information, see our way through the clutter of experience, and persuade one another of the best way to do things. We have
said a great deal about market myths in chapter 6, but, in a way, this
entire book has been about myths—particularly the confining stories
we tell—about ethics, about communication, about work, and, ironically, about what makes us happy. By talking about ethics as if it is
something removed from daily life, we have greatly limited its appeal
and its capacity to affect our lives. Along the way, we have failed to
appreciate how we frame ethics, up front, even before confronting
specific issues or dilemmas.

By focusing our attention on the clearly ethical implications of
talk in our professional and work lives, we have sought to reframe

and reposition ethics so that it occupies a central, rather than periph-
eral, place in our own consciousness and in what we often call the
"real world." In this concluding chapter, we return to the broad topic
of ethics in this new light, exploring how our analysis suggests we
might change the way we talk about ethics, individually and culturally. Before we do so, however, we briefly revisit our arguments in
terms of both significant features of ethical talk and the main domains
in which such talk occurs. In addition, we want to explain further how
each of these domains is character forming for those in relationship
with it, and how each possesses a certain character in itself. In other
words, we should consider (1) how we, as characters, enter each of
these spheres; (2) how our character is affected by interactions and
experiences within each of these contexts; and (3) how we characterize each of these cultures and environments. As we focus on personal
character, we should remain aware of organizations, professions, the
market, and work contexts. Each of these domains features agency
and responsibility. Agency and responsibility, in turn, are grounded
in and transcend individual action.

As we've argued throughout this book, our mythical view of ethics is a limited one, unnecessarily restricted by three common ways
of speaking. We *compartmentalize* ethics by circumscribing distinct
spheres of our lives in which ethics do and do not apply, or at least
where different, and limited, ethical standards play a role. For example, we say, "It's not personal, it's business" or "Out there, it's a dog-
eat-dog world." We *essentialize* ethics when we reduce them to the
character(istics) of a person (good or bad) and locate ethics only in
unusual situations. For example, we think, "Look at that great hero"
and "What would Kant do?" We *abstract* ethics when we appeal exclusively to theories or procedures meant to help us reason our way out
of such quandaries, using such prescriptive theories as the categorical imperative and utilitarianism. In cases of commodification, we
further abstract ethics by removing from view the ethical notions of
"value" and substituting for them the narrower notions of "market
value." In all these ways, we prevent ethics from doing the full range
of wonderful work that it can do in our lives.

We're accustomed to these modes of thinking and speaking
about ethics, even though—or, perhaps, because—they avoid a lot
of the ethical complexities of work and life. These devices of thought
and language are appealing partly because we need them to manage
our complex worlds. They become problematic, however, when we
mistake their linguistic handiness for universal relevance. There are
moments where resorting to the colloquialism "It's not personal, it's

business" might be helpful, whether it is to offer strong but appropriate criticism or to make tough hiring (or firing) decisions. But when the colloquialism implies a mandate and is applied to all kinds of situations, it obscures how business *is* personal and thus allows us to exclude people's needs from all of our business deliberations. In other words, when compartmentalization, essentialism, and abstraction become substitutes for deeper reflection on ethical conduct, they prevent us from seeing important connections between varied situations, from understanding ethical pursuits in process, and from seeing how lived experience should be in constant conversation with ethical theory (however formal or informal). In this closing chapter, we would like to revisit three sets of core ideas from this book. We will then return to each of the domains we have discussed—work, professions, organizations, and markets.

The first set of core ideas concerns ethics. At its heart is the need for ongoing engagement with ethics in our work and in our lives. Typically, people position ethics as a sort of grand regulative ideal, or more colloquially, as a kind of utopia. This is one reason that George's students (discussed in the preface) were reluctant to engage the topic of ethics in the first place; they saw ethics as unrealistic, constraining, or isolating. This is also why business and communication students regularly show little interest in ethics courses and view compassion as largely irrelevant to the world of commerce (though, encouragingly, a 2009 *New York Times* article highlighted the efforts undertaken by MBA students at top programs such as Harvard and Columbia to integrate ethics into their education above and beyond one course in the curriculum; 20 percent of Harvard's 2009 MBA class signed the voluntary, student-led ethics pledge, "The M.B.A. Oath" [Wayne, 2009, May 29]). And even though these students held fast to their concerns about living moral lives, ethics seemed to belong to a distant universe. To the contrary, ethics lives as a fundamental and compelling feature of everyday life that is interwoven with issues of how we work, how we treat others, and how we strive to make the little societies we inhabit better while finding our best place within them. We are suggesting a complete reorientation toward ethics, with people not so much avoiding unethical acts as embracing ethical pursuits.

The second sets of core ideas concerns communication. As demonstrated in this book, communication has an ethical inherency. Likewise, we orient our communication to promote reflection, to question assumptions, and to raise paths to betterment that are often submerged in the culture at large. Because our ethical imagination is shaped and limited by how we speak (or don't speak) of ethics, it is crucial that we consider new ways to introduce, highlight, and transform ethical practice. If we talk of ethics as a burden, a cost, or an exception to a rule, then we are unlikely to think about ethics until we are confronted by blatant misdeeds. If we relegate the application of ethics to special cases or refer to ethics only when we are in trouble, then we miss the ways that ethics are part of the fabric of our lives. If we describe ethics as work, mainly using the negative sense of the word, we will miss opportunities for inspiration and fulfillment. With regard to ethical practice, communication is central.

The third and final set of core ideas concerns professional life, that the professional is the personal. Our innumerable actions, taken at the behest of the innumerable roles assumed in a lifetime (sometimes including that of a "professional"), ultimately contribute a single, aggregate identify. Our single lifetime *is* the real world. Rather than conceding that demonstrating ethics at work is "unrealistic," we insist that an ethical view of work, professions, organizations, and the market is the ultimate form of realism. Simply put, society doesn't work well any other way. If the economic collapse of 2008 taught us nothing else, it certainly showed that illusions, in this case the assertion that the market needs no regulation, can lead a lot of people astray. Despite our faith in that particular market illusion, trusting in the truthfulness of that assertion, we created a market that failed even to serve strict financial objectives, let alone social goals. This is precisely why the market is being reevaluated in many parts of the world: in the form that it has commonly taken since the late 1970s, it is neither as efficient nor as wondrous as had been assumed. By focusing our attention on how we talk about ethics, especially in our professional and work lives, we move ethics from the edges of our personal awareness and what we conventionally call the "real world" and into a central place of consciousness.

Now, from *that* central place, let us consider how ethics, communication, and work are interrelated, before turning to consider how a transformation in our view of ethics might look and sound, across the domains of work, profession, organization, and market. We begin by rethinking just what we mean when we talk about ethics.

Hints of a New Perspective on Professional Ethics

The heart of the approach to ethics that we have outlined in this book seeks not to offer a guide of how (not) to think or act when encountering specific ethical dilemmas, but instead to open up the question of ethics itself, by challenging how we speak about ethics and, how we, consequently, conceive of its potentialities in our work and lives. Our point is not to be pre/proscriptive, except in a very broad sense. Instead, we are most concerned with the status we accord ethics in our professional lives, and that means starting with questions about how we think and talk about ethics, if and when we do so. For example, while higher education training for business and other careers now routinely includes ethics, particularly ethical decision-making routinely faced in particular career paths, rarely, if ever, do we discuss career choice itself as an ethical endeavor. Although professional schools may increasingly pay attention to issues such as legal or medical ethics, colleges and universities rarely provide students with the space and the tools to consider, from an ethical perspective, the decision to become a lawyer or a doctor in the first place. Without thus enlisting the help of ethics, our efforts to solve problems on an issue-by-issue basis are likely to remain isolated and ultimately unsatisfying. What's more, unless we release ethics from its confinement and invite it into the living room of our lives, we are not going to see how it relates to our ultimate happiness, as individuals and as a society. This book is about reframing ethics—rethinking our common mythology of ethics—so that we can flourish in our work and in other spheres of our lives.

First, ethics are not just about specific decisions but about entire ways of being and doing. When organizations promote their own standards, as in ethics codes, we find ourselves zeroing in on particular issues, such as conflicts of interest, disclosure, and the integrity of accounting procedures. All this is fine, but we also need a broader vision of the roles of ethics at work. The Wall Street Journal's column "Second Acts" features this wider vision, sharing stories of people who have left one job for another, and have done so with the kind of ethical deliberation we are advocating (even if they wouldn't recognize their decisions as ethical in this fashion). Sometimes these profiles feature workers who were deeply dissatisfied with their careers, leaving to find work that speaks to their passions; others feature workers who, confronted by changes in their industry, avail themselves of the opportunity to discover more meaningful work. In other cases, the profiles feature workers, such as Susanne Lyons, the marketing executive behind the "Life Takes Visa" campaign, who alter their work situation not out of frustration or desperation, but rather to better fit their evolving sense out of what they want out of life (Garone, 2008). The "Second Acts" stories remind us of the fundamentally ethical nature of work as a "calling," which, as the writer Thomas Moore (2008) observes, should not be seen as fixed and unchanging but rather as flexible and "polycentric." In other words, we ought to rise to the ethical imperative of continually reflecting on the role of work in our lives, and making adjustments—big or small—based on those reflections.

Second, ethics are not just about explicit attention to moments of ethical dilemma but also about situations in which the role of ethics isn't initially apparent. "Just a Job" and other colloquialisms about work (discussed in chapter 3) share an implicit intent to define us out of ethical situations. Each tries to mark the work world as a place where ethics applies rarely, if ever. As Kenneth Burke (1963) and many other theorists of language have taught us, we define things in terms of what they are not rather than what they are. Our common language for ethics is no exception. Thus, when we attempt to define the scope of an ethical situation, we do so by talking about what's out of scope rather than what's in scope. That's what such colloquial expressions as "It's not personal" or "It's just a job" do: they displace ethics to some other domain of our lives. To put the matter in terms of time rather than space, we might say that ethics becomes the thing we get to when we've taken care of all our other business; that is, except when a shocking breach of standards or a scandal shakes up our priorities. In other words, by marking only certain problematic moments as distinctly, we implicitly make the argument that the "rest" of our lives isn't the space or place to talk ethics.

Third, ethics are not "work" but certainly they are *about* work. Ethics and ethical conversation and judgments are not things we add to our lives because we have no choice, as when we find ourselves in moments of quandary. Rather, ethics are bound up with our pursuits of well-being, happiness, and our roles in the world. In *The Division of Labor in Society*, Durkheim (1964) asked, Of what purpose, ultimately, is our elaborate system of work and its various forms, if not to serve individual and collective happiness? He was careful, however, to caution against reducing happiness to the "sum total of pleasure" (p. 188), arguing that the increasing specialization of the modern work system has often detracted from levels of happiness. This is why, for example, Durkheim sees suicide as a distinguishing feature of civilization. Here, Durkheim's distinction suggests the notion of *eudaimonia* as an experience deeper and more robust than fleeting moments of pleasure. In other words, without a holistic view of ethics that both extends to our work and connects work with the "rest" of our lives, the possibility for human flourishing quickly begins to recede.

Fourth, ethics are not just about the heroic but also concern the ordinary. Perhaps because we predominantly view ethics as pertinent only in moments of quandary, we have a tendency to view ethical acts as heroic acts, as instances where, against overwhelming pressure, the ethical actor chooses to do the "right thing" (e.g., in the film *Schindler's List*). If, however, ethics is about the stream of life rather than just its turbulent moments, we will find ethics in the mundane as well. Consider the 2007 film *Lars and the Real Girl*. Set in a small town, the film tells the story of Lars Lindstrom, a socially awkward and emotionally troubled man who orders a sex doll named Bianca from an adult Web site. Lars introduces her to his brother Gus and sister-in-law Karin as if she were a Christian missionary from Brazil, his Internet-dating "girlfriend." Concerned, they take him to see a local doctor, also a psychiatrist, who convinces Lars to bring Bianca in weekly for her "health problem" to secretly arrange weekly therapy sessions for Lars. As a part of Lars's therapy, the doctor asks Gus and Karin to play along, treating Bianca as if she were real; soon the whole town is playing along as well, taking Bianca on shopping outings and to school board meetings. Eventually, Bianca "dies" and Lars emerges transformed, healed from the earlier trauma of his parents' death and ready to live a fully adult life, thanks to the mundane kindness of his family and community, who played along with his self-deceit until he was ready to let it go.

There are, of course, instances that fall between or blend the heroic and the mundane. Consider this powerful example related to a colleague by her friend: During the political repression and accompanying "disappearances" in Argentina in the late 1970s, the state police went to every school to examine schools records to identify and sometimes remove students who actively protested the dictatorship. In one high school, there was a capable but bureaucratic and not particularly well-liked principal. It was recently discovered that the principal made the decision to go to the school in the middle of the night and burn down the building, and with it all the students' records. This is a case of what might be called banal heroism, yet the situation marked a difficult ethical dilemma, especially for a rules-oriented administrator. The point is that we find ethics across the range of human activities, from the exceptional to the everyday.

Fifth, "just a job" becomes "just jobs," implying justice on all levels. As we move toward a richer notion of the roles of work in society, we start to think about the "justice" of various types of jobs and professions themselves. We mean this in both the sense of how the work is done and what the work is. Here, the work of groups like Jobs with Justice (see jwj.com), a nonprofit organization that seeks to link workers' rights campaigns with other pressing community issues, is instructive for the manner in which it encourages us to think about the deep connections between work itself and its context.

Similarly, Urban Habitat offered a 2007 special issue of its journal Race, Poverty, and the Environment entitled "JUST Jobs? Organizing for Economic Justice" (see B. J. Clarke, 2007), discussing the relationship between national and local economic policies and the quality of working life. Of course, one does not have to have as deep a commitment to social activism as Jobs with Justice or Urban Habitat to realize the impact of speaking about work in terms of "just jobs": all that is required is a greater sensitivity to the broader social implication of work.

All of these ideas lead us toward the revival and reformulation of Aristotelian virtue ethics, embracing the notion of human flourishing as the ultimate goal for both individuals and society. At the same time, we are interested in the unexplored connection between Aristotle's Ethics (2002) and his Rhetoric (1991) because he understood deeply that how issues are formulated and presented bears heavily on how compelling they will be for various audiences. Aristotle's key term for this was "persuasion," but he would be quite comfortable with the discussion of "framing" in politics and other arenas today.

Virtue ethics takes a long view of ethical issues, framing them not as merely momentary or episodic concerns but rather as issues relevant across all domains of life and one's entire lifespan. Importantly, the notion of lifespan can be applied to an organization, profession, or a society just as readily as to an individual. From this perspective, ethics involves process as much as it involves points of reference. Virtue ethics can help us reframe specific ethical decisions within a wider context, allowing us to ask, What does it mean to do ethics? Virtue ethics provides the "master reframe" (as we explained in chapter 2 and consider further below), encouraging us to ask probing questions about ourselves, who we are and the lives we would like to lead in the interest of truly flourishing. Here, both Appiah (2008) and Nussbaum (1999) argue that it is a mistake to read virtue ethics as a view at odds with deontological or teleological approaches. For Appiah, this was the error made by the advocates of the mid-twentieth-century revival of virtue ethics, who sought a return to Aristotelian thinking as a clear alternative to ethics of duty or consequence.

From a traditional standpoint, each major theory offers a question for the agent who is confronted with an ethical dilemma. Deontology asks, "What is my duty?" Teleological ethics probe, "What are the likely consequences of my actions?" And the traditional view of virtue ethics considers, "What would a virtuous person do?" Such a narrow casting of the role for virtue ethics misses the mark and diminishes its potential. Rather than offering a different question to choose from, the question of virtue ethics is of an entirely different magnitude: not one of acting, but rather one of functioning and being. As Appiah puts it, the "distinctive contribution" of virtue ethics is its "recognition that what we *are* matters for human flourishing as well as what we *do*"(p. 64).

Put another way, a virtuous person may sometimes apply a teleological approach, and other times a deontological approach; perhaps switch between kinds of moral agents, that is, the decider, the refiner, or the absolutist; or reconsider the application of other ethical features. Jan Steutel and David Carr (1999), in the introduction to their book on virtue ethics and moral education, note how virtue ethics complements other ethical systems. They observed that Kant himself "offers an account of virtue as a kind of resistance to the internal forces opposing moral attitude or will." They continue, "In brief, the virtuous person is depicted as the one with sufficient strength of mind to obey the moral law in the teeth of counter-inclinations" (p. 6). So, even when we think we're relying on internal values for our motive (as in the categorical imperative), as human beings we still rely on moral wisdom to hold us to that motive. It is with this observation that we can discount the criticism that virtue ethics is too abstract, that it fails to offer codified principles. That criticism has to do with its focus on ethics education rather than moral particulars. It is not surprising, then, that it would be perceived as abstract. Its focus on education is another reason that it complements rather than replaces consequentialist and deontological ethical theories. Each helps us see certain elements of a situation so we may better act out life.

Let's return to the experience of the classroom for a moment. In more than a decade of teaching courses on communication and work life, George has found that one of the real attractions for students is the research done on happiness. We have argued (in chapter 2) that if you had presented the same material in, say, the 1970s, not as many people would have taken the subject seriously. Now, it seizes everyone's attention. In fact, some of the most somber educational moments (for the three of us who teach) occur when we present the findings on individual and societal happiness. Why? Well, we would guess that one big reason is that a lot of people are questioning the meaning of their own lives and not necessarily taking for granted the traditional messages about happiness, worth, and success in today's world. In other words, by engaging them in discussions about happiness, we've found students from many walks of life willing to talk about such issues as the limits of the market, the dissatisfactions associated with a consumer lifestyle, the downsides of being a high-status professional, and the compromises that our employers often demand of us. The point here is not to bring students around to a particular policy position—or simply to depress them with talk about happiness not found—but to open up new avenues to consider how individual pursuits are connected to a larger whole. For our purposes, part of the task is to unite Aristotle's ancient ideas, with our ethical being in the present-day world. This is a reframing, or recovery, of ethics that transcends tired debates about self-interest versus altruism (as if one or the other could be somehow removed from human nature).

As we approach the end of our book, you may be left wondering what to do with the arguments and critiques we've outlined here. After all, compared to more traditional approaches to business, workplace, and professional ethics, ours has steered clear of offering ready-made prescriptions for working through ethical dilemmas. We suggest departing from situation-based "fast and frugal" moral heuristics (Appiah, 2008). Instead, we advocate an approach that anchors us where we can more fully consider how our actions fit with our broader understanding of how we would like to live our lives and what types of people we wish to be. So, rather than being devices that help us act in that cluttered, hectic, and confusing world while simultaneously reinforcing that world's sense of disconnection, isolation, and chaos, ethics becomes a touchstone to help us make greater sense of that world and our place in it.

In essence, what we are asking you to do is to consider ethics not as a solution to a problem but rather as an issue in itself. We're speaking of a more complete and positive sense of ethics, related more closely to puzzle solving than to crisis management. In this regard, we're again influenced by the advice of Slavoj Žižek (2008b) who warns against the rush to act when confronted with the urgency of a problem. Žižek's particular concern is with the problem frame "Every x [seconds/minutes] a y is z"—a frame that presents large social problems as small and immediate concerns. The problem with such a framing is that it encourages us to act immediately; after all, if we wait another x seconds, another y will be z'd. We then rush to solutions without fully understanding the problem. Our view of ethics parallels this argument: if ethics for us exists only in the moment-by-moment decision-making that responds to crises and quandaries, we don't develop a greater understanding of life as an ethical enterprise.

There's a second sense in which Žižek's observation speaks to the ethical approach we've advocated here. After all, in the over-the-top guilt-inducing nature of advertisements employing the xyz frame (the "every x seconds a child dies from z in Africa" genre of advertisements is a particularly egregious example), we can find the seeds of the same reluctance to engage ethics that we found in George's students and that served as the impetus for this book. When one is guilt-tripped to do the "right thing," she may do it but be far less likely to feel good about doing it than she would if she had decided of her own to do it. Rather than viewing ethics as exerting pressure to act in the moment, we instead suggest it be viewed in a longer-term, more contemplative mode as addressing broader questions about the kinds of people we want to be and the lives we'd like to lead, individually and collectively. In other words, we encourage a view of ethics that moves away from moral admonition and toward something that we engage, questions that we *want* to answer rather than *have* to answer. We want to get to a place where ethics is not work.

How Do We Get There from Here?

The subtitle for the international best-selling book *The 7 Habits of Highly Effective People* (Covey, 1989) is "Restoring the Character Ethic." Stephen Covey writes that success comes from learning and integrating principles into your basic character. He acknowledges Aristotle, who much earlier detailed the importance of habits in developing excellence in learning (Aristotle, 2002, pp. 111–13). Not surprisingly, we learn by consciously doing, something pointed out to us by artists, people we normally think of as "being moved" to create. The choreographer Twyla Tharp (2003), the writer Graham Greene (Hurn & Jay, 1997), and the photographer Josef Koudelka (Hurn & Jay, 1997) developed skills in order to succeed in the respective art forms to which each was called. Their success in their respective callings combines learned skills with the artists' innate nature. Tharp had to dance, Greene had to write, and Koudelka had to photograph. As noted in chapter 2, *phronesis*, or practical wisdom, provides the judgment necessary to balance reason and emotion. This wisdom comes from experience: we learn, or habituate ourselves (Dunne, 1999), to best apply ourselves through our virtues. Thus our virtue reflects our habits. As Aristotle notes, "It does not make a small difference whether people are habituated to behave in one way or in another way from childhood on, but a very great one; or rather, it makes all the difference in the world" (Aristotle, 2002, p. 112).

We mention habits because the ultimate effect of the suggestions that follow is directly related to taking them; knowing them is not enough.

Widening the Frame of Ethics

If we return for a moment to George's account of his students' responses to the terms "ethics" and "morality," we find that one way to explain the students' reluctance to engage ethics is by noting the typically negative way ethics is portrayed. That is, if ethics is a separate sphere one enters only when in trouble, it is not surprising that, under normal circumstances, most people don't want to go there. Here, we can rely upon the sociolinguist George Lakoff's ground-breaking work (2008) on the political effect of linguistic frames. A frame is a cognitive and linguistic device with which we approach an issue or a problem. It can be something as simple as thinking of one political party as "behind the times," or as complicated as considering "technology"—which itself is composed of a bundle of factors—as a solution to human problems. Lakoff's essential argument is that you cannot beat a particular frame or argument by arguing within it because in doing so you are always reinforcing that frame. For example, if the discussion is framed as being about tax "relief"—a term both major political parties in the United States regularly use—a big part of the debate is already lost. After all, who wouldn't want relief from an implied burden? In our case, if ethics is predominantly framed as a cost, as a problem, as an "add on," its negative aspects are reinforced. Nobody wants to confront these things unless and until forced to do so. In this sense, the definition of ethics that George heard in 1993 from a prominent business ethicist makes sense: "Acting ethically at work is determining where your legal responsibilities lie and then going one centimeter beyond that." Such views narrowly frame ethics as compliance, focusing on the technical adherence to rules and showing no concern for the ethical principles reflected by the rules.

As we consider both how ethics in general is framed and how people talk about and work through specific ethical decisions, these aspects of language and imagery are especially valuable. In other words, these are linguistic features that we should notice as much in everyday talk and in films and on Web sites as we do in academic settings.

First, we should note key terms, their ambiguities and their uses. A common term like "efficiency" may seem innocent enough, and, for most people hearing it, it certainly doesn't call ethics to mind.

Yet, efficiency, with its many definitions, partly involves the question of which resources, including time, we privilege, and how we use them (Barnard, 1968). Framing a colleague's proposal as "inefficient" is an attempt to stifle it; still, we seldom stop to consider what exactly is meant by "efficiency" in a given case, whether the perspective is short-term or long-term, and whether it is linked to satisfaction with the results. What does it really mean, for instance, to efficiently deliver services such as education, counseling, and health care, let alone to nurture efficiently relationships with coworkers, colleagues, collaborators, clients, and even competitors? Surely there are different logics of efficiency for different types of work.

Second, we should actually trace out the implications of aphorisms and folk wisdom, calling into question what normally passes for common sense. As we've argued, such talk can have profound implications for how it shapes our view of the world, but the everyday nature of such talk often leaves us blind to those implications. Colloquialisms like "It's not personal, it's business" are ubiquitous but often unseen in our discourse about work. Consider, for example, a scene from the 2009 DreamWorks animated film Monsters vs. Aliens. Having commandeered the video screens of a Dr. Strangelove–like war room, the alien Gallaxhar proclaims to the assembled political and military leaders: "Humans of earth: My quest has led me to your planet. Give it to me now! [pause] You should in no way take this personally. It's just business." It's not this particular appearance of the expression that we find remarkable; that's just a characteristically savvy nod to the film's adult audience. What is important here is the broadcast of this expression to young children. They will grow up having heard the phrase repeated so many times that it will become for them a mythological given, and limit their ethical perspective. The commonness of such expressions, then, makes it difficult to ask questions about the commonsense view of work and the business world that they present, yet it is precisely such "common" sense that we ought to be questioning.

Third, we should reflect on both our own and others' typical narratives, especially the excuses and justifications offered for unexpected or questionable actions. Here we need to listen across episodes and messages to discern patterns of penetrating narratives and accounts of praise and blame, and to see their patterns. Consider, for instance, the appearance in English of the term "NIMBY" (the acronym for "not in my back yard"). The 2008 *Oxford*

English Dictionary argues that the term made its first appearances in 1980 in articles in *Forbes* and the *Christian Science Monitor*, where it was used to denote "an attitude ascribed to persons who object to the siting of something they regard as detrimental or hazardous in their own neighbourhood, while by implication raising no such objections to similar developments elsewhere." The term has gained widespread popularity as a pejorative highlighting the ethical stance underlying convenient opposition to issues ranging from where to site hazardous-waste facilities (Portney, 1991), social services for the sick and homeless (Takahasi, 1998), and bioterrorism research labs (R. Smith, 2008). NIMBY is a convenient shorthand for the way people compartmentalize their ethics by agreeing with an issue or project in principle yet rejecting the same project when it affects them directly: the expression, and others like it, draws our attention to an ethical pattern that we would not have seen, or seen so clearly, otherwise.

Fourth, we should attend to the possibilities for shifts in preferred metaphors and the rise of alternative myths. As we've argued, ways of speaking about ethics through metaphors and narratives have a profound influence on our very conception of ethics, and thus how we conceive of the possibilities of acting ethically. This is why myths are necessarily influential but not necessarily delusional. We should be keenly aware of opportunities to shift our metaphors and narratives in ways that reveal new ethical prospects. Consider, for instance, the book *The Lazy Way to Success: How to Do Nothing and Accomplish Everything* by the entrepreneur Fred Gratzon (2003), who argues that success is a *process* rather than a goal (2008). Gratzon's work is interesting within the genre of business self-help literature for its explicitly calling attention to communication. For example, Gratzon begins his book by asking, "If work is such a good thing, why is it called a grind? Why is the worker referred to as a stiff? And the boss, a slave driver? The overall work environment, a rat race where, heaven forbid, dogs eat dogs? Why? Because work stinks, that's why" (2003, p. 24). Gratzon's arguments hinge on playful redefinitions of "work" and "laziness," where work becomes doing that which you do not want to do, and laziness is not doing it. Gratzon, in effect, positions *laziness* as a new term for *work* that you love rather than dread. If taken too literally, Gratzon's arguments seem rather facile; what they drive at, however, is the power of our predominant metaphors to shape our perspectives, and our ability to change perspective by changing how we talk.

Is Virtuousness Good (for) Business?

In the fields of management, organizational behavior, and leadership, virtue ethics has received growing attention in the last decade (e.g., Ciulla, 2005). This attention has coincided with scholarly and popular interest in the causal relationship between what's been called "corporate social responsibility" or "corporate social performance" and firms' fiscal performance. For management theorists, the uptick in interest hasn't done anything to clarify the best path to successful and moral enterprise. While some might decry the fact that all this theorizing and research hasn't resulted in a perfect picture of the virtuous leader, member, or organization, we suggest, as do others, that recent work demonstrates the complex and unexpected nature of developing collective moral agency (Tomasi, 1991). It also gives us a chance to reflect on how these four features of language can be used to assess and address ethics in business organizations.

Many authors have attempted to generate data that demonstrates unequivocally the relationship between virtuous organizational and professional behavior and fiscal performance, yet a definitive answer remains elusive. Theoretically, businesses capitalize on social needs, meeting those needs with a product or service—provided for a fee that generates profit, of course. As our discussion in chapter 6 demonstrates, mention of the market relationship between persons and firms usually concerns amorality. Because research remains inconclusive, it is best to recognize that ethical practice and economic activity can be, but are not necessarily, in tension with one another (Margolis & Walsh, 2003). Plus, it is necessary to realize that economic responses to social problems aren't inherently the best options. This is particularly true because of the variance not only across and within organizations but also across time and cultures (Svensson & Wood, 2003). Within limits, what is ethical and virtuous is relative—to the people involved and to the encompassing culture and collectivity. Still, authors such as Arjoon (2000) say that ethics and virtuousness are the ongoing "business of business" (p. 159). But it is also true that such guiding questions can divert attention from the fact that capitalist enterprises in capitalist markets are, in fact, rewarded most obviously for their pursuit of profit (Crook, 2005). Here's the rub: we might be too relativistic (in a way, abstracting ethics) when we say that ethics change in various contexts and across time, but we might be too myopic (essentializing ethics) when we assert either that virtuousness is the sole goal of an organization or that it is unrelated to its core purpose.

Business theorists' response has been to put virtue in conversation with other perspectives (as noted in chapter 2). Earlier work on business and management ethics was often centered on right and wrong acts, and adherence to the rules governing conduct, with little consideration of how people create and maintain social bonds (Dobson, 2007). Combining concern with action and with agency is the virtue ethicists' task, and it requires recognizing that people are *always* enacting ethics—even in compartmentalizing it *out* of the world of business, as if one could be a good business*person* without being a good person (Whetstone, 2001). But why must a business organization be concerned with the development of virtue? One reason is that corporations and entrepreneurial firms are now the most significant institutions in the world, where some of society's most important decisions are made (Deetz, 1992). As such, these organizations adopt linguistic frames and their accompanying trends, and propagate them as they wield their considerable economic, political, and social power. How leaders in these organizations frame and conduct conversations about ethics is important well beyond the boundary of business activity.

What's more, these processes have been heavily researched, and the results can be frightening. Empirical studies have demonstrated that those at the highest levels of business organizations tend to have substantial personal and demographic similarities. This means that the folks at the top are likely from the same groups and express similar types of preferences (what social scientists would call "value homogeneity"). Moreover, those business leaders in the top hierarchical ranks are also more likely to score highly on measures of social dominance orientation, meaning that they are more willing to believe that the dominance of one group over others is natural or necessary in society (Sidanius, Pratto, & Mitchell, 1994). High social dominance orientation has been shown to dispose people to racist, sexist, and other biased attitudes (Sidanius & Pratto, 2001). It is now clear that, in business settings, even persons in low-status groups tend to prefer the hiring, retention, and promotion of people affiliated with high-status groups (Umphress et al., 2007). Yes, members of disadvantaged groups in the business world have been shown to routinely act against their own group's interests—and this is often done to meet perceived business demands. This is not good news for advocates of diversity and social justice. Once a domain of work takes on this character, it can become so hostile that underrepresented groups self-select themselves out of the market, profession, or organization (see, e.g., Pratto et al., 1997).

An individual life's transformation into a life of virtuous practice must also mean the transformation of immoral or amoral contexts into moral communities. One path toward redressing this ambiguity and non-virtuousness has been proposed by Heugens, Kaptein, and van Oosterhout (2008). Their treatment of virtue meets organizations "where they are," so to speak. The authors note that it is unreasonable to claim that there is a universally applicable form for virtuous organizations, or that any one goal or act is the principle that dictates an organization's virtuousness. Their model charts a process of change that sees organizations evolve from being tools for ethical action to actual collective moral agents. For Heugens, Kaptein, and van Oosterhout, organizations can become an ethical force in themselves, a moral community evoking an ethical character. They suggest that empirical evidence demonstrates three types of organizations with three different connections between social performance and fiscal performance: nexus-of-contracts organizations, utilitarian organizations, and moral communities. The progression from the first to the last is dynamic, non-linear, and never certain. The chief difference is that the first two types intended to be good for something else, not good in themselves, per se. Still, as we know from experience with the nonprofit sector, organizations that are *premised* upon moral (self-) regulation are not inherently more upright than other organizations (p. 109).

Communication is central in Heugens, Kaptein, and van Oosterhout's model. Founders and top managers are central to the organization's sense of itself and its purpose, and collective moral development can be "crowd[ed] out" of moral conversation by an obsession with business expediency (p. 112). Crafting a vision for moral development must then be the work of employees such as middle managers, according to these authors, whose efforts can "help the organization meet the boundary conditions for collective moral agency" (p. 113). In a sense, this means providing the space for conversations about ethics, and matching moral commitments with what the business is skilled at providing. This simply can't happen in organizational settings like those described above, where people must abandon a sense of self, diversity, and moral purpose to be seen as excelling in their work.

But, again, moral communities aren't the only type of organization that can do good and be a good business. The connection between corporate social performance and corporate fiscal performance, what Heugens, Kaptein, and van Oosterhout (2008) call the "CSP–CFP link," is different for each organizational type. Nexus-of-contracts organizations and utilitarian organizations are often viewed with suspicion when they attempt to do good externally or attempt to control their members. This is because these organizations are generally centered on satisfying different individual interests or are designed to do something *else*. By comparison, moral communities "can...count on an 'authenticity bonus,' which helps them avoid the 'double-edged sword'" of collective ethical action (p. 114). The authors explain that the benefit, or "bonus," of moral action for an organization's image is "unlikely to accrue to nexus-of-contracts and utilitarian organizations" the way it does for moral communities (p. 114).

It may be true that you can "do well by doing good." This seems more likely, though, if the organizational form is something like a moral community, a community premised on ethical conduct. Leaders and laborers alike have to partake in ethical conversations for deeply good business to make good business sense. But, as we've noted throughout this book, there are many contemporary conventions in public discourse about ethics that would push ethics aside or partition it off from the core of our work, our profession, and our social relationships. These tendencies in our communication reinforce practices that make business rationality hostile to ethical reason. These patterns also prevent the transformation of organizations so that they might seek excellence in a more holistic and wholesome way. It is up to us, then, to seek out opportunities to keep alive conversations about ethics and drive them to the very center of who we are as individuals and as groups. Capitalist business organizations can be crafted to respond to such hostility, so that their purpose cannot escape the scope of ethical reflection and so that they are encouraged to take responsibility. Yet, many business organizations communicate that decisions based on ethical wisdom aren't what they "do." It is important to ask, What do we want? Who do we want to be? Do our answers suggest flourishing, or merely profiting? As a tentative response to these questions, in the next section we provide inspirational examples of people and groups that refused to "selectively disengage" (Bandura, 2002) ethics from broader discussions of professional life.

Telling New Ethical Stories

In looking for ways to speak about ethics that can better promote personal and social flourishing, we suggested in chapter 2 the metaphor of *conversation*. This metaphor, for us, has several things going for it. First, it directs our attention to the power of talk, which we usually dismiss as inconsequental. More importantly, conversation emphasizes the dynamic and interactive nature of talk: after all, a conversation is very different than a monologue. In a conversation, there is give and take, ebb and flow; the possibility for change is ever present as participants respond to one another. In short, the metaphor of conversation suggests to us how we might collectively imagine, rather than simply impose, the means by which we might flourish as individuals and as a society.

Much like our discussion of ethics above, the metaphor of conversation works for us at two levels: the conversations we as individuals have, where we navigate ethics in concrete, allegedly real-world situations; and the more metaphorical conversation we as a society have about the meaning and place of ethics in our collective social life. The second set of conversations includes how we relate to theories, but it also refers more generally to how we place ourselves in the ongoing ethical conversations that characterize our society and to how we can be more conscious of those conversations.

In this book, we haven't said much about whistle blowing, although we've offered some examples of it. We pay comparatively little attention to the topic partly because it is the subject of numerous case studies and books. In addition, though, the typical framing of whistle blowing—in terms of spectacular incidents of corruption—can divert our attention from the everyday ways that ethics function (or don't function) at work. Still, whistle blowing is important not only because it represents a challenge to accustomed ways of doing things in business, government, or elsewhere but also because it signals places where the ethical rubber hits the road for individuals and institutions. Whistle-blowing acts are framed in various ways, depending on the particular point of view and the power relations involved. In the United States, there's even an Office of the Whistleblower Protection Program to institutionalize the handling of whistleblowers' actions. The heightened awareness surrounding most acts of whistle blowing highlights the tensions between various spheres, principles, and loyalties.

Whistle blowing, as a specific kind of ethical act, and ethical acts in general, can cut both ways. On one side, we take seriously who we think we are—a devoted father, an empathetic nurse, an honest procurement officer—and act and *express* our ethics accordingly. On the other side, our actions and reflections gather coherence, *incorporating* ethical character. In fact, we always work in these two directions simultaneously. This is a dynamic vision of *ethos*, or character, which Aristotle understood as the sum of impressions of one's depth of character that could be used as resources to persuade others. For Aristotle, the three artistic proofs—*ethos, pathos,* and *logos*—work in concert to create the complete context for the possibilities of persuasion (Grimaldi, 1998). The dynamic of character, or ethos, is intimately bound up with the rationality of the message, or logos, and the appeals to the emotions of the audience, or pathos. (Indeed, these categories hark back to the ethical features discussed in chapter 2.) One's character derives from past situations and is brought into new circumstances; it is neither static nor easily defined. The stories we tell about ourselves and others often represent attempts to settle on distinct roles for characters in our lives, but this tendency doesn't honor how narratives themselves develop and change along with the people who populate them.

Stories were a key mechanism for survival for Victor Frankl as he endured the confines and horrors of a German concentration camp in World War II. While interned, he grappled with the ethical question, "What gives life meaning?" Under a regime of suffering that only those who have experienced it can imagine, this psychiatrist-made-prisoner observed his own experiences and listened to the stories of those around him in order to explain how one can live amid death. As Frankl wrote, "The right example was more effective than words could ever be" (2006, p. 80). The model of the prisoner who finds meaning in suffering then becomes a story that may help other prisoners constitute their beliefs of how to live a life with meaning, that is, how to constitute ethical principles for life.

Throughout the book we have tried to anchor our arguments and analysis in specific examples found everywhere from business to popular culture; to this point, our examples have been primarily negative. That is, we have tended to use examples to illustrate what we see as problematic in the way we talk about ethics. In this section, we aim to point instead to examples illustrating positive changes in conceptions of ethics. We offer these narratives to show how we might actualize the richer sense of ethics we've been advocating, but we should be careful here to note that we don't hold these people and organizations—fictional or real—on a pedestal. They're not heroes; in fact, they are ordinary. Remember that part of our goal is to move beyond our heroes-and-scandals stories of ethical life. Virtue ethics isn't just for the pure, the great, or the mythological. In fact, virtues can be, and most often are, expressed in the most ordinary acts and lives.

Work

Of the domains we've covered, work is undoubtedly the most personal and, as such, the domain over which we have the most immediate control. This is neither to say that we have total control nor to suggest that we can transform our relationship to work in any way we choose. Moreover, as we step into certain cultures of work, with their pressures and their customs, we are guided, if not goaded, to act in specific ways. Certainly, we find ourselves constrained—by financial obligations, such as student loans, mortgages, and consumer debt; by financial and geographic responsibilities to our families; by the apparent limits of our education, class, gender, or race; and so on. It's easy for self-help authors to repeat the refrain that there are no limits, but to us such arguments are useful only as motivating devices. There are very real limits that we cannot control, even though we may hold out hope of transcending them. Such hopes, it is true, are sometimes realized, but that's the exception rather than the rule. Nevertheless, we do have more direct and individual choice over our ethical relationship to our work than we have in non-work domains, which require the increasingly complex coordination of the ethical choices of many, and often anonymous, others.

Even when working within these largely external limits, however, changing our relationship with our work can be quite difficult because of the significant psychological cost. Consider, for instance, the epiphany of the fictional character Andy Millman in the HBO series *Extras*. At the conclusion of the series finale, Andy finds himself on the set of "Celebrity Big Brother" with other C-list celebrities desperate for the fame they need to sustain their careers. Andy reached this point after struggling for years as a non-speaking extra in television and film who finally struck it big with his own BBC sitcom. The catch, for Andy, was that to do so he had to "sell out," trading his artistic vision of a moving, human comedy for one based entirely on the catchphrase, "Are you having a laugh?" *Extra's* second season outlines Andy's struggles with his selling out, as his life changes in his pursuit of fame. When Andy's "fifteen minutes of fame" begins to wane, he turns to reality TV in a desperate last-ditch effort to maintain his celebrity. After suffering the antics of his vapid flatmates, Andy finally has an epiphany, and launches into an impromptu rant against the entire celebrity industry, from producers to paparazzi to audiences, leaving the harshest criticism for himself:

Shame on me. I'm the worst of all, because I'm one of
these people that goes, "I'm an entertainer. It's in my
blood." Yea, it's in my blood because a real job's too hard.
I would love to be a doctor: too hard, I didn't want to
put the work in. Love to be a war hero: I'm too scared. So
I go, "Oh, it's what I do." And I have someone balled out
if my cappuccino's cold, or if they look at me the wrong
way. A friend of mine once said, they said I'd never be
happy because I'd never be famous enough. And they were
right.

Andy comes to realize that the instrumental path he's taken to
achieve career success has done great damage to his character. He's
lived in a manner artificial and foreign to his former self, cater-
ing to celebrities at the expense of his relationships with friends
and colleagues from his similarly humble origins. He voluntarily
changed himself for the benefit of his career, but at a tremendous
cost.

Andy's revelation suggests one way we might transform
our ethical relationship to our work within the process of critical
reflection leading to personal revelation. But what then? Consider
the approach of the Portland, Oregon–based company Vocation
Vacations (see vocationvacations.com). Marketing itself to potential
clients as offering an opportunity to "test drive [their] dream job,"
the business connects individuals contemplating a second career
with mentors working in industries that speak to the client's passion, from bakeries to breweries, and dog training to dude ranching.
Of course, we should be careful to note that at $1,000-plus a pop,
such vacations represent an actual path to vocational transformation
only for those who can afford it. Nevertheless, there's an important
spirit behind the company, a certain adventurousness toward work
through which one can find the exploration of new types of work as
a rewarding vacation. What souvenirs might these working tourists
return with? One hopes they'll cherish more than photographs and
an enhanced understanding on the art of brewing beer. Minimally,
they would have a clearer sense of the duties associated with their
objectives, now having observed an assumed master of the task.
Better still, with this understanding they might better understand
how this work could them take where they wish to go in their lives,
and what doing the work contributes to their identity and their
character.

Profession

The possibility that seemingly idiosyncratic choices and behaviors can spread throughout a profession is at the heart of the case of Dr. Hunter "Patch" Adams. Adams was made famous by the 1998 film based on his career. Patch Adams, in his medical career, has challenged the established ways of doing things by promoting free medical care, by trying to bring physicians down from their pedestals in U.S. society, and by injecting humor into a range of health care services. Patch Adams is an inspiring, charismatic figure, and his life is actually far richer and more complex than was portrayed in the movie, where the story ends with his graduation from the Medical College of Virginia in 1971.

After recovering from a suicidal depression and committing himself to service in his early twenties, Adams set about questioning medical practice, even as he trained for it. From the time he was a medical student, he would occasionally dress up in a clown costume and visit hospitalized children. Adams believes in the healing powers of love, compassion, and especially laughter. This commitment is closely related to his beliefs in sharing information with patients rather than disseminating knowledge, in fostering intimacy and not cool professionalism, and in promoting collaborative approaches to healing and health.

After more than a decade of working at free clinics in Virginia and West Virginia, in 1983 Adams began work on his dream of a free hospital with diverse health services and embodying the ideals discussed above. Adams's organization, the Gesundheit! Institute, supports the development of the hospital and serves to spread transformative visions of health care. Adams regularly travels to Russia to visit children's hospitals and he has been prominent on the U.S. lecture circuit since the film's release.

Adams is probably best known for his humorous approach to health care. A good example of his humor can be seen in his own family interactions. Trying to lift his mother's spirits after her leg was amputated, Adams told her, "Well, you've got just one foot in the grave, Mom." Not just anyone can get away with this, as Adams's friends and colleagues note. Nor has Adams succeeded in getting large numbers of American Medical Association members to try things his way. But, through his example, writings (e.g., Adams, 1998), speeches, workshops, and the movie, Adams has caused many people to think about the deficiencies of a highly professionalized, bureaucratized, and marketized health care system.

Adams's story returns us to several issues: the dark side of what we usually think of as professionalism, the power of reframing what we do at work and with others, and the complex role of agency in ethical pursuits. Because a great deal of Adams's efforts revolve around his own charisma and personal energy (not to mention quirks), it's easy to see his work as unattainably exceptional or, worse, as impossibly eccentric. But this would confine the lessons from Adams's story. Rather, we should recognize that there are multiple paths to appropriate reform of professional practice—even when the profession is resistant to the ideas. Looking to our own experience and initiative, we can reframe and revive ethical practice at work. We can reconceive what it means to practice well our profession. Seeing or creating certain windows of opportunity, we may not become Hollywood material (i.e., a marketable story) but we can make a difference. In this case a profession was partially transformed to focus on the happiness of others.

Organization

One especially poignant, even haunting, example of the kind of ethical transformation we're advocating may be seen in the environmental awakening of Ray Anderson, who was the CEO of Interface, Inc., the world's largest manufacturer of soft-surface tiles. In the 2004 documentary *The Corporation*, and in his own book *Mid-Course Correction* (1999), Anderson tells the story of his "spear in the chest" conversion upon reading Paul Hawken's *Ecology of Commerce* (1994). As the head of a corporation in a notoriously high-polluting industry, Anderson, when asked to present his environmental vision for the company to a group of engineers rethinking the company's environmental practices, realized, to his dismay, that he didn't have one. That realization led to the company's adoption of "Mission Zero," a commitment to eliminate its negative environmental impact by 2020. What this meant, for Interface, was "completely reimagining and redesigning everything [they did]," including how they defined their business ("Sustainability Overview," n.d.). Here, Interface engages in a radically communicative act, changing its self-definition to free it to imagine how it might otherwise be. This imagination has radically changed Interface's organizational practices as it tackles what it terms the "seven fronts" of the challenge of climbing "Mt. Sustainability":

- Eliminate waste
- Benign emissions

- Closing the loop
- Resource-efficient transportation
- Sensitizing stakeholders
- Redesign commerce ("Seven Steps," n.d.)

While only the last two fronts—sensitizing stakeholders and redesigning commerce—are explicitly communication-related, the origins of every item on the list lie in an imaginative act of communication, in a redefinition of what it means to be a business. The reimagining itself is linked to another innovative act of communication: Hawken's book placed "ecology" and "commerce," two terms not normally found near each other, in a relationship to create a space for Interface's transformation.

Of course, Interface's transformation is not simply corporate or organizational. The fact that it drew its inspiration from Hawken's (1994) arguments suggests that Interface sees its organizational role as a change agent in the broader market as well. Its vision statement expresses its goal of effecting change throughout the economy: "To be the first company that, by its deeds, shows the entire industrial world what sustainability is in all its dimensions: People, process, product, place and profits—by 2020—and in doing so we will become restorative through the power of influence" ("Our Vision," n.d., para. 1). Here, we see an organization that is not only aware of itself as a concrete, individual entity, but also embedded in and responsible to a broader "community." Consequently, the organization espouses an obligation to transform not only itself but also its "environment," in both literal and metaphorical senses.

Market

Achieving the broadly environmental changes that Anderson envisioned requires transforming how we conceive of the market itself. The global economic crisis that started in 2008 provoked deep questioning about the nature of the market in the United States and beyond. In considering these issues, we might ask, What would a transformed market look like? One way to begin imagining such a transformed market is by exploring the growing worldwide interest in so-called alternative economies. These initiatives arise outside of free trade regimes and usually apart from taxable commerce as well. Sometimes they appear in direct opposition or as a countervailing force to free trade regimes. At other times, they represent creative responses to local necessity, as when striking workers maintain their support network long after a strike. In every case, a group effort is involved. Unlike the most prominent cases of socially responsible business, these alternative economies rely more heavily on group solidarity than on individual charismatic leadership. The promise of such alternative economies is suggested by their growing popularity, particularly in the wake of the 2008 economic downturn (Dokoupil, 2008). Organizations such as worker cooperatives and micro-finance institutions may also be included here, although these tend to be more closely linked to the conventional economy at large.

The gift economy is deliberately counter-posed to conventional notions of exchange and may well involve the idea of paying it forward to both the community and the recipient, along with counter-conventional expectations for returns. Some gift systems have been inspired by two famous books, both titled *The Gift*, one written by the cultural anthropologist Marcel Mauss (1950/1990), the other by the cultural critic Lewis Hyde (1983). Both books describe the extraordinary (or so it often seems) acts of generosity and kindness that are often obscured in the celebrations of self-interest that characterize our usual conceptions of the economy.

Gift economies, especially involving women, have recently been created on several continents. In Northwest Wales, for example, the Bangor Forest Garden Network promotes "freeconomics," including a give-and-take free shop, a give-and-take warehouse, and community give-and-take events, all aimed at keeping more good stuff out of landfills and recycling centers and instead circulating them in the community for the benefit of local people. South African *stokvels*, or women's gift collectives, periodically distribute to one woman the bounty in a kitty to which the many poor members contribute a small sum. Some *stokvels* now have men as members; there are also men-only *stokvels*. But, traditionally, these associations are by and for women. Members can borrow from this kitty, such as for illness, health, or tuition. The collective works together to help members in times of need (Muthien, 2008).

One of the most elaborate and longest-running cases of a gift economy can be seen in Lima, Peru, where women have been offering free labor in self-managed, self-sustaining kitchens since the late 1970s. Originally developed as direct support to teachers striking against the state, this Federation of Women Organized in Committees of Self-Sustaining Kitchens now counts over 1,800 collective kitchens in its network. Together with several other similar associations, these collective kitchens feed more than 7 percent of Lima's population, or 7.5 million people. There are no paid positions and no designated heads; cooks receive meals as compensation for their work; about 18 percent of meals are sold to paying customers from the surrounding neighborhood. Although there are a few cases of negligence and theft, there is an overwhelming commitment to the enterprise and to the neighborhoods being served. The story of the growth of the collective kitchens is one of example, inspiration, and organizational learning.

Critical to the expansion of the collective kitchens (Zibechi, 2008) has been the linkage of domestic functions to the public sphere. By seeing and discussing their work as part of the general public good, these largely undereducated women have become empowered and now understand their efforts as critical to the maintenance of Peru's economy. "This activity increases their self-esteem and their identification with popular sectors in the neighborhood, in addition to the training that projects offer them" (Zibechi, 2008, p. 1). What began as a small-group effort to respond to situations of need and injustice is now woven into the fabric of Peruvian life. Organizational learning by those persons participating in an enterprise is one way of reframing and reconfiguring the market, returning the notion to its historical roots in social connections, and rescuing it from the atomized nature of contemporary industrial society.

Talking about the *Character* of Self, Work, and Society

Each year in Davos, Switzerland, business and political leaders gather to discuss the global economy. These "Davos Men" (Huntington, 2004), it's fair to say, generally value individual interests and agency over those of the collective; that is, they maintain that the market works best when it is governed least. One might expect that at the 2009 gathering, amid a global economic crisis, the individual and individual responsibility would rule. Yet, examine the following statements by those Davos men and Davos women in attendance: "We are all guilty, and the scope of attrition is large"; "the banking industry [has] something to apologize for"; "There are six billion people on the face of the earth, and probably about five billion participated in what went on" (Copetas & Harper, 2009). One gets the sense that the individual doesn't have agency, that individuals got carried away by the system.

In response to the economic crisis of 2008–9, governments around the world mortgaged the future to socialize the losses brought about by individuals acting in self-interest. And they poured out public funds again to capitalize the continuation of failed financial enterprises. Government leaders justified both actions as necessary for the collective good. President Barack Obama, in his inauguration speech on January 20, 2009, spoke directly to the relationship between individual and collective good: "This crisis has reminded us that without a watchful eye, the market can spin out of control. The nation cannot prosper long when it favors only the prosperous" (para. 16). And yet, the stories of $1,400 wastebaskets, $50 million corporate jet purchases, and billions in bonuses—by, and for the benefit of, Davos men in corporations that had received money from the public purse—bring us full circle—from the economy and back to the domains of work, professionalism, and the market.

We have argued for ethical transformation as necessary to happiness. The transformation we speak of in this book must be at both the individual and collective levels. If bailout money intended to benefit the collective is seen by corporate managers as instead abstract—as capital and as without demands of ethical transformation—then the bailouts will likely fail to have the intended effect. They will pay for the bonuses and lavish parties of the few, rather than be re-circulated in the social corpus for the benefit of all. As another Davos attendee noted, "This moment requires a real humility about the fact that we built these systems and are responsible for them" (Copetas & Harper, 2009). It is in this time of crisis that the personal, the organizational, the professional, and in the market, that the doors of transformative possibilities most easily open. Conversations at every level are critical components of this transformation. Rhetoric reveals, and rhetoric transforms.

Each narrative outlined above is a type of story we might tell about ethics to move it out of a box and fully into our lives. These stories have both their exceptional and their workaday aspects. The point is not to valorize these people, characters, groups, or organizations. Rather, it is to glimpse the broader horizon of possibility for ethics that can come with another look and a reframing of what really counts in our lives and our institutions. This is where ethics and communication meet on the territory of happiness. What, then, can we do to make ethics compelling rather than something that we feel compelled to do; that is, how can we make ethics not seem like "work"? The prevailing way of talking about ethics, especially in professional contexts in the United States, ignores its potential to foster creativity, inspiration, and joy. And this is as true in popular culture as it is in the boardroom as it is in academia. As we listen for new stories to tell about ethics, the idea of character comes to the forefront.

Stories use at least two meanings of the word "character." The first pertains to the actors in the story. We are the main characters in any story about ourselves. The second meaning pertains to the qualities of the character. These may range from heroic qualities, such as those portrayed by Odysseus as he made his ten-year journey home, depicted in Homer's epic poem *The Odyssey*, to mundane attributes, such as those of the traveling salesman Willy Loman, from Arthur Miller's 1949 play, *Death of a Salesman* (1998). Our personal stories change over time, and so does our identity as we reflect upon stories old and integrate stories new. Like these stories, a personal ethical system is always in a state of becoming. Still, we must be careful not to confuse these two meaning of character, lest we start accounting for behavior as arising from character, rather than recognizing that it is character that (partly) reflects behavior. In social psychology, overemphasizing character in narrative accounts is termed a "fundamental attribution error," and character-based ethics are just as prone to this error (Harmon, 1999). However, this myopic affection for essentialized character reflects a shortcoming of the practitioner(s) not a deficiency of virtue ethics. Virtue ethics, with its notion of practical wisdom, highly values accurate perception and comprehension of situations and agents' capacities. To account for behavior by character alone is a form of prejudice.

Another argument against claims that virtue ethics essentializes character is that this second sense of character does not refer to individuals alone; we use it to refer to the character of a culture or a society as well. These two levels—and their characters—are intimately linked, and thus accounts of individual behavior must take into account the society in which individuals operate; essentialized character becomes an illogical account for behavior. After all, we cannot flourish as individuals separate from others who, like us, are striving for excellence. In other words, part of the experience of *eudaimonia* is the struggle for the pursuit of excellence of character by both the collective and the individual. There is a great degree of interdependence between the two levels, where the character of the individual and that of society depend on each other, and as a result, they are reliant on each other to flourish. This perspective returns us to a very old but enduring sense of "integrity," referring to the integral whole of something. In the view of the philosopher and sociologist William M. Sullivan (1995), integrity is what mediates the tensions between personal achievement and social relationship. Integrity is about wholeness, balance, and ongoing reflection—but always in the company of others (even when they aren't actually present to voice their aspirations or concerns). We need to find ways of speaking that help us cooperate in the flourishing of all. It is with such cooperation as the fabric of our everyday individual and collective lives, not only in moments of crisis, that we ultimately find ethics.

References

Abbott, A. 1988. *The system of professions: An essay on the division of expert labor.* Chicago: University of Chicago Press.

Abuse of Iraqi POWs by GIs probed: 60 Minutes II has exclusive report on alleged mistreatment. 2004. *60 Minutes II/CBS News,* April 28, 2004. http://www.cbsnews.com/stories/2004/04/27/60II/main614063.shtml (accessed September 25, 2008).

Adams, P. 1998. *House calls: How we can all heal the world one visit at a time.* San Francisco: Robert D. Reed.

Aden, S. 2005. Protect pro-life druggists. *USA Today,* April 5, 2005, p. 14A.

Agger, B. 2003. *Speeding up fast capitalism: Cultures, families, schools, bodies.* Boulder, CO: Paradigm.

Akieda, M. and S. Sato, producers. H. Koreeda, writer/director. 1998. *After life.* DVD. Tokyo: Engine Film Inc. and TV Man Union.

Alberty, E. 2008. Employee's suit: Company used waterboarding to motivate workers. *Salt Lake City Tribune,* February 27, 2008 (accessed April 20, 2008, from ProQuest database).

Allen, B. J. 1995. "Diversity" and organizational communication. *Journal of Applied Communication Research* 23:143–55.

Allen, B. J. 1996. Feminist standpoint theory: A black woman's review of organizational socialization. *Communication Studies* 47:257–71.

Allen, B. J. 2007. Theorizing communication and race. *Communication Monographs* 74:259–64.

Allen, C. 2008. A study of business networks for responsibility and sustainability in New Zealand. PhD diss., University of Waikato, Hamilton, NZ.

Almond, G. A. 1991. Capitalism and democracy. *Political Science and Politics* 24: 467–74.

Alperovitz, G. 2005. *America beyond capitalism: Reclaiming our wealth, our liberty, and our democracy.* Hoboken, NJ: John Wiley & Sons.

Amid furor, Pentagon kills terrorism futures market. 2003. *CNN: Inside Politics*, July 30, 2003. http://www.cnn.com/2003/ALLPOLITICS/07/29/terror.market/index.html (accessed August 29, 2008).

Andersen, J. A. 2008. An organization called Harry. *Journal of Organizational Change Management* 21: 174–87.

Anderson, J. A., and E. E. Englehardt. 2001. *The organizational self and ethical conduct*. Fort Worth, TX: Harcourt Brace.

Anderson, P. T., writer. 2008. *There will be blood*. DVD. Directed by P. T. Anderson. Los Angeles: Paramount Home Entertainment.

Anderson, R. 1999. *Mid-course correction: Toward a sustainable enterprise: The interface model*. Atlanta, GA: Peregrinzilla Press.

Anielski, M., and J. Rowe. 1999. *The genuine progress indicator: 1998 update. Redefining progress/The nature of economics*. San Francisco, CA: Redefining Progress.

Appiah, K. A. 2005. *The ethics of identity*. Princeton, NJ: Princeton University Press.

Appiah, K. A. 2008. *Experiments in ethics*. Cambridge, MA: Harvard University Press.

Applebaum, H. 1992. *The concept of work: Ancient, medieval, modern*. Albany: SUNY Press.

Applebaum, H. 1995. The concept of work in Western thought. In *Meanings of work: Considerations for the twenty-first century*, ed. F. C. Gamst, 46–78. Albany: SUNY Press.

Arendt, H. 1994. *Eichmann in Jerusalem: A report on the banality of evil*. New York: Penguin.

Arendt, H. 1998. *The human condition*. Chicago: University of Chicago Press.

Aristotle. 1991. *On rhetoric: A theory of civic discourse*. Trans. G. A. Kennedy. New York: Oxford University Press.

Aristotle. 1996. *The politics and the constitution of Athens*. Trans. S. Everson. Cambridge, UK: Cambridge University Press.

Aristotle. 2002. *Nichomachean ethics*. Trans. S. Broadie and C. Rowe. Oxford, UK: Oxford University Press.

Arjoon. S. 2000. Virtue theory as a dynamic theory of business. *Journal of Business Ethics* 28:159–78.

Ashcraft, K. L. 2000. Empowering "professional" relationships: Organizational communication meets feminist practice. *Management Communication Quarterly* 13:347–92.

Ashcraft, K. L. 2007. Appreciating the "work" of discourse: Occupational identity and difference as organizing mechanisms in the case of commercial pilots. *Discourse & Communication* 1:9–36.

Ashcraft, K. L. Forthcoming. Dominance in flight: The cultural production of U.S. airline pilots. Unpublished manuscript, Salt Lake City: University of Utah.

Ashcraft, K. L., and Allen, B. J. 2003. The racial foundation of organizational communication. *Communication Theory* 13:5–38.

Ashcraft, K. L., and D. K. Mumby. 2004. *Reworking gender: A feminist communicology of organization.* Thousand Oaks, CA: Sage.

Aune, J. A. 2001. *Selling the free market: The rhetoric of economic correctness.* New York: Guilford.

Austin, J. L. 1975. *How to do things with words.* Cambridge, MA: Harvard University Press.

Ayer, A. J. 1946. *Language, truth, and logic.* 2nd ed. New York: Dover. Original work published 1936.

Bakan, J. 2004. *The corporation: The pathological pursuit of profit and power.* New York: Free Press.

Bakan, J., writer. 2004. *The corporation.* DVD. Directed by M. Achbar and J. Abbott. Vancouver, British Columbia, CA: Big Picture Media Corporation.

Bakken, T., and T. Hernes. 2006. Organizing is both a verb and a noun: Weick meets Whitehead. *Organization Studies* 27:1599–616.

Ballard, D. I. 2007. Chronemics at work: Using socio-historical accounts to illuminate contemporary workplace temporality. In *Research in the sociology of work: Vol. 17, Workplace temporalities,* ed. R. Rubin, 29–54. Cambridge, MA: Elsevier.

Ballard, R. 2008. An ethnographic and philosophical investigation into patrol officers: Communication ethics as critical work. PhD diss., University of Denver, Colorado.

Bandura, A. 2002. Selective moral disengagement in the exercise of moral agency. *Journal of Moral Education* 31:101–19.

Barley, S. R., and G. Kunda. (2004). *Gurus, hired guns, and warm bodies: Itinerant experts in a knowledge economy.* Princeton, NJ: Princeton University Press.

Barley, S. R., and G. Kunda. 2006. Contracting: A new form of professional practice. *Academy of Management Perspectives* 20:45–66.

Barnard, C. I. 1968. *The functions of the executive.* Cambridge, MA: Harvard University Press. Original work published 1938.

Barrett, R. 1998. *Liberating the corporate soul: Building a visionary organization.* Woburn, MA: Butterworth-Heinemann.

Bartlett, D. L., and J. B. Steele. 2006. *How health care in America became big business—and bad medicine.* New York: Broadway Books.

Bauman, Z. 1989. *Modernity and the Holocaust.* Ithaca, NY: Cornell University Press.

Bauman, Z. 2008. *Does ethics have a chance in a world of consumers?* Cambridge, MA: Harvard University Press.

Baumeister, R. F., and M. R. Leary. 1995. The need to belong: Desire for interpersonal attachments as a fundamental human motivation. *Psychological Bulletin* 11:497–529.

BBC News. 2004. Bush appoints Texas ally to key post. *BBC News,* November 10, 2004. http://news.bbc.co.uk/2/hi/americas/4000679.stm (accessed November 13, 2008).

Beder, S. 2000. *Selling the work ethic: From the Puritan pulpit to corporate PR.* London: Zed.

Belk, R., writer. 2007. *Personal organizers*. DVD. Produced and directed by R. Belk. Salt Lake City: University of Utah.

Bellah, R., R. Madsen, W. M. Sullivan, A. Swidler, and S. M. Tipton. 1985. *Habits of the heart: Individualism and commitment in American life*. Berkeley and Los Angeles: University of California Press.

Bellah, R., R. Madsen, W. M. Sullivan, A. Swidler, and S. M. Tipton. 1991. *The good society*. New York: Vintage.

Berenson, A., and D. B. Henriques. 2008. S.E.C. says it missed signals on Madoff fraud case. *New York Times*. December 16, 2008, http://www.nytimes.com/2008/12/17/business/17madoff.html (accessed January 10, 2009).

Berry, W. 1993. *Sex, economy, freedom and community*. New York: Pantheon.

Berry, W. 2000. *Life is a miracle: Essays against modern superstition*. Washington, DC: Counterpoint.

Beyer, J. M., and D. Nino. 1999. Ethics and cultures in international business. *Journal of Management Inquiry* 8:287–97.

Bigelow, G. 2005. Let there be markets. *Harper's*, May 2005, pp. 33–38.

Billig, M., and K. Macmillan. 2005. Metaphor, idiom and ideology: The search for "no smoking guns" across time. *Discourse & Society* 16:459–80.

Bing, S. 2002. *What would Machiavelli do? The ends justify the meanness*. New York: Collins Business.

Bird, K., and M. J. Sherwin. 2005. *American Prometheus: The triumph and tragedy of J. Robert Oppenheimer*. New York: Knopf.

Bohm, D. 2003. *On dialogue*. Ed. L. Nichol New York: Routledge.

Boihem, H., director/producer. 1997. *The ad and the ego*. Rancho Santa Margarita, CA: Parallax Pictures.

Bok, S. 1988. Kant's arguments in support of the maxim "Do what is right though the world should perish." *Argumentation* 2:7–25.

Borge, C. 2007. Basic instincts: The science of evil. *ABC News*, January 3, 2007. http://abcnews.go.com/Primetime/story?id=2765416&page=1 (accessed September 13, 2008).

Borsook, P. 2000. *Cyberselfish: A critical romp through the terribly libertarian culture of high tech*. New York: PublicAffairs.

Boselovic. L. 1994. Steeled for the future: Weirton Steel enters its second decade with CEO Elish at the helm and employees at the rudder. *Pittsburgh Post Cazette*, September 18, 1994, Business, p. C-1.

Boss, S. 2007. Even in a virtual world, stuff matters. *New York Times*, September 9, 2007, Business, p. 1.

Bourdieu, P. 1972. *Outline of a theory of practice*. Cambridge, UK: Cambridge University Press.

Bordieu, P. 1990. *The logic of practice*. Trans. R. Nice. Stanford, CA: Stanford University Press.

Boushey, H., and C. E. Weller. 2005. What the numbers tell us. In *Inequality matters: The growing economic divide in America and its poisonous consequences*, ed. J. Lardner and D. A. Smith, 27–40. New York: New Press.

Bouville, M. 2008. Whistle-blowing and morality. *Journal of Business Ethics* 81: 579–85.

Bowe, J. 2007. *Nobodies: Modern American slave labor and the dark side of the new global economy*. New York: Random House.

Boyte, H. 2004. *Everyday politics: Reconnecting citizens and public life*. Philadelphia: University of Pennsylvania Press.

Boyton, L. A. 2002. Professionalism and social responsibility: Foundations of public relations ethics. In *Communication yearbook 26*, ed. W. B. Gudykunst, 230–65. Thousand Oaks, CA: Sage.

Brabham, D. C. 2008. Survey data on motivations, demographics, and professionalism from the member community at iStockphoto.com. Unpublished raw data. http://www.darenbrabham.com/istock.html (accessed April 12, 2008).

Brooks, J. L., M. Groening, A. Jean, I. Maxtone-Graham, G. Meyer, D. Mirkin, M. Reiss, M. Scully, M. Selman, J. Swartzwelder, and J. Vitti, writers. 2007. *The Simpsons movie*. DVD. Directed by D. Silverman. Los Angeles: Twentieth Century Fox.

Brown, M. 1989. Ethics in organizations. *Issues in Ethics* 2. http://www.scu.edu/ethics/publications/iie/v2n1/homepage.html (accessed June 4, 2009).

Brown, M. H. 1990. Defining stories in organizations: Characteristics and functions. In *Communication yearbook 13*, ed. J. A. Anderson, 162–90. Newbury Park, CA: Sage.

Browning, L. D. 1992. Lists and stories as organizational communication. *Communication Theory* 2:281–302.

Bruhn, J. G. 2002. *Trust and the health of organizations*. New York: Kluwer Academic/Plenum.

Buber, M. 2004. *I and thou*. Trans. R. G. Smith. London: Continuum. Original work published 1923.

Burke, K. 1984. *Permanence and change*. Berkeley: University of California Press. Orginal work published 1935.

Burke, K. 1937. *Attitudes toward history*. Berkeley: University of California Press.

Burke, K. 1945. *A grammar of motives*. Berkeley: University of California Press.

Burke, K. 1969. *A rhetoric of motives*. Berkeley: University of California Press. Orginal work published 1950.

Burke, K. 1966. *Language as symbolic action: Essays on life, literature, and method*. Berkeley: University of California Press.

Burke, K. 1970. *The rhetoric of religion: Studies in logology*. Berkeley: University of California Press.

Burke, K. 1973. *The rhetorical situation*. In *Communication: Ethical and moral issues*, ed. L. Thayer, 263–75. London: Gordon & Breach.

Burke, K. 1974. *Philosophy of literary form*. Berkeley: University of California Press.

Burnett, M., and D. Trump, executive producers. 2004. Ethics, schmethics [Television series episode]. *The Apprentice*, January 28, 2004. New York: NBC.

Burr, T. 2008. Top aide politicized judge hires. *Salt Lake Tribune*, July 29, 2008, pp. A-1, 4.

Burrell, G., and G. Morgan. 1979. *Sociological paradigms and organizational analysis: Elements of the sociology of corporate life.* London: Heinemann.

Bush, G. W. 2001. Address to a joint session of Congress and the American people. September 20, 2001. http://www.whitehouse.gov/news/releases/2001/09/20010920-8.html (accessed September 23, 2008).

Bush, G. W. 2006a. Bush: "I'm the decider" on Rumsfeld. *CNN.com*, April 18, 2006. http://www.cnn.com/2006/POLITICS/04/18/rumsfelhttp://www.cnn.com/2006/POLITICS/04/18/rumsfeld (accessed November 14, 2008).

Bush, G. W. 2006b. President's Radio Address. September 30, 2006. http://www.whitehouse.gov/news/releases/2006/09/20060930.html (accessed January 10, 2009).

Butler, J. 1993. *Bodies that matter: On the discursive limits of "sex."* London: Routledge.

Buzzanell, P. M., ed. 2000. *Rethinking organizational and managerial communication from feminist perspectives.* Thousand Oaks, CA: Sage.

Buzzanell, P. M. 2007. Career and work-life survey. Unpublished manuscript, West Lafayette, IN: Purdue University.

Buzzanell, P. M., and S. R. Goldzwig. 1991. Linear and nonlinear career models: Metaphors, paradigms, and ideologies. *Management Communication Quarterly* 4:466–505.

Canary, H. E., and M. M. Jennings. 2008. Principles and influence in codes of ethics: A centering resonance analysis comparing pre- and post-Sarbanes-Oxley codes of ethics. *Journal of Business Ethics* 80:263–78.

Carey, B. 2006. Lady Macbeth not alone in her quest for spotlessness. *New York Times*, September 12, 2006. http://www.nytimes.com/2006/09/12/health/psychology/12macbeth.html?_r=1 (accessed December 15, 2008).

Carr, D. 2007. Thousands are laid off. What's New? *New York Times*, April 2, 2007, pp. C-1, 7.

Carroll, A. B. 1979. A three-dimensional conceptual model of corporate social responsibility performance. *Academy of Management Review* 4:497–505.

Cassirer, E., and C. W. Hendel. 1946. *The myth of the state.* New Haven, CT: Yale University Press.

Castells, M. 1996. *The rise of network society.* Malden, MA: Blackwell.

Cather, W. 2002. *Alexander's bridge.* Mineola, NY: Dover. Original work published 1912.

Chaplinsky v. State of New Hampshire, 315 U.S. 568 (1942).

Charles, M., and D. B. Grusky. 2004. *Occupational ghettos: The worldwide segregation of women and men.* Stanford, CA: Stanford University Press.

Cheney, G. 1982. A field study of organizational identification. Master's thesis, West Lafayette: IN: Purdue University.

Cheney, G. 2004a. Arguing about the "place" of values in market-oriented discourse. In *New directions in rhetorical criticism*, ed. P. Sullivan and S. Goldzwig, 61–88. Thousand Oaks, CA: Sage.

Cheney, G. 2004b. Bringing ethics in from the margins. *Australian Journal of Communication* 31:35–40.

Cheney, G. 2005. The united consumers of America. Or, is there a citizen in the house? Paper presented at the 2nd Annual Humanities Lecture, University of Utah, Salt Lake City, March 2005.

Cheney, G. 2008a. Bureaucracy. In *Encyclopedia of Communication*. Ed. W. Donsbach. http://www.communicationencyclopedia.com/public/ (accessed June 5, 2009).

Cheney, G. 2008b. The cooperatives facing the economic crisis: Responsibilities and opportunities in the future global market. Presentation. Arizmendi Topaketak, Arrasate-Mondragón, Basque Country, Spain. November 27, 2008.

Cheney, G., and K. L. Ashcraft. 2007. Considering "the professional" in communication studies: Implications for theory and practice within and beyond the boundaries of organizational communication. *Communication Theory* 17:146–75.

Cheney, G., L. T. Christensen, T. E. Zorn Jr., and S. Ganesh. 2004. *Organizational communication in an age of globalization: Issues, reflections and practices.* Prospect Heights, IL: Waveland.

Cheney, G., T. E. Zorn Jr., S. Planalp, and D. J. Lair. 2008. Meaningful work and personal/social well-being: Organizational communication engages the meanings of work. In *Communication yearbook 32*, ed. C. Beck, 137–86. Thousand Oaks, CA: Sage.

Chouinard, Y. 2006. *Let my people go surfing: The education of a reluctant businessman.* New York: Penguin.

Christensen, L. T., M. Morsing, and G. Cheney. 2008. *Challenging corporate communications: Convention, complexity, and critique.* London: Sage.

Chugh, D., M. H. Bazerman, and M. R. Banaji. 2005. Bounded ethicality as a psychological barrier to recognizing conflicts of interest. In *Conflicts of interest: Problems and solutions from law, medicine and organizational settings*, ed. D. A. Moore, D. M. Cain, G. F. Loewenstein, and M. H. Bazerman. London: Cambridge University Press.

Ciulla, J. B. 2000. *The working life: The promise and betrayal of modern work.* Pittsburg: Three Rivers Press.

Ciulla, J. B. 2005. The state of leadership ethics and the work that lies before us. *Business Ethics: A European Review* 14:323–35.

Clair, R. P. 1993. The use of framing devices to sequester organizational narratives: Hegemony and harassment. *Communication Monographs* 60:113–36.

Clair, R. P. 1996. The political nature of the colloquialism, "a real job": Implications for organizational socialization. *Communication Monographs* 63:249–67.

Clarke, B. J. 2007. About this issue. *Race, Poverty and the Environment* 14:3.

Clarke, T. 2008. *The last campaign: Robert F. Kennedy and 82 days that inspired America.* New York: Henry Holt.

Clemetson, L. 2007. The racial politics of speaking well. *New York Times*, February 4, 2007, sec. 4, pp. 1–4.

Cloud, D. L. 2001. Laboring under the sign of the new: Cultural studies, organizational communication, and the fallacy of the new economy. *Management Communication Quarterly* 15:259–78.

Code of ethics. 2000. Archived Enron Web page. January 2000. http://www.thesmokinggun.com:80/graphics/packageart/enron/enron.pdf(accessed September 18, 2008).

Cohen, E., and J. Cohen, writers. 2007. *No Country for Old Men*. DVD. Produced and directed by E. Cohen and J. Cohen. Los Angeles: Paramount Vantage.

Cohen, L. G. 2001. Just doing my job. *Journal of General Internal Medicine* 16:501–4.

Collins, B. 2008. Hot commodities, stuffed markets, empty bellies: What's behind higher food prices? *Dollars & Sense* (July/August): 10–12, 21.

Condit, C., and J. L. Lucaites. 1990. *Crafting equality*. Chicago: University of Chicago Press.

Conrad, C. Ed. 1993. *The ethical nexus: Values, communication and organizational decisions*. Norwood, NJ: Ablex.

Conrad, D. 2003. Setting the stage. *Management communication quarterly* 171:5–19.

Cooper, A. 2008. Culprits of the collapse [Television series episode]. *AC360*. New York: CNN.

Copetas, A. C., and Harper, C. 2009. Davos delegates in "denial" as $25 trillion of wealth vanishes. *Bloomberg News*, January 30, 2009. http://www.bloomberg.com/apps/news?pid=newsarchive&sid=abAA1ieh6wTk (accessed January 30, 2009).

Costanza, R., J. Erikson, K. Fligger, A. Adams, A. Christian, B. Atschuler, S. Balter, B. Fisher, J. Hike, J. Kelly, T. Kerr, M. McCauley, K. Montone, M. Rauch, K. Schmiedeskamp, D. Saxton, L. Sparacino, W. Tusinski, and L. Williams. 2004. Estimates of the genuine progress indicator GPI for Vermont, Chittenden County and Burlington, from 1950 to 2000. *Ecological Economics* 51: 139–55.

Cotts, C., K. Burton, and E. Logutenkova. 2009. Credit Suisse urged clients to dump Madoff funds. *Bloomberg News*, January 7, 2009. http://www.bloomberg.com/apps/news?pid=newsarchive&sid=a7Ei7.DM8DHc (accessed January 7, 2008).

Coulehan, J., and P. C. Williams. 2001. Vanquishing virtue: The impact of medical education. *Academic Medicine* 76:598–605.

Covey, S. 1989. *The 7 habits of highly effective people: Restoring the character ethic*. New York: Simon & Schuster.

Cox, A., writer. 1984. *Repo man*. DVD. Directed by A. Cox. Troy, MI: Anchor Bay Entertainment.

Cox, H. 1999. The market as God: Living in the new dispensation. *The Atlantic* (March): 18–22.

Crainer, S. 1998. In search of the real author. *Management Today* (May): 50–54.

Crane, D. 1972. *Invisible colleges: Diffusion of knowledge in scientific communities*. Chicago: University of Chicago Press.

Crook, C. 2005. The good company. *Economist* (January 22, 2005): 3–4.

Csikszentmihalyi, M. 1991. *Flow: The psychology of optimal experience*. New York: Harper & Row.

Cummings, S., and T. Thanem. 2002. Essai: The ghost in the organism. *Organization Studies* 235:817–39.

Daly, H. E. 1977. *Steady-state economics: The economics of biophysical equilibrium and moral growth*. New York: W. H. Freeman.

Daly, H. E. 1996. *Beyond growth: The economics of sustainable development*. Boston: Beacon.

Daly, H. E., and J. Cobb. 1989. *For the common good: Redirecting the economy towards community, the environment, and a sustainable future*. Boston: Beacon.

Damasio, A. R. 1994. *Descartes's error: Emotion, reason, and the human brain*. New York: G. P. Putnam's Sons.

Damon, W. 2008. *The path to purpose: Helping our children find their calling in life*. New York: Free Press.

Davidson, E. A. 2000. *You can't eat GNP: Economics as if ecology mattered*. Cambridge, MA: Perseus.

Deal, T., and A. Kennedy. 1982. *Corporate cultures: The rites and rituals of corporate life*. Reading, MA: Addison Wesley.

Deetz, S. 1992. *Democracy in an age of corporate colonization*. New York: SUNY Press.

de Graaf, J., ed. 2003. *Take back your time: Fighting overwork and time poverty in America*. San Francisco: Berrett-Koehler.

Denhardt, R. B. 1981. *In the shadow of organization*. Lawrence: University Press of Kansas.

Desmond, J. 1995. Reclaiming the subject: Decommodifying marketing knowledge? *Journal of Marketing Management* 11:721–46.

De Waal, F. 2005. *Our inner ape*. New York: Riverhead.

Dickens, C. 2006. *A Christmas carol*. Cambridge, MA: Candlewick. Original work published 1843.

Diener, E., and S. Oishi. 2000. Money and happiness: Income and subjective well-being across nations. In *Culture and subjective well-being*, ed. E. Diener and E. M. Suh, 185–218. Cambridge, MA: MIT Press.

Diener, E., and M. E. Seligman. 2002. Very happy people. *Psychological Science* 131:81–84.

Diener, E., and E. M. Suh, eds. 2000. *Culture and subjective well-being*. Cambridge, MA: MIT Press.

Dirks, K. T., and D. L. Ferrin. 2002. Trust in leadership: Meta-analytic findings and implications for research and practice. *Journal of applied psychology* 874:611–28.

Dobson, J. 2007. Applying virtue ethics to business: The agent-based approach. *Electronic Journal of Business Ethics and Organization Studies* 12. http://ejbo.jyu.fi/ (accessed June 5, 2009).

Dokoupil, T. 2008. A plan for hard times: Print cash. *Newsweek*, December 1, 2008, p. 9.

Donkin, R. 2001. *Blood, sweat, and tears: The evolution of work*. New York: TEXERE LLC.

Douglas, M. 1986. *How institutions think*. Syracuse, NY: Syracuse University Press.

du Gay, P. 2000. *In praise of bureaucracy: Weber, organization, ethics*. London: Sage.

du Gay, P., ed. 2005. *The values of bureaucracy*. Oxford, UK: Oxford University Press.

Dunne, J. 1999. Virtue, phronesis and learning. In *Virtue ethics and moral education*, ed. D. Carr & J. Steutel, 49–63. London: Routledge.

Durkheim, E. 1964. *The division of labor in society*. New York: Free Press. Original work published 1893.

Durkheim, E. 1996. *Professional ethics and civic morals*. London: Routledge. Original work published 1900.

Dylan, B. 1991. Who killed Davey Moore? *The bootleg series*. Vols. 1–3. CD. New York: Sony.

Dzur, A. W. 2008. *Democratic professionalism: Citizen participation and the reconstruction of professional ethics, identity, and practice*. University Park: Pennsylvania State University Press.

Economist. 2008. Trust: The faith that moves Mammon. *Economist*, October 16, 2008. http://www.economist.com/finance/displaystory.cfm?story_id=12436122&fsrc=rss (accessed January 4, 2009).

Edelstein, L. 1966. *The meaning of stoicism*. London: Oxford University Press.

Edminston, B. 2000. Drama as ethical education. *Research in Drama Education* 51:63–84.

Eichenwald, Kurt. 2005. *Conspiracy of fools: A true story*. New York: Broadway.

Emerson, R. W. 1983. *Essays*. Boston: Houghton Mifflin. Original work published 1841.

Emmison, M. 2003. Social class and cultural mobility: Reconfiguring the cultural omnivore thesis. *Journal of Sociology* 39:211–30.

Epstein, E. 2005. Boxer eyes prescription protection. *San Francisco Chronicle*, April 19, 2005, p. A1.

Ewen, S. 1976. *Captains of consciousness: Advertising and the roots of consumer culture*. New York: McGraw-Hill.

Ewen, S. 1984. *All-consuming images*. New York: Basic.

Farrell, C. 2002. The other side of Adam Smith. *Business Week*, November 15, 2002. http://www.businessweek.com/bwdaily/dnflash/nov2002/nf20021115_2141.htm (accessed June 9, 2008).

Faulconbridge, J., and D. Muzio. 2008. Globalization and the professions. *Work, employment and society* 22:7–26.

Ferguson, K. A. 1984. *The feminist case against bureaucracy*. Philadelphia: Temple University Press.

Feuer, L.S., ed. 1959. *Marx and Engels: Basic writings on politics and philosophy*. New York: Anchor.

Fischman, W., B. Solomon, D. Greenspan, and H. Gardner. 2004. *Making good: How young people cope with moral dilemmas at work*. Cambridge, MA: Harvard University Press.

Fish, S. 2008. None of the answers. *New York Times*, August 10, 2008. http://fish.blogs.nytimes.com/2008/08/10/none-of-the-answers (accessed August 10, 2008).

Flader, S. L. 1974. *Thinking like a mountain: Aldo Leopold and the evolution of an ecological attitude toward deer, wolves, and forests.* Madison: University of Wisconsin Press.

Fleming, P., and A. Spicer. 2007. *Contesting the corporation: Struggle, power and resistance in organizations.* Cambridge, UK: Cambridge University Press.

Forster, S. 2005. Pharmacist rebuked. *Milwaukee Journal Sentinel,* April 14, 2005, p. B1.

Foucault, M. 1984. *The Foucault reader.* Ed. P. Rabinow. New York: Pantheon.

Fradon, D. 1992. Corporate leaders gather in a field. *The New Yorker,* June 8, 1992. http://www.cartoonbank.com/product_details.asp?mscssid=XU559BG 3DABU8NDQ2E81PQHB2QKQ0F91&sitetype=1&did=4&sid=28931 (accessed October 9, 2008).

Frankena, W. K. 1973. *Ethics.* 2nd ed. Englewood Cliffs, NJ: Prentice-Hall.

Frankenreiter, D. 2004. Heading home. On *Donavon Frankenreiter.* MP3. Mango Tree, HI: Brushfire Records.

Frankl, V. 2006. *Man's search for meaning.* Boston: Beacon Press.

Franklin, B. 1986. *Poor Richard's almanack: Being the choicest morsels of wisdom, written during the years of the almanack's publication.* White Plains, NY: Peter Pauper. Original work published 1732.

Friedman, M. 1970. The social responsibility of business is to increase its profits. *New York Times Magazine,* September 13, 1970, pp. 32–33, 122, 126.

Fromm, E. 1961. *Marx's concept of man.* New York: Free Press.

Frye, N. 1957. *Anatomy of criticism.* Princeton, NJ: Princeton University Press.

Fukuyama, F. 2006a. After neoconservativism. *New York Times Magazine,* February 19, 2006. http://www.nytimes.com/2006/02/19/magazine/neo .html?pagewanted=all (accessed September 3, 2008).

Fukuyama, F. 2006b. *America at the crossroads.* New Haven, CT: Yale University Press.

Galtung, J. 2006. Keynote address to the International Peace Research Association, Calgary, Alberta, Canada, January 7, 2006.

Gardner, H. 2008. What is good work? Tanner Humanities Lecture, University of Utah, Salt Lake City, April 10, 2008.

Gardner, H., M. Csikszentmihalyi, and W. Damon. 2001. *Good work: When excellence and ethics meet.* New York: Basic.

Garone, E. 2008. An executive downshifts from marketing fast lane. *Wall Street Journal Online,* October 7, 2008. http://online.wsj.com/article/SB12 2334618369310373.html (accessed November 10, 2008).

Gibbs, R. 2000. *Why ethics? Signs of responsibilities.* Princeton, NJ: Princeton University Press.

Gibney, A., writer. 2005. Enron: The smartest guys in the room. DVD. Directed by A. Gibney. New York: Jigsaw Productions.

Gibney, A., writer. 2008. *Taxi to the dark side.* DVD. Directed by A. Gibney. New York: Jigsaw Productions.

Gibson, R. 1999. For Pizza Hut, a new pie-in-the-sky strategy. *Wall Street Journal,* September 3, 1999 (accessed June 1, 2008, from ProQuest database).

Gibson-Graham, J. K. 2006. *A post-capitalist politics*. Minneapolis: University of Minnesota Press.

Gilbert, D. T., and T. D. Wilson. 2000. Miswanting: Some problems in the forecasting of future affective states. In *Feeling and thinking*, ed. J. P. Forgas, 178–97. New York: Cambridge University Press.

Gill, R. 2006. The work-life relationship for "people with choices:" Entrepreneurs as crystallized selves? *Electronic Journal of Communication 16* (3 & 4). http://www.cios.org/www/ejc/v16n34.htm (accessed September 24, 2008).

Gill, R. Forthcoming. The discourse and practice of entrepreneurship and enterprising. PhD diss., University of Utah.

Gilligan, C. 1982. *In a different voice: Psychological theory and women's development*. Cambridge, MA: Harvard University Press.

Gilroy, T., writer. 2008. *Michael Clayton*. DVD. Directed by T. Gilroy. Los Angeles: Warner Bros. Pictures.

Gini, A. 2001. *My job, my self: Work and the creation of the modern individual*. New York: Routledge.

Gladwell, M. 2005. *Blink: The power of thinking without thinking*. New York: Little, Brown.

Gladwell, M. 2008. *Outliers: The story of success*. Boston: Little, Brown.

Golden, A. G., E. L. Kirby, and J. Jorgenson. 2006. Work-life research from both sides now: An integrative perspective for organizational and family communication. In *Communication yearbook 30*, ed. C. Beck, 143–95. Mahwah, NJ: Lawrence Erlbaum.

Goldgar, A. 2007. *Tulipmania: Money, honor and knowledge in the Dutch Golden Age*. Chicago: University of Chicago Press.

Goldsteen, R. L., K. Goldsteen, J. H. Swan, and W. Clemeña. 2001. Harry and Louise and health care reform: Romancing public opinion. *Journal of Health Politics, Policy and Law* 26:1325–52.

Goodpaster, K. 2007. Conscience and corporate culture. Malden, MA: Blackwell.

Goodwyn, W. 2008. The perilous path of FAA whistle-blowers. *National Public Radio's All Things Considered*, June 12, 2008. http://www.npr.org/templates/story/story.php?storyId=91428378 (accessed December 12, 2008).

Gopnik, A. 1997. Trouble at the tower. *New Yorker*. August 4, 1997, p. 80.

Government in an 'ethics crisis,' survey finds. 2008. *Washington Times*, January 30, 2008. http://washingtontimes.com/news/2008/jan/30/government-in-an-ethics-crisis-survey-finds (accessed September 16, 2008).

Greene, R. W., and D. Hicks. 2005. Lost convictions: Debating both sides and the ethical self-fashioning of liberal citizens. *Cultural Studies* 19:100–26.

Greider, W. 1998. *One world ready or not: The manic logic of global capitalism*. New York: Simon & Schuster.

Grimaldi, W. M. A. 1998. Studies in the philosophy of Aristotle's *Rhetoric*. In *Landmark essays on Aristotelian rhetoric*, ed. R. L. Enos and L. P. Agnew, 15–160. Mahwa, NJ: Lawrence Erlbaum.

Grant, D., and C. Oswick, eds. 1996. *Metaphor and organization*. London: Sage.

Grant S., writer. 2000. *Erin Brockovich*. DVD. Directed by S. Soderbergh. Los Angeles: Universal Pictures.

Grant, S. 2005. A case study in charismatic leadership and corporate social responsibility: Anita Roddick and the Body Shop. PhD diss., University of Waikato, Hamilton, NZ.

Gratzon, F. 2003. *The lazy way to success: How to do nothing and accomplish everything*. Fairfield, IA: Soma.

Gratzon, F. 2008. The lazy way to success: Definition of success. http://lazyway. blogs.com/lazy_way/2008/01/definition-of-s.html (accessed December 11, 2008).

Greenhouse, S. 2008. *The big squeeze: Tough times for the American worker*. New York: Knopf.

Habermas, J. 1972. *Knowledge and human interests*. Boston: Beacon.

Habermas, J. 1979. *Communication and the evolution of society*. Boston: Beacon.

Hafen, S. 2004. Organizational gossip: A revolving door of regulation and resistance. *Southern Communication Journal* 69:223–40.

Hallett, T. 2003. Symbolic power and organizational culture. *Sociological Theory* 21:128–149.

Hamilton, C. 2004. *Growth fetish*. London: Pluto.

Hammer, M. 1997. *Beyond reengineering: How the process-centered organization is changing our work and our lives*. New York: HarperCollins.

Hammer, M., and J. Champy. 1995. *Reengineering the corporation: A manifesto for business revolution*. New York: HarperCollins.

Hardwick, M. 2003. *Mall maker: Victor Gruen, architect of an American dream*. Philadelphia: University of Pennsylvania Press.

Harmon, G. 1999. Moral philosophy meets social psychology: Virtue ethics and the fundamental attribution error. *Proceedings of the Aristotelian Society* 993:315–31.

Harré, R., and P. F. Secord. 1972. *The explanation of social behaviour*. Malden, MA: Blackwell.

Hart, K. 2005. *The hitman's dilemma: Or business, personal and impersonal*. Chicago: University of Chicago Press.

Hasian Jr., M. A. 1996. *The rhetoric of eugenics in Anglo-American thought*. Athens: University of Georgia Press.

Hasian Jr., M., and E. Croasmun. 1992. The legitimizing function of judicial rhetoric in the eugenics controversy. *Argumentation & Advocacy* 28:123–34.

Hawes, L. C. 1974. Social collectivities as communication. *Quarterly Journal of Speech* 60:497–502.

Hawken, P. 1994. *The ecology of commerce: A declaration of sustainability*. New York: HarperBusiness.

Hawken, P., A. Lovins, and L. L. Lovins. 1999. *Natural capitalism: Creating the next industrial revolution*. New York: Back Bay Books.

Hedges, C. 2002. *War is a force that gives us meaning*. New York: PublicAffairs.

Hedges, J. 2008. The expressions and transformations of identity in Alcoholics Anonymous: A multi-method study of individual, group and organization. PhD diss., University of Utah.

Heilbroner, R. L. 1972. *The worldly philosophers: The lives, times, and ideas of the great economic thinkers.* 4th ed. New York: Simon & Schuster.

Heugens, P. P. M. A. R., M. Kaptein, and J. H. van Oosterhout. 2008. Contracts to communities: A processual model of organizational virtue. *Journal of Management Studies* 45:100–21.

Hirschman, A. O. 1970. *Exit, voice, and loyalty: Responses to decline in firms, organizations, and states.* Cambridge, MA: Harvard University Press.

Hobbes, T. 1997. *Leviathan* R. E. Flathman and D. Johnston, eds. New York: Norton. Original work published in 1651.

Hochschild, A. R. 1989. *The second shift: Working families and the revolution at home.* New York: Viking.

Hochschild, A. R. 1997. *The time bind: When work becomes home and home becomes work.* New York: Metropolitan.

Hodgson, G. M. 1999. *Economics and utopia: Why the learning economy is not the end of history.* London: Routledge.

Hoffman, J. 2008. The language of loss for the jobless. *New York Times*, May 18, 2008, sec. SS, pp. 1–2.

Hofstede, G. 1980. *Culture's consequences: International differences in work-related values.* Newbury Park, CA: Sage.

Holmer-Nadesan, M., and A. Trethewey. 2000. Performing the enterprising subject: Gendered strategies for success? *Text and Performance Quarterly* 20:223–50.

Horowitz, D. 2006. *The professors: The 101 most dangerous academics in America.* Washington, DC: Regnery.

Horwitz, M. J. 1977. *The transformation of American law, 1780–1860.* Cambridge, MA: Harvard University Press.

Huczynski, A. 1993. *Management gurus.* London: Routledge.

Huntington, S. 2004. Dead souls: The denationalization of American elite. *National Interest* 75:5–19.

Hurn, D., and B. Jay. 1997. *On being a photographer.* Anacortes, WA: LensWork.

Hutchinson, D. S. 1995. Ethics. In *The Cambridge companion to Aristotle,* ed. J.Barnes, 195–232. New York: Cambridge University Press.

Hyde, L. 1983. *The gift: Imagination and the erotic life of property.* New York: Vintage/Random House.

Ignatius, A. 2002. Wall Street's Top Cop. *Time,* December 30, 2002. http://www.time.com/time/magazine/article/0,9171,1003960,00.html (accessed September 21, 2008).

Insurance recruiter n.d. Job description. http://28374.jobs.monster.com/getjob.asp?JobID=55726336&AVSDM=2008–10–03+10%3A03%3A30&Logo=0&pg=2&sort=rv&tm=30d&rad=5&aj=28374 (accessed October 15, 2008).

Intergovernmental Panel on Climate Change. 2007. Summary for Policymakers. In *Climate change 2007: The physical science basis. Contribution of Working*

Group I to the fourth assessment report of the Intergovernmental Panel on Climate Change, ed. S. D. Solomon, D. Quin, M. Manning, Z. Chen, M. Marquis, K. B. Averyt, M. Tgnor, and H. L. Miller. Cambridge, UK: Cambridge University Press. http://ipcc-wg1.ucar.edu/wg1/Report/AR4WG1_Print_SPM.pdf (accessed September, 22, 2008)

Jackall, R. 1988. *Moral mazes: The world of corporate managers.* New York: Oxford University Press.

Jackson, B. 1996. Re-engineering the sense of self: The manager and the management guru. *Journal of Management Studies* 33:571–90.

Jackson, B. 2001. *Management gurus and management fashions: A dramatistic inquiry.* London: Routledge.

Jacobs, J. S. 2006. Tim Robbins and Derek Luke: The two sides of *Catch a Fire. Popentertainment.com*, October 27, 2006. www.popentertainment.com/robinsluke.htm (accessed November 14, 2008).

Jacobs, M. 1997. "How about some meat?": The Office of Price Administration, consumption politics, and state building from the bottom up, 1941–1946. *Journal of American History* 84:910–41.

Johannesen, R. L., K. S. Valde, and K. E. Whedbee. 2008. *Ethics in human communication.* 6th ed. Long Grove, IL: Waveland.

Johnson, C. 2008. A backlog of cases alleging fraud: Whistle-blower suits languish at Justice. *Washington Post*, July 2, 2008, p. A1.

Johnson, D. 2007. *Tree of smoke.* Yew York: Farrar, Straus & Giroux.

Johnson, J. D. 1992. Approaches to organizational communication structure. *Journal of Business Research* 25:99–113.

Jones, C., M. Parker, and R. Ten Bos. 2005. *For business ethics.* London: Routledge.

Jung, C. G. 1953. The development of personality: Collected works of C. G. Jung. V01.17. Trans. G. Adler and R. F. C. Hull. Princeton, NJ: Princeton University Press.

Kant, I. 1993. *Grounding for the metaphysics of morals: On a supposed right to lie because of philanthropic concerns.* 3rd ed. Trans. J. W. Ellington. Indianapolis, IN: Hackett Publishing. Original work published in 1785.

Kant, I. 1996. *The metaphysics of morals.* 2nd ed. Ed. and trans. M. Gregor. New York: Cambridge University Press. Original work published 1797.

Kanter, R. M. 1977a. *Men and women of the corporation.* New York: Basic.

Kanter, R. M. 1977b. *Work and family in the United States: A critical review and policy agenda.* New York: Russell Sage Foundation.

Kashima, Y., and V. Callan. 1994. The Japanese work group. In *Handbook of Industrial and Organizational Psychology* 2nd ed. Vol. 4. Ed. M. D. Dunnette, L. M. Hough, and H. C. Triandis, 610–46. Palo Alto, CA: Consulting Psychologists Press.

Kassing, J. W., and T. A. Avtgis. 1999. Examining the relationship between organizational dissent and aggressive communication. *Management Communication Quarterly* 13:100–15.

Katz, D., and R. Kahn. 1978. *The social psychology of organizations.* 2nd ed. New York: John Wiley.

Keen, S. 1988. *Faces of the enemy: Reflections of the hostile imagination*. New York: Harper & Row.

Kellaris, J. J., B. A. Boyle, and R. F. Dahlstrom. 1994. Framing and situational ethics. *Marketing Letters* 5:69–75.

Kendall, B. E., R. Gill, and G. Cheney. 2007. Consumer activism and corporate social responsibility: How strong a connection? In *The debate over corporate social responsibility*, ed. S. May, J. Roper, and G. Cheney, 241–64. New York: Oxford University Press.

Kennedy, R. F. 1968. Address, University of Kansas, Lawrence, March 18, 1968.

Kipphardt, H. 1968. *In the matter of J. Robert Oppenheimer*. New York: Hill & Wang.

Kirby, A. 2005. Analysis: Anglican schism nears reality. *BBC News*, February 25, 2005. http://news.bbc.co.uk/1/hi/uk/4296373.stm (accessed September 25, 2008).

Kirby, E. L., A. G. Golden, C. E. Medved, J. Jorgenson, and P. M. Buzzanell. 2003. An organizational communication challenge to the discourse of work and family research: From problematics to empowerment. In *Communication yearbook 27*, ed. P. Kalbfleisch, 1–43. Mahwah, NJ: Lawrence Erlbaum.

Klein, N. 1999. *No logo*. New York: Picador.

Knight, J. 2006. *Just doing my job*. Sydney, Australia: Hachette Livre.

Knoke, D., and J. H. Kuklinski. 1982. *Network analysis*. Beverly Hills, CA: Sage.

Koernberger, M., and A. D. Brown. 2007. "Ethics" as a discursive resource for identity work. *Human Relations* 60:497–518.

Kohlberg, L. 1981. *The philosophy of moral development: Moral stages and the idea of justice*. Cambridge, MA: Harper & Row.

Kostof, S. ed. 1986. *The architect: Chapters in the history of the profession*. New York: Oxford University Press.

Kotz, D. M. 2008. Shocked disbelief. *Truthout.org—Perspective*, November 2, 2008. http://www.truthout.org/110208B (accessed November 2, 2008).

Kuttner, R. 1997. *Everything for sale: The virtues and limits of markets*. New York: Knopf.

Krugman, P. 2006. U.S. Inequality driven by massive income gains by tiny minority. *Salt Lake Tribune*, February 28, 2006, p. A-9.

Lair, D. J. 2007. "Survivor for business people": A critical-rhetorical engagement of The Apprentice as popular management discourse. PhD diss., University of Utah.

Lair, D. J., K. Sullivan, and G. Cheney. 2005. Marketization and the recasting of the professional self. *Management Communication Quarterly* 18: 307–343.

Lakoff, G. 2002. *Moral politics: How liberals and conservatives think*. 2nd ed. Chicago: University of Chicago Press.

Lakoff, G. 2008. *The political mind: Why you can't understand 21st century American politics with an 18th century brain*. New York: Penguin.

Lal, V. 2005. Witch hunts in the academy. *Economic and Political Weekly*, May 7, 2005, pp. 1932–34.

Lane, R. E. 2000. *The loss of happiness in market democracies*. New Haven, CT: Yale University Press.

Lardner, J., and D. A. Smith. eds. 2005. *Inequality matters: The growing economic divide in America and its poisonous consequences.* New York: New Press.

Larson, M. S. 1977. *The rise of professionalism: A sociological analysis.* Berkeley and Los Angeles: University of California Press.

Laufer, R., and C. Paradeise. 1990. *Marketing democracy.* New Brunswick, NJ: Transaction.

Lee, J. 8. 2003. Neighbors of vast hog farms say foul air endangers their health. *New York Times,* May 11, 2003. http://query.nytimes.com/gst/fullpage.ht ml?res=9E04EFDE123FF932A25756C0A9659C8B63&scp=1&sq=Neighbor s%200f%20Vast%20Hog%20Farms&st=cse (accessed December 15, 2008).

Leopold, A. 1949/1968. *A Sand County almanac and sketches here and there.* London: Oxford University Press.

Levinas, E. 1989. Ethics as first philosophy. Trans. S. Hand and M. Temple. In *The Levinas reader,* ed. S. Hand, 75–87. Oxford, UK: Blackwell.

Lévi-Strauss, C. 1995. *Myth and meaning: Cracking the code of culture.* New York: Schocken.

Lewis, M., and D. Einhorn. 2009. The end of the financial world as we know it. *New York Times,* January 4, 2009, sec. O, pp. 9–10.

Life & Times transcript. 2005. Television show. July 21, 2005. http://www.kcet. org/lifeandtimes/archives/200507/20050721.php (accessed September 13, 2008).

Liu, B. F., and J. S. Horsley. 2007. The government communication decision wheel: Toward a public relations model for the public sector. *Journal of Public Relations Research* 19:377–93.

Lyon, A. 2008. The mis/recognition of Enron executives' competence as cultural and social capital. *Communication Studies* 59:371–87.

Macdonald, K. M. 1995. *The sociology of the professions.* London: Sage.

MacIntyre, A. 1984. *After virtue: A study in moral theory.* 2nd ed. Notre Dame, IN: University of Notre Dame Press.

Marcuse, H. 1964. *One-dimensional man: Studies in the ideology of advanced industrial society.* Boston: Beacon.

Margolis, J. D., and J. P. Walsh. 2003. Misery loves companies: Rethinking social initiatives by business. *Administrative Science Quarterly* 48:268–305.

Marx, K. 1844/1961. *Economic and philosophical manuscripts.* In *Marx's concept of man,* by E. Fromm. New York: Free Press.

Marx, K. 1976. *Capital, Volume 1.* London: Verso. Original work published 1867.

Mauss, M. 1950/1990. *The Gift.* New York: Norton. Original work published 1950.

May, S., G. Cheney, and J. Roper, eds. 2007. *The debate over corporate social responsibility.* New York: Oxford University Press.

May, S. K. In press. Activating ethical engagement in organizations. In *Communication activism* 3, ed. L. Frey and K. Carragee. Creskill, NJ: Hampton.

Mayer, C. J. 1990. Personalizing the impersonal: Corporations and the Bill of Rights. *Hastings Law Journal* 41:580–667.

Mazzetti, M. 2008. '03 memo approved harsh interrogations. *New York Times*, April 2, 2008. http://www.nytimes.com/2008/04/02/washington/02terror. html (accessed December 15, 2008).

McCain: "I Know What's Right For America." 2007. *CBS News/Face the Nation*, August 19, 2007. http://www.cbsnews.com/stories/2007/08/19/ftn/main 3182562.shtml (accessed June 1, 2009).

McClellan, S. 2008. *What happened: Inside the Bush White House and Washington's culture of deception*. New York: Public Affairs.

McCloskey, D. N. 1985. *The rhetoric of economics*. Madison: University of Wisconsin Press.

McKibben, B. 2007. *Deep economy: The wealth of communities and the durable future*. New York: Times Books.

McMillan, J, J., & Cheney, G. 1996. The student as consumer: Implications and limitations of a metaphor. *Communication Education* 45:1–15.

McPhee, R. D. 1985. Formal structure and organizational communication. In *Organizational communication: Traditional themes and new directions*, ed. R. D. McPhee and P. K. Tompkins, 149–77. Beverly Hills, CA: Sage.

Mead, R. 2003. The Marx brother: how a philosopher from Slovenia became an international star. *New Yorker*, May 5, 2003. http://www.lacan.com/ziny. htm (accessed June 9, 2008).

Meeker-Lowry, S. 1996. Community money: The potential of local currency. In *The case against the global economy and for a turn toward the local*, ed. J. Mander and E. Goldsmith, 446–59. San Francisco: Sierra Club Books.

Meithe, T. D., and J. Rothschild. 1994. Whistleblowing and the control of organizational misconduct. *Sociological Inquiry* 64:322–47.

Merton, R. K. 1940. Bureaucratic structure and personality. *Social Forces* 18: 560–68.

Mertz, E. 2007. The language of US law schools. *Researching Law* 18 (4):1–7.

Meyer, J. W., and B. Rowan. 1977. Institutionalized organizations: Formal structure as myth and ceremony. *American Journal of Sociology* 83:340–63.

Microsoft. n.d. About Microsoft: Your potential. Our passion. http://www. microsoft.com/about/brandcampaigns/innovation/yourpotential/ main.html (accessed February 4, 2009).

Military subpoenas CBS Haditha video. 2008. *CBS News*, February 22, 2008. http://www.cbsnews.com/stories/2008/02/22/iraq/main3862292.shtml (accessed May 30, 2008).

Mill, J. S. 2002. Utilitarianism. In *The Basic Writings of John Stuart Mill*, 233–301. New York: Modern Library. Original work published 1863.

Miller, A. 1949/1998. *Death of a salesman*. New York: Penguin.

Miller, K. I., and J. Koesten. 2008. Financial feeling: An investigation of emotion and communication in the workplace. *Journal of Applied Communication Research* 36:8–32.

Mills, C. W. 1940. Situated actions and vocabularies of motive. *American Sociological Review* 5:904–913.

Moore, G. E. 2004. *Principia ethica*. New York: Dover. Original work published 1903.

Moore, M., writer. 2007. *Sicko*. DVD. Directed by M. Moure New York: Weinstein Co. Home Entertainment.

Moore, T. 2008. *A life at work: The joy of discovering what you were born to do*. New York: Broadway.

Morgan, G. 1986. *Images of organization*. 1st ed. Newbury Park, CA: Sage.

Morgan, G. 1997. *Images of organization*. 2nd ed. Thousand Oaks, CA: Sage.

Morgenson, G. 2008. Given a shovel, Americans dig deeper. *New York Times*, July 20, 2008 (accessed September 20, 2008, from ProQuest database).

Morris, E., writer. 1999. *Mr. Death: The Rise and Fall of Fred A. Leuchter, Jr*. DVD. Directed by E. Morris. London: Channel Four Films.

Mouffe, C. 1999. Deliberative democracy or agonistic pluralism? *Social Research* 66:745–58.

Moyers, B. 2008. Wall Street woes. *Bill Moyers Journal*, September 19, 2008. http://www.pbs.org/moyers/journal/09192008/profile2.html (accessed October 12, 2008).

Muirhead, R. 2004. *Just work*. Cambridge, MA: Harvard University Press.

Muller, J. Z. 2002. *The mind and the market: Capitalism in Western thought*. New York: Anchor.

Mumby, D. K. 1987. The political function of narrative in organizations. *Communication Monographs* 54:113–27.

Mumby, D. K. 1997. The problem of hegemony: Rereading Gramsci for organizational communication studies. *Western Journal of Communication* 61:343–75.

Munshi, D. 2005. Through the subject's eye: Situating the other in discourses of diversity. In *International and multicultural organizational communication*, ed. G. Cheney and G. A. Barnett, 45–70. Cresskill, NJ: Hampton.

Muthien, B. 2008. Gift giving circles: African stokvels. *Globalpolecon*. http://groups.yahoo.com/group/globalpolecon/message/576 (accessed January 14, 2009).

Myers, D. G. 1992. *The pursuit of happiness: Discovering the pathway to fulfillment, well-being, and enduring personal joy*. New York: Avon.

Myers, D.G., and E. Diener. 1995. Who is happy? *Psychological Science*, 6:10–19.

Nagel, T. 1978. *The possibility of altruism*. Princeton, NJ: Princeton University Press.

Naughton, K., and M. Peyser. 2004. The world according to TRUMP. *Newsweek*, March 1, 2004, pp. 48–55. Retrieved March 20, 2004, from ABI/INFORM database.

Newton, L. 2006. *Permission to steal: Revealing the roots of corporate scandal*. Malden, MA: Blackwell.

Nussbaum, M. C. 1999. Virtue ethics: A misleading category? *Journal of Ethics* 3:163–201.

Obama, B. H. 2009. Inaugural address, January 20, 2009. http://www.whitehouse.gov/blog/inaugural-address (accessed February 2, 2009).

Olson, P. 2008. The world's hardest-working countries. In *Forbes.com Workforce*, May 21, 2008, pp. 1–2. http://www.forbes.com/2008/05/21/labor-market-workforce-lead-citizen-cx_po_0521countries.html (accessed June 3, 2008).

Ortony, A. Ed. 1993. *Metaphor and thought*. Cambridge, UK: Cambridge University Press.

Orwell, G. 1970. Politics and the English language. In *A Collection of essays*, 156–70. New York: Mariner.

Ouichi, W. G., and A. L. Wilkins. 1985. Organizational culture. *Annual review of sociology* 11:457–83.

Our vision. n.d. Interface, Inc. webpage. http://www.interfaceglobal.com/ Sustainability/Our-Journey/Vision.aspx (accessed June 3, 2009).

Owens, M. 2007. Personal communication, May 27, 2007, Salt Lake City, UT.

Oxford English Dictionary. 1989. Entry for "Career." 2nd ed. http://diction-ary.oed.com/cgi/entry/50033428?query_type=word&queryword=caree r&first=1&max_to_show=10&sort_type=alpha&result_place=1&search_id=KJkU-OHtMNo-4203&hilite=50033428 (accessed August 31, 2008).

Oxford English Dictionary. 2008. Entry for "NIMBY." http://0-dictionary.oed.com. bianca.penlib.du.edu/cgi/entry/00324851?single=1&query_type=word&qu eryword=NIMBY&first=1&max_to_show=10 (accessed December 15, 2008).

Pacanowsky, M., and N. O-Donnell-Trujillo. 1982. Communication and organi-zational cultures. *Western Journal of Communication* 46:115–30.

Palmer, P. 1999. *Let your life speak: Listening for the voice of vocation*. Hoboken, NJ: Jossey-Bass.

Papert, D. 2002. Hard fun. http://www.papert.org/articles/HardFun.html (accessed August 5, 2008).

Pascarella, S. 2005. Top five destinations for a working vacation. *USA Today*, September 14, 2005. http://www.usatoday.com/travel/deals/ inside/2005-09-14-column_x.htm (accessed September 13, 2008).

Pasinetti, L. 2005. Paradoxes of happiness in economics. In *Economics and happi-ness: Framing the analysis*, ed. L. Bruni, and P. L. Porta, 336–44. Oxford, UK: Oxford University Press.

Patchen, M. 1970. *Participation, achievement, and involvement on the job*. Upper Saddle River, NJ: Prentice-Hall.

Perrucci, R., R. M. Anderson, D. E. Schendel, and L. E. Tractman. 1980. Whistle-blowing: Professionals' resistance to organizational authority. *Social Problems* 28:149–67.

Peters, T., and R. Waterman. 1982. *In search of excellence: Lessons from America's best-run companies*. New York: Harper & Row.

Pfanner, E. 2008. In flailing Iceland, disbelief and regret. *New York Times*, October 9, 2008, p. B1.

Pfeffer, J. 2006. Working alone: Whatever happened to the idea of organizations as communities? In *America at work: Choices and challenges*, ed. E. E. Lawler III and J. O'Toole, 3–22. New York: Palgrave Macmillan. http://articles. latimes.com/2007/may/11/business/fi-pasadena11 (accessed September 19, 2008).

Planalp, S. 1999. *Communicating emotion: Social, moral, and cultural processes*. Cambridge, UK: Cambridge University Press.

Plato. 1987. Euthypro. In *Plato: Euthyphro, Apology, Crito*, trans. F. J. Church, 1–20. New York: Prentice Hall.

Plato. 1990a. Gorgias. Trans. W. R. N. Lamb. In *The rhetorical tradition: Readings from classical times to the present*, ed. P. Bizzell and B. Herzberg, 61–112. Boston: Bedford/St. Martin's.

Plato. 1990b. Phaedrus. Trans. H. N. Fowler. In *The rhetorical tradition: Readings from classical times to the present*, ed. P. Bizzell and B. Herzberg, 113–43. Boston: Bedford/St. Martin's.

Polanyi, K. 2001. *The great transformation: The political and economic origins of our time*. Boston: Beacon. Original work published 1944.

Pollan, M. 2008. *In defense of food: An eater's manifesto*. New York: Penguin.

Pollin, R. 2005. *Contours of descent: U.S. economic fractures and the landscape of global austerity*. London: Verso.

Pool, R. 2006. An offer he couldn't refuse. *Research in Review Magazine*. http://www.rinr.fsu.edu/summer2006/features/coverstory.html (accessed September 16, 2008).

Porter, M. E. 2003. Strategic corporate philanthropy. Keynote address to the European Academy for Business and Society, Copenhagen, Denmark, September 2003.

Portney, K. E. 1991. *Siting hazardous waste treatment facilities: The NIMBY syndrome*. New York: Auburn House.

Pratto, F., L. M. Stallworth, J. Sidanius, and B. Siers. 1997. The gender gap in occupational role attainment: A social dominance approach. *Journal of Personality and Social Psychology* 72:37–53.

Pritchard, M. 2006. *Professional integrity: Thinking ethically*. Lawrence: University Press of Kansas.

Purdy, K. 2004. Some Buffalo, N.Y.-area workers learn from business-based reality TV show. *Knight Ridder Tribune Business News*, March 10, 2004, p. 1 (accessed March 20, 2004, from ABI/INFORM database).

Putnam, R. D. 2000. *Bowling alone: The collapse and revival of American community*. New York: Simon & Schuster.

Rand, A. 1996. *Atlas shrugged*. New York: Signet. Original work published 1957.

Rand, A. 2000. *The fountainhead*. New York: Scribner Classics. Original work published 1943.

Rawls, J. 1999. *A theory of justice*. Rev. ed. Cambridge, MA: Harvard University Press. Original work published 1971.

Readings, B. 1996. *The university in ruins*. Cambridge, MA: Harvard University Press.

Reese, L. 2004. *Auschwitz: A new history*. New York: Public Affairs.

Rich, C. O. 2009. The longings of labor and working identities: Gender, sexuality, and the organization of barbers and hairstylists. PhD diss., Salt Lake City: University of Utah.

Ritz, D. 2003. When rights collide: Free speech, corporations, and moral rights. *Ethical Space* 11:39–45.

Ritz, D. 2007. Can corporate personhood be socially responsible? In *The debate over corporate social responsibility*, ed. S. May, J. Roper, and G. Cheney, 190–204. New York: Oxford University Press.

Rorty, R. 1979. *Philosophy and the mirror of nature*. Princeton, NJ: Princeton University Press.

Rusbult, C. E. 1987. Responses to dissatisfaction in close relationships: The exist–voice–loyality–neglect model. In *Intimate relationships: Development, dynamics, and deterioration*, ed. D. Perelman & S. Duck, 109–238. London: Sage.

Sabini, J., and M. Silver. 1982. *Moralities of everyday life*. New York: Oxford University Press.

Safransky, S. 2006. Sy Safransky's notebook. *Sun Magazine* 369:47.

Sayer, D. 1991. *Capitalism and modernity: An excursus on Marx and Weber*. London: Routledge.

Schmidt, J. 2000. *Disciplined minds: A critical look at salaried professionals and the soul-battering system that shaped their lives*. Lanham, MD: Rowman & Littlefield.

Schmidt, M. S. 2007. Pettitte admits he used H.G.H. "for two days." *New York Times*, December 16, 2007.

Schmookler, A. B. 1993. *The illusion of choice: How the market economy shapes our destiny*. Albany: SUNY Press.

Schor, J. B. 1992. *The overworked American: The unexpected decline of leisure*. New York: HarperCollins.

Schor, J. B. 1997. *The overspent American: Why we want what we don't need*. New York: HarperCollins.

Schor, J. B. 2004. *Born to buy: The commercialized child and the new consumer culture*. New York: Scribner.

Schumacher, E. F. 1973. *Small is beautiful: Economics as if people mattered*. New York: Harper & Row.

Schutz, A. 1967. *The phenomenology of the social world*. Evanston, IL: Northwestern University Press.

Schwartzman, H. B. 1989. *The meeting: Gatherings in organizations and communities*. New York: Plenum.

Scott, J. C. 1986. *Domination and the arts of resistance: Hidden transcripts*. New Haven, CT: Yale University Press.

Scott, M. B., and S. M. Lyman. 1968. Accounts. *American Sociological Review* 33:46–62.

Searle, J. R. 1995. *The construction of social reality*. New York: Free Press.

Seeger, M., and T. Kuhn. In press. Communication, ethics and organization. In *The international communication handbook of communication ethics*, ed. G. Cheney, S. May, and D. Munshi. New York: Routledge/Erlbaum.

Sen, A. K. 1992. *Inequality reexamined*. Cambridge, MA: Harvard University Press.

Sen, A. K. 2006. *Identity and violence: The illusion of destiny*. London: Sage.

Sennett, R. 1980. *Authority*. New York: Knopf.

Sennett, R. 1998. *The corrosion of character: The personal consequences of work in the new capitalism*. New York: W. W. Norton.

Sennett, R. 2006. *The culture of the new capitalism*. New Haven, CT: Yale University Press.

Seven steps. n.d. Interface, Inc. webpage. http://www.interfacesustainability.com/ seven.html (accessed August 19, 2008).

Sewell, G., and J. Barker. 2005. Max Weber and the irony of bureaucracy. In *Social theory at work*, ed. M. Korczynski, R. Hodson, and P. Edwards, 56–87. Oxford, UK: Oxford University Press.

Shakespeare, W. 1998. *As you like it*. Ed. A. Brissenden. London: Oxford University Press.

Shane, S., and M. Mazzetti. 2008. Report blames Rumsfeld for detainee abuse. *New York Times*, December 11, 2008. http://www.nytimes.com/2008/12/12/ washington/12detainee.html?scp=4&sq=rumsfeld%20torture&st=cse (accessed December 19, 2008).

Shanker, T. 2005. Pentagon sets new policies on reporting sex assaults at academies. *New York Times*, March 19, 2005 (accessed June 11, 2008, from ProQuest database).

Shelley, M. 1994. *Frankenstein*. Ed. D. L. Macdonald and K. Scherf. Orchard Park, NY: Broadview. Original work published 1818.

Sidanius, J., and F. Pratto. 2001. *Social dominance: An intergroup theory of social hierarchy and oppression*. Cambridge, UK: Cambridge University Press.

Sidanius, J., F. Pratto, and M. Mitchell. 1994. Group identity, social dominance orientation, and intergroup discrimination: Some implications of social dominance theory. *Journal of Social Psychology* 134:151–67.

Simon, H. A. 1997. *Administrative behavior: A study of decision-making processes in administrative organizations*. 4th ed. New York: Free Press.

Sinclair, U. 1927. *Oil! A novel*. New York: A. & C. Boni.

Singer, P. 2004. *The president of good and evil*. New York: Dutton.

Smircich, L. 1983. Concepts of culture and organizational analysis. *Administrative Science Quarterly* 28:339–58.

Smith, A. 1976a. *The theory of moral sentiments*. Ed. A. L. Macfie and D. D. Raphael. Oxford, UK: Oxford University Press. Original work published 1759.

Smith, A. 1976b. *The wealth of nations* Ed. R. H. Campbell and A. S. Skinner. Oxford, UK: Oxford University Press. Original work published 1776.

Smith, R. 2008. Will "NIMBY" syndrome kill N.C.'s chances for bioterror lab? *WRAL.com*, January 9, 2008. http://localtechwire.com/business/local_tech_ wire/opinion/blogpost/2275140 (accessed December 11, 2008).

Smith, R. C., and E. M. Eisenberg. 1987. Conflict at Disneyland: A root-metaphor analysis. *Communication Monographs* 54:367–80.

Smith, V. 2001. *Crossing the great divide: Worker risk and opportunity in the new economy*. Ithaca, NY: Cornell University Press.

Snodgrass, M., writer. 1989. The ensigns of command [Television series episode]. Directed by C. Bole. In *Star trek: The next generation*, prod. by R. Berman and G. Roddenberry. Los Angeles: CBS Paramount Television.

Solnit, R. 2008. News from nowhere. *Harper's*, October 2008, pp. 47–53.

Solomon, R. C. 1999. *A better way to think about business*. New York: Oxford University Press.

Soros, G. 2000. *Open society: Reforming global capitalism*. New York: Public Affairs.

Stark, J. 2001. Startup.com. *Salon.com*, May 11, 2001. http://archive.salon.com/ent/movies/review/2001/05/11/startup (accessed September 24, 2008).

Stearns, P. 1994. *American cool*. New York: New York University Press.

Stearns, P. 2006. *Consumerism in world history*. 2nd ed. London: Routledge.

Stein, H. F. 2001. *Nothing personal, just business: A journey into organizational darkness*. Westport, CT: Quorum.

Steutel, J., and D. Carr. 1999. Virtue ethics and the virtue approach to moral education. In *Virtue ethics and moral education*, ed. D. Carr and J. Steutel, 3–18. London: Routledge.

Stevens, B. 2008. Corporate ethical codes: Effective instruments for influencing behavior. *Journal of Business Ethics* 78: 601–9.

Stewart, B. 2007. I know I can never return to this hell. http://findarticles.com/p/articles/mi_qn4176/is_20070519/ai_n19165487/?tag=content;c011 (accessed October 15, 2008).

Stewart, C. S., 2004. A question of ethics: How to teach them? *New York Times*, March 21, 2004, sec. 3, p. 11.

Stewart, J. 2007. Alan Greenspan. *Daily Show with Jon Stewart*, September 18, 2007. http://www.thedailyshow.com/video/index.jhtml?videoId=102970&title=Alan-Greenspan (accessed October 12, 2008).

Stiglitz, J. E. 2008. Reversal of fortune. *Vanity Fair*, November 1, 2008. http://www.truthout.org/103108R (accessed November 1, 2008).

Stolberg, S. G. 2004. Past defeat and personal quest shape long-shot Kucinich bid. *New York Times*, January 2, 2004. http://query.nytimes.com/gst/fullpage.html?res=9C00E1DC1631F931A35752C0A9629C8B63 (accessed April 4, 2008).

Sullivan, K. R. 2007. Embodied tensions: navigating the contours of sexuality at work. PhD diss., Salt Lake City: University of Utah.

Sullivan, W. 1995. *Work and integrity*. New York: HarperCollins.

Sunstein, C. 2003. *Why societies need dissent*. Cambridge, MA: Harvard University Press.

Sustainability overview. n.d. Interface, Inc. webpage. http://www.interfaceinc.com/goals/sustainability_overview.html (accessed August 19, 2008).

Svensson, G., and G. Wood. 2003. The dynamics of business ethics: A function of time and culture—Cases and models. *Management Decision* 41:350–61.

Takahashi, L. M. (1998) *Homelessness, AIDS, and stigmatization*. Oxford, UK: Clarendon Press.

Talberth, J., C. Cobb, and N. Slattery. 2006. *The genuine progress indicator 2006: A tool for sustainable development*. Oakland, CA: Redefining Progress/The Nature of Economics. http://www.environmental-expert.com/Files%5C24200%5Carticles%5C12128%5CGPI202006.pdf (accessed January 15, 2009).

Taylor, A., writer/Directed by A Taylor. 2006. *Žižek!* DVD. New York: Zeitgeist Films.

Telecommunications Act, 47 U.S.C. §332[c] (1996)

Telecommuting and the working mom. n.d. Lewis & Clark College webpage. http://www.lclark.edu/~soan370/global/at&tvirtualmom.html (accessed September 13, 2008).

Tenbrunsel, A. E., and K. Smith-Crowe. 2008. Ethical decision making: Where we've been and where we're going. *The Academy of Management Annals* 21:545–607.

Thackaberry, J. A. 2003. Mutual metaphors of *Survivor* and office politics: Images of work in popular *Survivor* criticism. In *Survivor lessons: Essays on communication and reality television*, ed. M. J. Smith and A. F. Wood, 153–81. New York: McFarland.

Tharp, T. 2003. *The creative habit: Learn it and use it for life.* New York: Simon & Schuster.

Thompson, C. 2004. The E-infectors. *New York Times Magazine*, February 8, 2004, pp. 28–33.

Thompson, E. P. 1967. Time, work-discipline, and industrial capitalism. *Past & Present* 38:56–97.

Tomasi, J. 1991. Individual rights and community virtues. *Ethics* 101:521–36.

Tracy, S. J. 2000. Becoming a character for commerce: Emotion labor, self-subordination, and discursive construction of identity in a total institution. *Management Communication Quarterly* 14:790–827.

Tracy, S. J., and C. Scott. 2006. Sexuality, masculinity, and taint management among firefighters and correctional officers: Getting down and dirty with "America's heros" and the "scum of law enforcement." *Management Communication Quarterly* 20:6–38.

Treviño, L. K., and D. Weaver. 2003. *Managing ethics in business organizations: Social scientific perspectives.* Palo Alto, CA: Stanford University Press.

Tschumi, B. 1996. *Architecture and disjunction.* Cambridge, MA: MIT Press.

Tugend, A. 2008. Job hunting is, and isn't, what it used to be. *New York Times*, September 27, 2008. http://www.nytimes.com/2008/09/27/business/yourmoney/27shortcuts.html (accessed October 12, 2008).

Tumulty, K. 2002. Spitzer's spectacle. *Time*, June 10, 2002. http://www.time.com/time/magazine/article/0,9171,1002604,00.html (accessed September 21, 2008).

Turner, B. S. 1996. Preface. In *Professional ethics and civic morals*, by E. Durkheim, 2nd ed. London: Routledge.

Twain, M. 2008. *The adventures of Tom Sawyer.* New York: Puffin. Original work published 1876.

Umphress, E. E., K. Smith-Crowe, A. P. Brief, J. Dietz, and M. B. Watkins. 2007. When birds of a feather flock together and when they do not: Status composition, social dominance orientation, and organizational attractiveness. *Journal of Applied Psychology* 92:396–409.

United States Securities and Exchange Commission. 2003. Disclosure required by sections 406 and 407 of the Sarbanes-Oxley Act of 2002; Correction. May 7, 2003. http://sec.gov/rules/final/33–8177a.htm (accessed September 21, 2008).

Updike, N., and I. Glass. Producers. 1998. Numbers [Radio series episode]. In *This American Life*. http://www.thisamericanlife.org/Radio_Episode.aspx?sched=1277 (accessed January 10, 2009).

Van Buren, C. 2001. Teaching hackers: School computing culture and the future of cyber-rights. *Journal of Information Ethics* 10:51–72.

Vande Berg, L., and N. Trujillo. 1989. *Organizational life on television*. Norwood, NJ: Ablex.

Vatz, R. E. 1973. The myth of the rhetorical situation. *Philosophy & Rhetoric* 6:154–61.

Veblen, T. 1935. *The theory of the leisure class: An economic study of institutions*. New York: Mentor. Original work published 1899.

Virilio, P. 1977. *Speed and politics*. Trans. M. Polizzotti. Los Angeles: Semiotexte.

Vogel, D. 2006. *The market for virtue: The potential and limits of corporate social responsibility*. Washington, DC: Brookings Institution.

Von Bertalanffy, L. 1968. *General systems theory: Foundations, development, applications*. New York: George Braziller.

Wallace, D. F. 1999. *Brief interviews with hideous men*. Boston: Little, Brown.

Warrick, J. 2008. CIA tactics endorsed in secret memos: Waterboarding got White House nod. *Washington Post*, October 15, 2008, p. A1.

Wayne, L. (2009). A promise to be ethical in an era of immortality. *New York Times*, May 29, 2009. http://www.nytimes.com/2009/05/30/business/300ath. html (accessed June 4, 2009).

Weaver, G. B., L. K. Treviño, and P. L. Cochran. 1999. Corporate ethics practices in the mid-1990s: An empirical study of the Fortune 1000. *Journal of Business Ethics* 18:283–294.

Weber, M. 1978. *Economy and Society*. 2 vols. Ed. G. Roth and C. Wittich. Berkeley and Los Angeles: University of California Press.

Weber, M. 2002. *The Protestant ethic and the spirit of capitalism*. New York: Penguin. Original work published 1905.

Welch, D. 1998. Our market, which art in heaven. *New Zealand Listener*, July 11, 1998, p. 25.

Wells, J. T. 2000. *Frankensteins of fraud: The 20th century's top ten white-collar criminals*. Austin, TX: Obsidian.

Werhane, P. 1985. *Persons, rights, and corporations*. Englewood Cliffs, NJ: Prentice-Hall.

Werhane, P. C. 1991. *Adam Smith and his legacy for modern capitalism*. New York: Oxford University Press.

Whetstone, J. T. 2001. How virtue fits within business ethics. *Journal of Business Ethics* 33:101–14.

White, H. 1981. Where do markets come from? *American Journal of Sociology* 87:519–47.

Whyte, W. H. 1956. *The organization man*. New York: Doubleday.

Williams, W. C. 2000. The use of force. In *The Norton anthology of short fiction*. 6th ed. Ed. R. V. Cassill and R. Bausch, 904–7. New York: W. W. Norton.

Willmott, H. 1998. Towards a new ethics? The contributions of poststructuralism and posthumanism. In *Ethics and organizations*, Ed. M. Parker, 76–121. London: Sage.

Wilson, S. 1955. *Man in the gray flannel suit*. London: Remploy.

Wittgenstein, L. 1999. *Philosophical investigations*. New York: Prentice Hall. Original work published 1953.

Wolgast, E. 1992. *Ethics of an artificial person: Lost responsibility in professions and organizations*. Stanford, CA: Stanford University Press.

Working life. n.d. Amazon.com commentary. http://www.amazon.com/Working-Life-Promise-Betrayal-Modern/dp/0609807374/ref=pd_bbs_sr_1?ie=UTF8&s=books&qid=1212445019&sr=8-1 (accessed June 2, 2008).

Younger, B., writer. 2001. *Boiler room*. DVD. Directed by B. Younger. Los Angeles: New Line Cinema.

Zbracki, M. J. 1998. The rhetoric and reality of Total Quality Management. *Administrative Science Quarterly* 43:602–636.

Zibechi, R. 2008. Lima's community kitchens: Combating hunger and loneliness. Trans. M. Roof. *Americas program*, January 14, 2008. http://americas.irc-online.org/am/4889 (accessed January 15, 2009).

Zimbardo, P. G. 2004. The situationist perspective on the psychology of evil: Understanding how good people are transformed into perpetrators. In *The social psychology of good and evil*, ed. A. G. Miller, 21–50. New York: Guilford Press.

Žižek, S. 1994. The spectre of ideology. In *Mapping ideology*, 1–33. London: Verso.

Žižek, S. 2006. Jack Bauer and the ethics of urgency. *In These Times* http://lacan.com/zizbauer.htm (accessed June 5, 2008).

Žižek, S. 2008a. Don't just do something, talk. *London Review of Books*, October 9, 2008. http://www.lrb.co.uk/v00/n03/zize01_.html (accessed October 10, 2008).

Žižek, S. 2008b. *Violence*. New York: Picador.

Zorn, T., and E. Collins. 2007. Is sustainability sustainable? Corporate social responsibility, sustainable business, and management fashion. In *The debate over corporate social responsibility*, Ed. S. May, G. Cheney, and J. Roper, 405–15. New York: Oxford University Press.

Index

LaVergne, TN USA
26 April 2010
180645LV00002B/24/P